SPANISH

PHRASE BOOK
& DICTIONARY

CONTENTS

Hi, I'm Rick Steves.

I'm the only monolingual speaker I know who's had the nerve to design a series of European phrase books. But that's one of the things that makes them better.

You see, after more than 30 years of travel through Europe, I've learned firsthand: (1) what's essential for communication in another country, and (2) what's not. I've assembled the most important words and phrases in a logical, no-frills format, and I've worked with native Europeans and seasoned travelers to give you the simplest, clearest translations possible.

But this book is more than just a pocket translator. The words and phrases have been carefully selected to help you have a smarter, smoother trip in Spain without going broke. Spain used to be cheap and chaotic. These days it's neither. It's better organized than ever—and can be as expensive as France or Germany. The key to getting more out of every travel dollar is to get closer to the local people, and to rely less on entertainment, restaurants, and hotels that cater only to foreign tourists. This book will not only help you order a meal at a locals-only Sevilla restaurant—it will help you talk with the family who runs the place...about their kids, travel dreams, and favorite música. Long after your memories of museums had faded, you'll still treasure the personal encounters you had with your new Spanish friends.

A good phrase book should help you enjoy your travel experience—not just survive it—so I've added a healthy dose of humor. A few phrases are just for fun and aren't meant to be used at all. But most of the phrases are for real and should be used with "please" (*por favor*). I know you can tell the difference.

While I've provided plenty of phrases, you'll find it just as effective to use even just a word or two to convey your meaning, and rely on context, gestures, and smiles to help you out. To make harried postal clerks happy, don't say haltingly in Spanish: "I would like to buy three stamps to mail these postcards to the United States." All you really need is *sellos* (stamps), *Estados Unidos* (USA), *por favor* (please). Smile, point to the postcards, hold up three fingers...and you've got stamps. (For more advice, see Tips for Hurdling the Language Barrier on page 407.)

To get the most out of this book, take the time to practice my Spanish pronunciation tips. But don't worry too much about memorizing grammatical rules, like the gender of a noun—the important thing is to communicate!

This book has a nifty menu decoder and a handy dictionary. You'll also find tongue twisters, international words, telephone tips, and two handy "cheat sheets." Tear out the sheets and keep them in your pocket, so you can easily memorize key phrases during otherwise idle moments. As you prepare for your trip, you may want to read this year's edition of my *Rick Steves' Spain* guidebook.

While a number of Spanish people speak fine English, many don't. The language barrier can seem high in Spain, but locals are happy to give an extra boost to any traveler who makes an effort to communicate.

My goal is to help you become a more confident, extroverted traveler. If this phrase book helps make that happen, or if you have suggestions for making it better, I'd love to hear from you at rick@ricksteves.com. I value your feedback.

¡Buen viaje! Have a good trip!

Rick Steves

GETTING
STARTED

Spanish opens the door to the land of siestas and fiestas, fun and flamenco. Imported from the Old World throughout the New, Spanish is the most widely spoken Romance language in the world. With its straightforward pronunciation, Spanish is also one of the simplest languages to learn.

Here are some tips for pronouncing Spanish words:

C usually sounds like C in cat.
> But C followed by E or I sounds like the soft TH in think.

D sounds like the soft D in soda.

G usually sounds like G in go.
> But G followed by E or I sounds like the guttural
> J in Baja.

H is silent.

J sounds like the guttural J in Baja.

LL sounds like Y in yes.

Ñ sounds like NI in onion.

R is trrrilled.

V usually sounds like B in bit.

Z sounds like the soft TH in think.

Spanish vowels are pronounced like this:

A sounds like A in father.

E can sound like E in get or AY in play.

I sounds like EE in seed.

O sounds like O in note.

U sounds like OO in moon.

Spanish has a few unusual signs and sounds. The Spanish add extra punctuation to questions and exclamations, like this: *¿Cómo está?* (How are you?) *¡Fantástico!* (Fantastic!) You've probably seen and heard the Spanish *ñ:* Think of *señor* and *mañana*. Spanish has a guttural sound similar to the J in Baja California. In the phonetics, the symbol for this clearing-your-throat sound is the italicized *h*.

Spanish words that end in a consonant are stressed on the last syllable, as in **Madrid.** Words ending in a vowel are generally stressed on the second-to-last syllable, as in **amigo.** To override these rules, the Spanish sometimes add an accent mark to the syllable that should be stressed, like this: **rápido** (fast) is pronounced **rah**-pee-doh.

When you're speaking a Romance language, sex is unavoidable. Even the words are masculine or feminine, and word endings can change depending on gender. A man is **simpático** (friendly), a woman is **simpática.** In this book, we sometimes show bisexual words like this— **simpático[a]**—to remind you. If you're speaking of a woman (which includes women speaking about themselves), use the **a** ending. It's always pronounced "ah." If a word ends in **r,** just add an **a** to make it feminine. For instance, an **autor** is a male **author** while an **autora** is female. Words ending in **e,** such as **amable** (kind), apply to either sex.

The endings of Spanish nouns and adjectives agree. Cold weather is **tiempo frío,** and a cold shower is a **ducha fría.**

Plurals are a snap. Add **s** to a word that ends in a vowel, like **pueblo** (village) and **es** to a word that ends in a consonant, like **ciudad** (city). Visit a mix of **pueblos** and **ciudades** to get the full flavor of Spain.

In northern and central Spain, Spanish sounds as if it's spoken with a lisp. **Gracias** (thank you) sounds like **grah-thee-ahs.** As you head farther south, you'll notice a difference in pronunciation. In southern Spain, along the coast, people thpeak without the lisp: **Gracias** sounds like **grah**-see-ahs. Listen to and imitate the Spanish people around you.

You can communicate a lot with only a few key Spanish words: **hay, vale,** and **esto**. Here's how:

Hay (which is pronounced "eye" and means "There is") is a handy all-purpose word that can be used as a statement (**No hay problema,** No problem) or a question (**¿Hay cerveza?** Do you have beer?). In a tapas bar, you might see a sign that says **Hay caracoles** (We have snails).

Spaniards use the word **vale** (**bah**-lay, meaning "OK") all the time. When you're pleased about something, you can say **vale.** When the vendor at the market gives you just the right amount, say **vale.** It even works as a question: If you're not sure whether you're getting on the right train, show your ticket to the conductor and ask **¿Vale?**

When combined with pointing, *esto* (**eh**-stoh, meaning "this") conveys worlds of meaning. If you can't remember the word for what you want at the market, just point to it and say *esto* with a smile.

You'll often hear the Spanish say ***por favor*** (por fah-**bor**, meaning "please"). The Spanish are friendly, polite people. Please use ***por favor*** whenever you can.

Here's a quick guide to the phonetics used in this book:

ah	like A in father
ay	like AY in play
ee	like EE in seed
eh	like E in get
ehr	sounds like "air"
g	like G in go
h	like the guttural J in Baja
ī	like I in light
oh	like O in note
or	like OR in core
oo	like OO in moon
ow	like OW in now
oy	like OY in toy
s	like S in sun

SPANISH BASICS

Be creative! You can combine the phrases in this chapter to say: "Two, please," or "No, thank you," or "Open tomorrow?" or "Please, where can I buy a ticket?" "Please" is a magic word in any language. If you want to buy something, you can point at it and say, *Por favor* (Please). If you know the word for what you want, such as the bill, simply say *La cuenta, por favor* (The bill, please).

HELLOS AND GOODBYES

Pleasantries

Hello.	Hola. **oh**-lah
Do you speak English?	¿Habla usted inglés? **ah**-blah oo-**stehd** een-**glays**
Yes. / No.	Sí. / No. see / noh
I don't speak Spanish.	No hablo español. noh **ah**-bloh eh-spahn-**yohl**
I'm sorry.	Lo siento. loh see-**ehn**-toh
Please.	Por favor. por fah-**bor**
Thank you (very much).	(Muchas) gracias. (**moo**-chahs) **grah**-thee-ahs
Excuse me.	Perdone. pehr-**doh**-nay
OK?	¿Vale? **bah**-lay
OK. (two ways to say it)	Vale. / De acuerdo. **bah**-lay / day ah-**kwehr**-doh
Good.	Bien. bee-**ehn**
Very good.	Muy bien. **moo**-ee bee-**ehn**
Excellent.	Excelente. ehk-seh-**lehn**-tay
You are very kind.	Usted es muy amable. oo-**stehd** ehs **moo**-ee ah-**mah**-blay
It's (not) a problem.	(No) hay problema. (noh) ī proh-**bleh**-mah
It doesn't matter.	No importa. noh eem-**por**-tah

| You're welcome. | De nada. day **nah**-dah |
| Goodbye. | Adiós. ah-dee-**ohs** |

Meeting and Greeting

Hello.	Hola. **oh**-lah
Good morning.	Buenos días. **bweh**-nohs **dee**-ahs
Good afternoon / evening.	Buenas tardes. **bweh**-nahs **tar**-dehs
Good night.	Buenas noches. **bweh**-nahs **noh**-chehs
Welcome!	¡Bienvenido! bee-ehn-beh-**nee**-doh
Mr.	Señor sehn-**yor**
Mrs.	Señora sehn-**yoh**-rah
Miss	Señorita sehn-yoh-**ree**-tah
My name is ____.	Me llamo ____. may **yah**-moh ____
What's your name?	¿Cómo se llama? **koh**-moh say **yah**-mah
Pleased to meet you.	Mucho gusto. **moo**-choh **goo**-stoh
How are you?	¿Cómo está? **koh**-moh eh-**stah**
How's it going? (informal)	¿Qué tal? kay tahl
Very well, thank you.	Muy bien, gracias. **moo**-ee bee-**ehn grah**-thee-ahs
Fine, thanks.	Bien, gracias. bee-**ehn grah**-thee-ahs
And you?	¿Y usted? ee oo-**stehd**
Where are you from?	¿De dónde es usted? day **dohn**-day ehs oo-**stehd**
I am from ____.	Soy de ____. soy day ____
I am / We are...	Soy / Somos... soy / **soh**-mohs
Are you...?	¿Está usted...? eh-**stah** oo-**stehd**
...on vacation	...de vacaciones day bah-kah-thee-**oh**-nehs
...on business	...de negocios day neh-**goh**-thee-ohs

The greeting **buenas días** (good morning) switches to **buenas tardes** (good afternoon/evening) starting about 2:00 p.m. You won't hear **buenas noches** (good night) until around 10 p.m.

Moving On

I'm going to _____.	Voy a _____.	boy ah _____
How do I go to _____?	¿Cómo voy a _____?	**koh**-moh boy ah _____
Let's go!	¡Vamos! **bah**-mohs	
See you later!	¡Hasta luego! **ah**-stah loo-**eh**-goh	
See you tomorrow!	¡Hasta mañana! **ah**-stah mahn-**yah**-nah	
Goodbye.	Adiós. ah-dee-**ohs**	
Good luck!	¡Buena suerte! **bweh**-nah **swehr**-tay	
Happy travels!	¡Buen viaje! bwehn bee-**ah**-hay	

STRUGGLING WITH SPANISH

Who Speaks What?

Spanish	español eh-spahn-**yohl**
English	inglés een-**glays**
Do you speak English?	¿Habla usted inglés? **ah**-blah oo-**stehd** een-**glays**
A teeny weeny bit?	¿Ni un poquito? nee oon poh-**kee**-toh
Please speak English.	Hable en inglés, por favor. **ah**-blay ehn een-**glays** por fah-**bor**
Speak slowly, please.	Hable despacio, por favor. **ah**-blay dehs-**pah**-thee-oh por fah-**bor**
Repeat?	¿Repita? reh-**pee**-tah
I understand.	Comprendo. kohm-**prehn**-doh
I don't understand.	No comprendo. noh kohm-**prehn**-doh
Do you understand?	¿Comprende? kohm-**prehn**-day

You speak English well.	Usted habla bien el inglés. oo-**stehd ah**-blah bee-**ehn** ehl een-**glays**
Does somebody nearby speak English?	¿Hay alguien por aquí que hable inglés? ī **ahlg**-ee-ehn por ah-**kee** kay **ah**-blay een-**glays**
I don't speak Spanish.	No hablo español. noh **ah**-bloh eh-spahn-**yohl**
I speak a little Spanish.	Hablo un poco de español. **ah**-bloh oon **poh**-koh day eh-spahn-**yohl**
What does this mean?	¿Qué significa esto? kay seeg-**nee**-fee-kah **eh**-stoh
How do you say this in Spanish?	¿Cómo se dice esto en español? **koh**-moh say **dee**-thay **eh**-stoh ehn eh-spahn-**yohl**
Write it for me?	¿Me lo escribe? may loh eh-**skree**-bay

Strictly Spanish Expressions

Vale. **bah**-lay	OK. / That's good. / I understand. / Uh-huh.
Diga(me). ("Talk to me") **dee**-gah(-may)	Hello. (answering phone) / Can I help you?
Mira. **mee**-rah	Look.
¿De veras? /¿De verdad? day **behr**-ahs / day behr-**dahd**	Really?
¡Caray! kah-**rī**	Wow!
De nada. ("It's nothing") day **nah**-dah	You're welcome.
¡Salud! sah-**lood**	Cheers! / Bless you! (after sneeze)
No hay problema. noh ī proh-**bleh**-mah	No problem.

De acuerdo. day ah-**kwehr**-doh	OK.
A ver... ah behr	Let's see...
Pues... pwehs	Well...
O sea... oh **seh**-ah	I mean...
¡Qué lástima! kay **lah**-stee-mah	What a pity!
¡Qué pena! kay **peh**-nah	How embarrassing!
Así es la vida. ah-**see** ehs lah **bee**-dah	That's life.
Que será, será. kay seh-**rah** seh-**rah**	What will be, will be.
¡Preciosa! preh-thee-**oh**-sah	Precious!
¡Buena suerte! bweh-nah **swehr**-tay	Good luck!
Venga. **behn**-gah	Come on.
¡Vamos! **bah**-mohs	Let's go!

REQUESTS

The Essentials

Can you help me?	¿Puede ayudarme? **pweh**-day ī-yoo-**dar**-may
Do you have _____?	¿Tiene _____? tee-**ehn**-ay _____
I'd / We'd like...	Me / Nos gustaría... may / nohs goo-stah-**ree**-ah

...this / that.	...esto / eso. eh-stoh / eh-soh
How much does it cost?	¿Cuánto cuesta? kwahn-toh kweh-stah
Is it free?	¿Es gratis? ehs grah-tees
Is it included?	¿Está incluido? eh-stah een-kloo-ee-doh
Is it possible?	¿Es posible? ehs poh-see-blay
Yes or no?	¿Sí o no? see oh noh
Where are the toilets?	¿Dónde están los servicios? dohn-day eh-stahn lohs sehr-bee-thee-ohs
men	hombres / caballeros ohm-brehs / kah-bah-yehr-ohs
women	mujeres / damas moo-hehr-ehs / dah-mahs

To prompt a simple answer, ask ¿Sí o no? (Yes or no?). To turn a word or sentence into a question, ask it in a questioning tone. An easy way to ask "Where are the toilets?" is to say ¿Servicios? Toilets are marked servicios or aseos; you can also ask for the baño (bathroom).

Where?

Where?	¿Dónde? dohn-day
Where is the...?	¿Dónde está la...? dohn-day eh-stah lah
...tourist information office	...oficina de turismo oh-fee-thee-nah day too-rees-moh
...train station	...estación de trenes eh-stah-thee-ohn day trehn-ehs
Where is a cash machine?	¿Dónde hay un cajero automático? dohn-day ī oon kah-hehr-oh ow-toh-mah-tee-koh
Where can I buy _____?	¿Dónde puedo comprar _____? dohn-day pweh-doh kohm-prar _____
Where can I find _____?	¿Dónde puedo encontrar _____? dohn-day pweh-doh ehn-kohn-trar _____

Spanish makes it easy if you're looking for a *banco, farmacia, hotel, restaurante,* or *supermercado.*

How Much?

How much does it cost?	¿Cuánto cuesta? **kwahn**-toh **kweh**-stah
Write it for me?	¿Me lo escribe? may loh eh-**skree**-bay
I'd like...	Me gustaría... may goo-stah-**ree**-ah
...a ticket.	...un billete. oon bee-**yeh**-tay
...the bill.	...la cuenta. lah **kwehn**-tah
This much. (gesturing)	Así. ah-**see**
More. / Less.	Más. / Menos. mahs / **meh**-nohs
Too much.	Demasiado. deh-mah-see-**ah**-doh

When?

When?	¿Cuándo? **kwahn**-doh
What time is it?	¿Qué hora es? kay **oh**-rah ehs
At what time?	¿A qué hora? ah kay **oh**-rah
_____ o'clock	las / la _____ lahs / lah _____
open / closed	abierto / cerrado ah-bee-**ehr**-toh / thehr-**ah**-doh
What time does this open / close?	¿A qué hora abren / cierran? ah kay **oh**-rah **ah**-brehn / thee-**ehr**-ahn
Is this open daily?	¿Abren a diario? **ah**-brehn ah dee-**ah**-ree-oh
What day is this closed?	¿Qué día está cerrado? kay **dee**-ah eh-**stah** thehr-**ah**-doh
On time?	¿Puntual? poon-too-**ahl**
Late?	¿Tarde? **tar**-day
Just a moment.	Un momento. oon moh-**mehn**-toh

now / soon / later	ahora / pronto / más tarde
	ah-**oh**-rah / **prohn**-toh / mahs **tar**-day
today / tomorrow	hoy / mañana oy / mahn-**yah**-nah

For tips on telling time, see "Time and Dates" on page 31.

How Long?

How long does it take?	¿Cuánto tiempo lleva?
	kwahn-toh tee-**ehm**-poh **yeh**-bah
How many minutes / hours?	¿Cuántos minutos / horas?
	kwahn-tohs mee-**noo**-tohs / **oh**-rahs
How far?	¿A qué distancia?
	ah kay dees-**tahn**-thee-ah

Just Ask

Why?	¿Por qué? por kay
Why not?	¿Por qué no? por kay noh
Is it necessary?	¿Es necesario?
	ehs neh-theh-**sah**-ree-oh
Can I / Can we...?	¿Puedo / Podemos...?
	pweh-doh / poh-**deh**-mohs
...borrow that for a moment	...tomar prestado eso un momento
	toh-**mar** preh-**stah**-doh **eh**-soh oon moh-**mehn**-toh
...use the toilet	...usar el servicio
	oo-sar ehl sehr-**bee**-thee-oh
Next? (in line)	¿El siguiente? ehl seeg-ee-**ehn**-tay
The last? (in line)	¿El último? ehl **ool**-tee-moh
What? (didn't hear)	¿Cómo? **koh**-moh
What is this / that?	¿Qué es esto / eso?
	kay ehs **eh**-stoh / **eh**-soh
What's going on?	¿Qué pasa? kay **pah**-sah

SIMPLY IMPORTANT WORDS

Numbers

0	cero **thehr**-oh
1	uno **oo**-noh
2	dos dohs
3	tres trehs
4	cuatro **kwah**-troh
5	cinco **theen**-koh
6	seis says
7	siete see-**eh**-tay
8	ocho **oh**-choh
9	nueve **nweh**-bay
10	diez dee-**ehth**
11	once **ohn**-thay
12	doce **doh**-thay
13	trece **treh**-thay
14	catorce kah-**tor**-thay
15	quince **keen**-thay
16	dieciséis dee-eh-thee-**says**
17	diecisiete dee-eh-thee-see-**eh**-tay
18	dieciocho dee-eh-thee-**oh**-choh
19	diecinueve dee-eh-thee-**nweh**-bay
20	veinte **bayn**-tay

You'll find more to count on in the "Numbers" section (page 24).

The Alphabet

If you're spelling your name over the phone, you can use the nouns in the third column to help make yourself understood. I'd say my name as: *R...Ramón, I...Italia, C...Carlos, K...Kilo*.

A	ah	América	ah-**may**-ree-kah
B	bay	Barcelona	bar-theh-**loh**-nah
C	thay	Carlos	**kar**-lohs
D	day	Dinamarca	dee-nah-**mar**-kah
E	ay	España	eh-**spahn**-yah
F	**eh**-fay	Francia	**frahn**-thee-ah
G	hay	Gerona	heh-**roh**-nah
H	**ah**-chay	Holanda	oh-**lahn**-dah
I	ee	Italia	ee-**tahl**-yah
J	hoh-tah	Jota	**hoh**-tah
K	kah	Kilo	**kee**-loh
L	**ehl**-ay	Lola	**loh**-lah
M	**ehm**-ay	Madrid	mah-**dreed**
N	**eh**-nay	Noruega	nor-**weh**-gah
O	oh	Oslo	**oh**-sloh
P	pay	Portugal	por-too-**gahl**
Q	koo	Queso	**keh**-soh
R	**ehr**-ay	Ramón	rah-**mohn**
S	**ehs**-ay	Sevilla	seh-**vee**-yah
T	tay	Toledo	toh-**leh**-doh
U	oo	Uruguay	oo-roo-**gwī**
V	**oo**-bay	Valencia	bah-**lehn**-thee-ah
W	oo-bay-**doh**-blay	Washington	**wah**-sheeng-tohn
X	eh-**khees**	Equix	eh-**keeks**
Y	ee-gree-**yeh**-gah	Yoga	**yoh**-gah
Z	**theh**-tah	Zamora	thah-**moh**-rah

Days and Months

Sunday	domingo doh-**meen**-goh
Monday	lunes **loo**-nehs
Tuesday	martes **mar**-tehs
Wednesday	miércoles mee-**ehr**-koh-lehs
Thursday	jueves **hweh**-behs
Friday	viernes bee-**ehr**-nehs
Saturday	sábado **sah**-bah-doh
January	enero eh-**nehr**-oh
February	febrero feh-**brehr**-oh
March	marzo **mar**-thoh
April	abril ah-**breel**
May	mayo **mī**-oh
June	junio **hoo**-nee-oh
July	julio **hoo**-lee-oh
August	agosto ah-**goh**-stoh
September	septiembre sehp-tee-**ehm**-bray
October	octubre ohk-**too**-bray
November	noviembre noh-bee-**ehm**-bray
December	diciembre dee-thee-**ehm**-bray

Big Little Words

I	yo yoh
you (formal)	usted oo-**stehd**
you (informal)	tú too
we	nosotros noh-**soh**-trohs
he	él ehl
she	ella **ay**-yah
it (m / f; varies by gender of noun)	el / la ehl / lah
they (m / f)	ellos / ellas **ay**-yohs / **ay**-yahs

and	y ee
at	a ah
because	porque por-**kay**
but	pero **pehr**-oh
by (train, car, etc.)	en ehn
for	para / por **pah**-rah / por
from	de day
here	aquí ah-**kee**
if	si see
in	en ehn
it	ello **ay**-yoh
not	no noh
now	ahora ah-**oh**-rah
of	de day
only	solo **soh**-loh
or	o oh
out	fuera **fwehr**-ah
that	eso **eh**-soh
this	esto **eh**-stoh
to	a ah
too	también tahm-bee-**ehn**
very	muy **moo**-ee

Opposites

good / bad	bueno / malo **bweh**-noh / **mah**-loh
best / worst	mejor / peor meh-**hor** / peh-**or**
a little / a lot	un poco / mucho oon **poh**-koh / **moo**-choh
more / less	más / menos mahs / **meh**-nohs
cheap / expensive	barato / caro bah-**rah**-toh / **kah**-roh

big / small	grande / pequeño **grahn**-day / peh-**kehn**-yoh
hot / cold	caliente / frío kah-lee-**ehn**-tay / **free**-oh
warm / cool	cálido / fresco **kah**-lee-doh / **freh**-skoh
open / closed	abierto / cerrado ah-bee-**ehr**-toh / thehr-**ah**-doh
entrance / exit	entrada / salida ehn-**trah**-dah / sah-**lee**-dah
push / pull	empuje / tire ehm-**poo**-hay / **tee**-ray
arrive / depart	llegar / salir yeh-**gar** / sah-**leer**
early / late	temprano / tarde tehm-**prah**-noh / **tar**-day
soon / later	pronto / más tarde **prohn**-toh / mahs **tar**-day
fast / slow	rápido / despacio **rah**-pee-doh / dehs-**pah**-thee-oh
here / there	aquí / allí ah-**kee** / ī-**yee**
near / far	cerca / lejos **thehr**-kah / **leh**-hohs
inside / outside	dentro / fuera **dehn**-troh / **fwehr**-ah
mine / yours	mío / suyo **mee**-oh / **soo**-yoh
this / that	esto / eso **eh**-stoh / **eh**-soh
easy / difficult	fácil / difícil **fah**-theel / dee-**fee**-theel
left / right	izquierda / derecha eeth-kee-**ehr**-dah / dehr-**eh**-chah
up / down	arriba / abajo ah-**ree**-bah / ah-**bah**-hoh
above / below	encima / debajo en-**thee**-mah / deh-**bah**-hoh
young / old	joven / viejo **hoh**-behn / bee-**eh**-hoh
new / old	nuevo / viejo **nweh**-boh / bee-**eh**-hoh
heavy / light	pesado / ligero peh-**sah**-doh / lee-**hehr**-oh
dark / light	oscuro / claro oh-**skoo**-roh / **klah**-roh
happy / sad	feliz / triste feh-**leeth** / **tree**-stay

beautiful / ugly	bonito / feo boh-**nee**-toh / **feh**-oh
nice / mean	simpático/ antipático seem-**pah**-tee-koh / ahn-tee-**pah**-tee-koh
smart / stupid	listo / estúpido **lee**-stoh / eh-**stoo**-pee-doh
vacant / occupied	libre / ocupado **lee**-bray / oh-koo-**pah**-doh
with / without	con / sin kohn / seen

Remember that adjectives ending in *o*, like *listo*, are masculine. If you're describing a female, swap the *o* for an *a*. A smart man is *listo*, while a smart woman is *lista*. Some adjectives don't change with the gender. A man or a woman can be *triste* or *feliz*.

SIGN LANGUAGE
Here are common signs you'll see in your travels.

Abierto	Open
Abierto de ____ a ____	Open from ____ to ____
Acceso libre	Free entry
Agua no potable	Undrinkable water
Agua potable	Drinkable water
Alarma de incendio	Fire alarm
Alquilo / Se alquila	For rent
Aseos	Toilets
Bajo su propia responsabilidad	At your own risk
Baños	Bathrooms
Caballeros	Gentlemen (men's room)
Cajero	Cashier
Camas	Vacancy ("beds")
Cambio exacto	Exact change
Centro (de la ciudad)	(Town) Center
Cerrado	Closed
Cerrado por obras	Closed for restoration
Cerrado por vacaciones	Closed for vacation

Coja su turno / número	Take a number
Completo	No vacancy
Cruce escolar	School crossing
Cuidado	Caution
Cuidado con el escalón	Watch your step
Damas	Ladies (women's room)
Dirección única	One-way street
Disculpen las molestias	Forgive the inconvenience
Disponible aquí	Available here
Emergencia	Emergency
Empujar	Push
En caso de emergencia	In case of emergency
En caso de emergencia no usar	Do not use in case of emergency
En venta aquí	Sold here
En venta / Se vende	For sale
Entrada	Entrance
Entrada libre	Free admission
Espere	Wait
Espere aquí por favor	Please wait here
Espere verde	Wait for green light (after pressing button at crosswalk)
Fuera de servicio	Out of service
Habitaciones	Vacancy ("rooms")
Horario	Schedule / Timetable / Opening times
Llamada urgente	Emergency call
Llegadas	Arrivals
Mediodía	Midday / Lunch break
Nivel	Level
(No) aceptamos tarjetas de crédito	We (do not) accept credit cards
No devuelve cambio	No change given (at a machine)
No fumar	No smoking
No molesten	Do not disturb
No pasar	No entry
No tocar	Don't touch
Ocupado	Occupied
Oferta	Sale / Special offer

Oficina de turismo	Tourist information office
Paso prohibido	No trespassing
Peatón, pulse	Pedestrian, press (button to change light)
Peligro	Danger
Perro peligroso	Mean dog
Planta	Floor
Prohibido	Forbidden
Prohibido aparcar	No parking
Reservado	Reserved
Salida	Exit
Salida de emergencia	Emergency exit
Salidas	Departures
Señoras	Women (women's room)
Señores	Men (men's room)
Servicios	Toilets
Sólo personal autorizado	Authorized personnel only
Taquilla	Ticket desk
Tenemos...	We have...
Tengan cuidado	Be careful
Tirar	Pull
Validar aquí	Validate here
Zona peatonal	Pedestrian zone

In addresses, *calle* (street) can be abbreviated as *c/*, and *paseo* (lane) is *P°*.

NUMBERS, MONEY & TIME

Y ou can count on this chapter to cover Spanish numbers, currency, credit and debit cards, time, dates, and major holidays and celebrations.

NUMBERS

0	cero **thehr**-oh
1	uno **oo**-noh
2	dos dohs
3	tres trehs
4	cuatro **kwah**-troh
5	cinco **theen**-koh
6	seis says
7	siete see-**eh**-tay
8	ocho **oh**-choh
9	nueve **nweh**-bay
10	diez dee-**ehth**
11	once **ohn**-thay
12	doce **doh**-thay
13	trece **treh**-thay
14	catorce kah-**tor**-thay
15	quince **keen**-thay
16	dieciséis dee-eh-thee-**says**
17	diecisiete dee-eh-thee-see-**eh**-tay
18	dieciocho dee-eh-thee-**oh**-choh
19	diecinueve dee-eh-thee-**nweh**-bay
20	veinte **bayn**-tay
21	veintiuno bayn-tee-**oo**-noh
22	veintidós bayn-tee-**dohs**
23	veintitrés bayn-tee-**trehs**
30	treinta **trayn**-tah
31	treinta y uno **trayn**-tah ee **oo**-noh
40	cuarenta kwah-**rehn**-tah

41	cuarenta y uno kwah-**rehn**-tah ee **oo**-noh
50	cincuenta theen-**kwehn**-tah
60	sesenta seh-**sehn**-tah
70	setenta seh-**tehn**-tah
80	ochenta oh-**chehn**-tah
90	noventa noh-**behn**-tah
100	cien thee-**ehn**
101	ciento uno thee-**ehn**-toh **oo**-noh
102	ciento dos thee-**ehn**-toh dohs
200	doscientos dohs-thee-**ehn**-tohs
300	trescientos treh-thee-**ehn**-tohs
400	cuatrocientos kwah-troh-thee-**ehn**-tohs
500	quinientos kee-nee-**ehn**-tohs
600	seiscientos says-thee-**ehn**-tohs
700	setecientos seh-teh-thee-**ehn**-tohs
800	ochocientos oh-choh-thee-**ehn**-tohs
900	novecientos noh-beh-thee-**ehn**-tohs
1000	mil meel
2000	dos mil dohs meel
2010	dos mil diez dohs meel dee-**ehth**
2011	dos mil once dohs meel **ohn**-thay
2012	dos mil doce dohs meel **doh**-thay
2013	dos mil trece dohs meel **treh**-thay
2014	dos mil catorce dohs meel kah-**tor**-thay
2015	dos mil quince dohs meel **keen**-thay
2016	dos mil dieciséis dohs meel dee-eh-thee-**says**
2017	dos mil diecisiete dohs meel dee-eh-thee-see-**eh**-tay
2018	dos mil dieciocho dohs meel dee-eh-thee-**oh**-choh

2019	dos mil diecinueve dohs meel dee-eh-thee-**nweh**-bay
2020	dos mil veinte dohs meel **bayn**-tay
million	millón mee-**yohn**
billion	mil millones meel mee-**yoh**-nehs
number one	número uno **noo**-mehr-oh **oo**-noh
first	primero pree-**mehr**-oh
second	segundo seh-**goon**-doh
third	tercero tehr-**thehr**-oh
once	una vez **oo**-nah behth
twice	dos veces dohs **beh**-thehs
a quarter	un cuarto oon **kwar**-toh
a third	un tercio oon **tehr**-thee-oh
half	mitad mee-**tahd**
this much	esta cantidad **eh**-stah kahn-tee-**dahd**
a dozen	una docena **oo**-nah doh-**theh**-nah
a handful	un puñado oon poon-**yah**-doh
enough	bastante bah-**stahn**-tay
not enough	no lo suficiente noh loh soo-fee-thee-**ehn**-tay
too much	demasiado deh-mah-see-**ah**-doh
more	más mahs
less	menos **meh**-nohs
50%	cincuenta por ciento theen-**kwehn**-tah por thee-**ehn**-toh
100%	cien por ciento thee-**ehn** por thee-**ehn**-toh

Learning how to say your hotel room number is a good way to practice Spanish numbers. You'll likely be asked for the number frequently (at breakfast, or to claim your key when you return to the room).

MONEY

Spain uses the euro currency. One euro (€) is divided into 100 cents (*céntimos*). When saying prices, Spaniards start with the number of euros, followed by *con* (with) and the number of cents—so €2.50 is *dos con cincuenta* ("two with fifty").

Use your common cents—cents are like pennies, and the euro has coins like nickels, dimes, and half-dollars. There are also €1 and €2 coins.

Cash Machines (ATMs)

Every cash machine has multilingual instructions. However, the keys might be marked in Spanish: *confirmar* means confirm, *continuar* or *anotación* is enter, *corregir* means change or correct, *cancelar* is cancel, and *borrar* means erase.

money	dinero dee-**nehr**-oh
cash	efectivo eh-fehk-**tee**-boh
card	tarjeta tar-**heh**-tah
PIN code	clave / número secreto / PIN **klah**-bay / **noo**-mehr-oh seh-**kreh**-toh / peen
Where is a...?	¿Dónde hay un...? **dohn**-day ī oon
...cash machine	...cajero automático kah-**hehr**-oh ow-toh-**mah**-tee-koh
...bank	...banco **bahn**-koh
My debit card has been...	Mi tarjeta de débito ha sido... mee tar-**heh**-tah day **day**-bee-toh ah **see**-doh
...demagnetized.	...desmagnetizada. dehs-mahg-neh-tee-**thah**-dah
...stolen.	...robada. roh-**bah**-dah
...eaten by the machine.	...tragada por el cajero. trah-**gah**-dah por ehl kah-**hehr**-oh
My card doesn't work.	Mi tarjeta no funciona. mee tar-**heh**-tah noh foon-thee-**oh**-nah

Key Phrases: Money

euro(s) (€)	euro(s) **yoo**-roh(s)
cent(s)	céntimo(s) **thehn**-tee-moh(s)
cash	efectivo eh-fehk-**tee**-boh
Where is a...?	¿Dónde hay un...? **dohn**-day ī oon
...**cash machine**	...cajero automático kah-**hehr**-oh ow-toh-**mah**-tee-koh
...**bank**	...banco **bahn**-koh
credit card	tarjeta de crédito tar-**heh**-tah day **kray**-dee-toh
debit card	tarjeta de débito tar-**heh**-tah day **day**-bee-toh
Do you accept credit cards?	¿Se aceptan tarjetas de crédito? say ah-**thehp**-tahn tar-**heh**-tahs day **kray**-dee-toh

Credit and Debit Cards

Credit cards are widely accepted at larger businesses, though smaller shops, restaurants, and hotels might prefer cash. Even if they accept credit cards, some hotels might cut you a discount for paying cash.

credit card	tarjeta de crédito tar-**heh**-tah day **kray**-dee-toh
debit card	tarjeta de débito tar-**heh**-tah day **day**-bee-toh
receipt	recibo / ticket reh-**thee**-boh / tee-**keht**
sign	firmar feer-**mar**
pay	pagar pah-**gar**
cashier	cajero kah-**hehr**-oh
cash advance	adelanto de dinero ah-deh-**lahn**-toh day dee-**nehr**-oh

Do you accept credit cards?	¿Se aceptan tarjetas de crédito? say ah-**thehp**-tahn tar-**heh**-tahs day **kray**-dee-toh
Cheaper if I pay cash?	¿Es más barato si pago en efectivo? ehs mahs bah-**rah**-toh see **pah**-goh ehn eh-fehk-**tee**-boh
I do not have a PIN.	No tengo un número secreto / PIN. noh **tehn**-goh oon **noo**-mehr-oh seh-**kreh**-toh / peen
Can I sign a receipt instead of entering the PIN?	¿Puedo firmar el recibo en vez de entrar el PIN? **pweh**-doh feer-**mar** ehl reh-**thee**-boh ehn behth day ehn-**trar** ehl peen
Print a receipt?	¿Imprime un recibo? eem-**pree**-may oon reh-**thee**-boh
I have another card.	Tengo otra tarjeta. **tehn**-goh **oh**-trah tar-**heh**-tah

Much of Europe is adopting a "chip-and-PIN" system. These credit cards are embedded with an electronic chip and require a PIN for authorization. If an automated payment machine won't take your card, look for a cashier who can swipe it instead, or find a machine that takes cash.

Paying with a Credit Card

If calling to reserve tickets or a hotel room, you may need to convey your credit-card information over the phone. Prepare in advance: To fill in the blanks, use the numbers, alphabet, and months on pages 14-16, and the years on pages 25-26.

| The name on the card is ____. | El nombre en la tarjeta es ____.
ehl **nohm**-bray ehn lah tar-**heh**-tah ehs ____ |
| The credit card number is ____. | El número de la tarjeta de crédito es ____.
ehl **noo**-mehr-oh day lah tar-**heh**-tah day **kray**-dee-toh ehs ____ |

| The expiration date is _____. | La fecha de caducidad es _____.
lah **feh**-chah day kah-doo-thee-**dahd** ehs _____ |
| The secret code (on the back) is _____. | El código secreto es _____.
ehl **koh**-dee-goh seh-**kreh**-toh ehs _____ |

Exchanging Money

exchange	cambio **kahm**-bee-oh
change money	cambiar dinero kahm-bee-**ar** dee-**nehr**-oh
exchange rate	tipo de cambio tee-**poh** day **kahm**-bee-oh
dollar(s)	dólar(es) **doh**-lar(-ays)
traveler's check	cheque de viajero **cheh**-kay day bee-ah-**hehr**-oh
buy / sell	comprar / vender kohm-**prar** / behn-**dehr**
commission	comisión koh-mee-see-**ohn**
Any extra fee?	¿Tienen alguna tasa extra? tee-**ehn**-ehn ahl-**goo**-nah **tah**-sah **ehk**-strah
I would like...	Me gustaría... may goo-stah-**ree**-ah
...small bills.	...billetes pequeños. bee-**yeh**-tehs peh-**kehn**-yohs
...large bills.	...billetes grandes. bee-**yeh**-tehs **grahn**-dehs
...a mix of small and large bills.	...algunos billetes grandes y otros pequeños. ahl-goo-**nohs** bee-**yeh**-tehs **grahn**-dehs ee **oh**-trohs peh-**kehn**-yohs
...coins.	...monedas. moh-**neh**-dahs

Can you break this? **(big bills into smaller** **bills)**	¿Me puede dar cambio más pequeño? may **pweh**-day dar **kahm**-bee-oh mahs peh-**kehn**-yoh
Is this a mistake?	¿Es esto un error? ehs **eh**-stoh oon eh-**ror**
This is incorrect.	Es incorrecto. ehs een-koh-**rehk**-toh
Where is the nearest **casino?**	¿Dónde está el casino más cercano? **dohn**-day eh-**stah** ehl kah-**see**-noh mahs thehr-**kah**-noh

Banks are generally open from about 9:00 to 2:00 Monday through Friday.

TIME AND DATES

Telling Time

In Spain, the 24-hour clock (or "military time") is used for setting formal appointments (for instance, arrival times at a hotel), for the opening and closing hours of museums and shops, and for train, bus, and boat schedules. Informally, the Spanish use the same 12-hour clock we do. So they might meet a friend at 3:00 *de la tarde* (in the afternoon), but catch a train at 15:15.

What time is it?	¿Qué hora es? kay **oh**-rah ehs
_____ o'clock	las / la _____ lahs / lah _____
(in the) morning	(de la) mañana (day lah) mahn-**yah**-nah
(in the) afternoon	(de la) tarde (day lah) **tar**-day
(in the) evening	(de la) noche (day lah) **noh**-chay
(at) night	(por la) noche (por lah) **noh**-chay
half	media **meh**-dee-ah
quarter	cuarto **kwar**-toh
minute	minuto mee-**noo**-toh
hour	hora **oh**-rah

Key Phrases: Time and Dates

What time is it?	¿Qué hora es?	kay **oh**-rah ehs
_____ o'clock	las / la _____	lahs / lah _____
minute	minuto	mee-**noo**-toh
hour	hora	**oh**-rah
It's 1:00.	Es la una.	ehs lah **oo**-nah
It's...	Son las...	sohn lahs
...7:00 in the morning.	...siete de la mañana.	see-**eh**-tay day lah mahn-**yah**-nah
...2:00 in the afternoon.	...dos de la tarde.	dohs day lah **tar**-day
At what time does this open / close?	¿A qué hora abren / cierran?	ah kay **oh**-rah **ah**-brehn / thee-**ehr**-ahn
day	día	**dee**-ah
today	hoy	oy
tomorrow	mañana	mahn-**yah**-nah
(this) week	(esta) semana	(**eh**-stah) seh-**mah**-nah
August 21	el veintiuno de agosto	ehl bayn-tee-**oo**-noh day ah-**goh**-stoh

It's... / At...	Son las... / A las...	sohn lahs / ah lahs
...8:00 in the morning.	...ocho de la mañana.	**oh**-choh day lah mahn-**yah**-nah
...4:00 in the afternoon.	...cuatro de la tarde.	**kwah**-troh day lah **tar**-day
...10:30 in the evening.	...diez y media de la noche.	dee-**ehth** ee **meh**-dee-ah day lah **noh**-chay
...a quarter past nine.	...nueve y cuarto.	**nweh**-bay ee **kwar**-toh
...a quarter to eleven.	...once menos cuarto.	**ohn**-thay **meh**-nohs **kwar**-toh

at 6:00 sharp	a las seis en punto ah lahs says ehn **poon**-toh
from 8:00 to 10:00	de ocho a diez day **oh**-choh ah dee-**ehth**
noon	mediodía meh-dee-oh-**dee**-ah
midnight	doce de la noche / medianoche **doh**-thay day lah **noh**-chay / meh-dee-ah-**noh**-chay
It's my bedtime.	Es la hora de acostarme. ehs lah **oh**-rah day ah-koh-**star**-may
I'll return / We'll return at 11:20.	Volveré / Volveremos a las once y veinte. bohl-beh-**ray** / bohl-beh-**reh**-mohs ah lahs **ohn**-thay ee **bayn**-tay
I'll arrive / We'll arrive by 6 o'clock.	Llegaré / Llegaremos antes de las seis de la tarde. yeh-gah-**ray** / yeh-gah-**reh**-mohs **ahn**-tehs day lahs says day lah **tar**-day

Timely Questions

When?	¿Cuándo? **kwahn**-doh
At what time?	¿A qué hora? ah kay **oh**-rah
opening time	hora de apertura **oh**-rah day ah-pehr-**too**-rah
At what time does this open / close?	¿A qué hora abren / cierran? ah kay **oh**-rah **ah**-brehn / thee-**ehr**-ahn
Is the train...?	¿Va el tren...? bah ehl trehn
Is the bus...?	¿Va el autobús...? bah ehl ow-toh-**boos**
...early	...adelantado ah-deh-lahn-**tah**-doh
...late	...con retraso kohn reh-**trah**-soh
...on time	...puntual poon-too-**ahl**
When is check-out time?	¿Cuándo es la hora de salida? **kwahn**-doh ehs lah **oh**-rah day sah-**lee**-dah

It's About Time

now	ahora ah-**oh**-rah
soon	pronto **prohn**-toh
later	más tarde mahs **tar**-day
in one hour	en una hora ehn **oo**-nah **oh**-rah
in half an hour	en media hora ehn **meh**-dee-ah **oh**-rah
in three hours	en tres horas ehn trehs **oh**-rahs
early	temprano tehm-**prah**-noh
late	tarde tar-**day**
on time	a tiempo ah tee-**ehm**-poh
anytime	a cualquier hora ah kwahl-kee-**ehr oh**-rah
immediately	inmediatamente ee-meh-dee-ah-tah-**mehn**-tay
every hour	cada hora **kah**-dah **oh**-rah
every day	cada día **kah**-dah **dee**-ah
daily	diario dee-**ah**-ree-oh
last	último[a] **ool**-tee-moh
this	esto **eh**-stoh
next	próxima **prohk**-see-mah
before	antes **ahn**-tehs
after	después dehs-**pwehs**
May 15	el quince de mayo ehl **keen**-thay day **mī**-oh
in the future	en el futuro ehn ehl foo-**too**-roh
in the past	en el pasado ehn ehl pah-**sah**-doh

The Day

day	día **dee**-ah
today	hoy oy
sunrise	amanecer ah-mah-neh-**thehr**

this morning	esta mañana **eh**-stah mahn-**yah**-nah
sunset	puesta de sol **pweh**-stah day sohl
tonight	esta noche **eh**-stah **noh**-chay
yesterday	ayer ah-**yehr**
tomorrow	mañana mahn-**yah**-nah
tomorrow morning	mañana por la mañana mahn-**yah**-nah por lah mahn-**yah**-nah
day after tomorrow	pasado mañana pah-**sah**-doh mahn-**yah**-nah

The wee hours of the morning are called *la madrugada*. It makes sense that the Spanish—who make use of this time—have a special word for it. Young people going out to party *(ir de marcha)* stay out *hasta la madrugada* (until the wee hours).

The Week

Sunday	domingo doh-**meen**-goh
Monday	lunes **loo**-nehs
Tuesday	martes **mar**-tehs
Wednesday	miércoles mee-**ehr**-koh-lehs
Thursday	jueves **hweh**-behs
Friday	viernes bee-**ehr**-nehs
Saturday	sábado **sah**-bah-doh
week	semana seh-**mah**-nah
last week	la semana pasada lah seh-**mah**-nah pah-**sah**-dah
this week	esta semana **eh**-stah seh-**mah**-nah
next week	la semana próxima lah seh-**mah**-nah **prohk**-see-mah
weekend	fin de semana feen day seh-**mah**-nah
this weekend	este fin de semana **eh**-stay feen day seh-**mah**-nah

The Months

month	mes mehs
January	enero eh-**nehr**-oh
February	febrero feh-**brehr**-oh
March	marzo **mar**-thoh
April	abril ah-**breel**
May	mayo **mī**-oh
June	junio **hoo**-nee-oh
July	julio **hoo**-lee-oh
August	agosto ah-**goh**-stoh
September	septiembre sehp-tee-**ehm**-bray
October	octubre ohk-**too**-bray
November	noviembre noh-bee-**ehm**-bray
December	diciembre dee-thee-**ehm**-bray

For dates, say **el** _____ [number] **de** _____ [month]. So the fourth of July is **el cuatro de julio**.

The Year

year	año **ahn**-yoh
season	temporada tehm-poh-**rah**-dah
spring	primavera pree-mah-**behr**-ah
summer	verano behr-**ah**-noh
fall	otoño oh-**tohn**-yoh
winter	invierno een-bee-**ehr**-noh

For a list of years, see the "Numbers" section, earlier.

Holidays and Happy Days

holiday	día festivo **dee**-ah feh-**stee**-boh
festival	festival feh-stee-**bahl**

Is today / tomorrow a holiday?	¿Es hoy / mañana un día festivo? ehs oy / mahn-**yah**-nah oon **dee**-ah feh-**stee**-boh
Is a holiday coming up soon?	¿Hay alguna fiesta pronto? ī ahl-**goo**-nah fee-**eh**-stah **prohn**-toh
When?	¿Cuándo? **kwahn**-doh
What is the holiday?	¿Qué fiesta es? kay fee-**eh**-stah ehs
Mardi Gras / Carnival	Martes de Carnaval / Carnaval **mar**-tehs day kar-nah-**bahl** / kar-nah-**bahl**
Holy Week	Semana Santa seh-**mah**-nah **sahn**-tah
Easter	Pascuas **pahs**-kwahs
April Fair (Sevilla)	Feria de Abril **feh**-ree-ah day ah-**breel**
May 1 / Labor Day	Uno de Mayo / Día del Trabajo **oo**-noh day **mī**-oh / **dee**-ah dehl trah-**bah**-hoh
Ascension	Ascensión ah-thehn-see-**ohn**
Pentecost	Pentecostés pehn-teh-kohs-**tays**
Corpus Christi	Corpus Christi kor-**poos kree**-stee
Running of the Bulls (July 6-14)	El Encierro / Fiesta de San Fermín ehl ehn-thee-**ehr**-oh / fee-**eh**-stah day sahn fehr-**meen**
Assumption (Aug 15)	Asunción de Maria ah-soon-thee-**ohn** day mah-**ree**-ah
Spanish National Day (Oct 12)	Día de la Hispanidad **dee**-ah day lah ees-pah-nee-**dahd**
All Saints' Day (Nov 1)	Día de Todos los Santos **dee**-ah day **toh**-dohs lohs **sahn**-tohs
Christmas Eve	Noche Buena **noh**-chay **bweh**-nah
Christmas	Navidad nah-bee-**dahd**
Merry Christmas!	¡Feliz Navidad! feh-**leeth** nah-bee-**dahd**
New Year's Eve	Noche Vieja **noh**-chay bee-**eh**-hah

New Year's Day	Día de Año Nuevo **dee**-ah day **ahn**-yoh **nweh**-boh
Happy New Year!	¡Feliz Año Nuevo! feh-**leeth ahn**-yoh **nweh**-boh
anniversary	aniversario ah-nee-behr-**sah**-ree-oh
Happy anniversary!	¡Feliz aniversario! feh-**leeth** ah-nee-behr-**sah**-ree-oh
birthday	cumpleaños koom-pleh-**ahn**-yohs
Happy birthday!	¡Feliz cumpleaños! feh-**leeth** koom-pleh-**ahn**-yohs

The Spanish sing "Happy Birthday" to the same tune we do, but they don't fill in the person's name. Here are the words: *Cumpleaños feliz, cumpleaños feliz, te deseamos todos cumpleaños, cumpleaños feliz.*

TRANSPORTATION

T his chapter includes the phrases you'll need for buying transit tickets and getting around by train, bus, subway, taxi, rental car, and foot—plus some handy route-finding phrases.

GETTING AROUND

train	tren trehn
city bus	autobús ow-toh-**boos**
long-distance bus	autocar ow-toh-**kar**
subway	metro **meh**-troh
taxi	taxi **tahk**-see
car	coche **koh**-chay
walk / by foot	caminar / a pie kah-mee-**nar** / ah pee-**ay**
Where is the...?	¿Dónde está el / la...? **dohn**-day eh-**stah** ehl / lah
...train station	...estación de tren eh-stah-thee-**ohn** day trehn
...bus station	...estación de autobuses eh-stah-thee-**ohn** day ow-toh-**boo**-sehs
...bus stop	...parada de autobús pah-**rah**-dah day ow-toh-**boos**
...subway station	...estación de metro eh-stah-thee-**ohn** day **meh**-troh
...taxi stand	...parada de taxi pah-**rah**-dah day **tahk**-see
I'm going / We're going to _____.	Voy / Vamos a _____. boy / **bah**-mohs ah _____
What is the cheapest / fastest / easiest way...?	¿Cuál es la manera más barata / rápida / fácil...? kwahl ehs lah mah-**neh**-rah mahs bah-**rah**-tah / **rah**-pee-dah / **fah**-theel
...to downtown	...al centro ahl **thehn**-troh

...to the train station	...a la estación de tren ah lah eh-stah-thee-**ohn** day trehn
...to my / our hotel	...a mi / nuestro hotel ah mee / **nweh**-stroh oh-**tehl**
...to the airport	...al aeropuerto ahl ah-eh-roh-**pwehr**-toh

TRAINS

For tips and strategies about rail travel and railpasses in Spain, see www
.ricksteves.com/rail. Note that many of the following train phrases work
for long-distance bus travel as well.

Ticket Basics

ticket	billete bee-**yeh**-tay
reservation	reserva reh-**sehr**-bah
ticket office	oficina de venta oh-fee-**thee**-nah day **behn**-tah
ticket machine	venta automática **behn**-tah ow-toh-**mah**-tee-kah
validate	validar bah-lee-**dar**
Where can I buy a ticket?	¿Dónde puedo comprar un billete? **dohn**-day **pweh**-doh kohm-**prar** oon bee-**yeh**-tay
Is this the line for...?	¿Es ésta la fila para...? ehs **eh**-stah lah **fee**-lah **pah**-rah
...tickets	...billetes bee-**yeh**-tehs
...reservations	...reservas reh-**sehr**-bahs
...information	...información een-for-mah-thee-**ohn**
One ticket (to _____).	Un billete (para _____). oon bee-**yeh**-tay (**pah**-rah _____)
Two tickets.	Dos billetes. dohs bee-**yeh**-tehs

Getting Tickets

When it comes to buying tickets for the bus, train, or subway, the following phrases will come in handy.

Where can I buy a ticket?	¿Dónde puedo comprar un billete? **dohn**-day **pweh**-doh kohm-**prar** oon bee-**yeh**-tay
How much (is a ticket to _____)?	¿Cuánto cuesta (el billete para _____)? **kwahn**-toh **kweh**-stah (ehl bee-**yeh**-tay **pah**-rah _____)
I want to go to _____.	Quiero ir a _____. kee-**ehr**-oh eer ah _____
One ticket / Two tickets (to _____).	Un billete / Dos billetes (para _____). oon bee-**yeh**-tay / dohs bee-**yeh**-tehs (**pah**-rah _____)
When is the next train / bus (to _____)?	¿Cuándo es el siguiente tren / autocar (a _____)? **kwahn**-doh ehs ehl seeg-ee-**ehn**-tay trehn / ow-toh-**kar** (ah _____)
What time does it leave?	¿A qué hora sale? ah kay **oh**-rah **sah**-lay
Is it direct?	¿Es directo? ehs dee-**rehk**-toh
Is a reservation required?	¿Se requiere reserva? say reh-kee-**ehr**-ay reh-**sehr**-bah
I'd / We'd like to reserve a seat.	Me / Nos gustaría reservar un asiento. may / nohs goo-stah-**ree**-ah reh-sehr-**bar**
Can I buy a ticket on board?	¿Puedo comprar el billete a bordo? **pweh**-doh kohm-**prar** ehl bee-**yeh**-tay ah **bor**-doh
Exact change only?	¿Cambio exacto? **kahm**-bee-oh ehk-**sahk**-toh

I want to go to ____.	Quiero ir a ____.
	kee-**ehr**-oh eer ah ____
How much (is a ticket to ____)?	¿Cuánto cuesta (el billete para ____)?
	kwahn-toh **kweh**-stah (ehl bee-**yeh**-tay **pah**-rah ____)
one-way	de ida day **ee**-dah
round-trip	de ida y vuelta day **ee**-dah ee **bwehl**-tah
today / tomorrow	hoy / mañana oy / mahn-**yah**-nah

Ticket Specifics

As trains and buses can sell out, it's smart to buy your tickets a day in advance even for short rides. For phrases related to discounts (such as children, families, or seniors), see page 46.

schedule	horario oh-**rah**-ree-oh
When is the next train / bus (to ____)?	¿Cuándo es el siguiente tren / autocar (a ____)?
	kwahn-doh ehs ehl seeg-ee-**ehn**-tay trehn / ow-toh-**kar** (ah ____)
What time does it leave?	¿A qué hora sale?
	ah kay **oh**-rah **sah**-lay
I'd / We'd like to leave...	Me / Nos gustaría salir...
	may / nohs goo-stah-**ree**-ah sah-**leer**
I'd / We'd like to arrive...	Me / Nos gustaría llegar...
	may / nohs goo-stah-**ree**-ah yeh-**gar**
...by ____ o'clock.	...antes de las ____.
	ahn-tehs day lahs ____
...at ____ o'clock...	..a las ____ ... ah lahs ____
...in the morning / afternoon / evening.	...por la mañana / tarde / noche.
	por lah mahn-**yah**-nah / **tar**-day / **noh**-chay

Is there a... train / bus?	¿Hay un tren / autocar...? T oon trehn / ow-toh-**kar**
...earlier	...más temprano mahs tehm-**prah**-noh
...later	...más tarde mahs **tar**-day
...overnight	...nocturno nohk-**toor**-noh
...cheaper	...más barato mahs bah-**rah**-toh
...express	...expreso ehk-**spreh**-soh
...direct	...directo dee-**rehk**-toh
Is it direct?	¿Es directo? ehs dee-**rehk**-toh
Is a transfer required?	¿Se requiere un transbordo? say reh-kee-**ehr**-ay oon trahns-**bor**-doh
How many transfers?	¿Cuantas conexiones? **kwahn**-tahs koh-nehk-see-**oh**-nehs
When? Where?	¿Cuándo? ¿Dónde? **kwahn**-doh / **dohn**-day
first / second class	primera / segunda clase pree-**mehr**-ah / seh-**goon**-dah **klah**-say
How long is this ticket valid?	¿Cuándo vence este billete? **kwahn**-doh **behn**-thay **eh**-stay bee-**yeh**-tay
Can you validate my railpass?	¿Puede validar el abono de tren? **pweh**-day bah-lee-**dar** ehl ah-**boh**-noh day trehn

Many large Spanish train stations have two sections—for suburban *cercanías* trains and for high-speed trains (such as *AVE*). Once you're in the right section, survey the different ticket lines or windows (marked *venta de billetes*). For example, you might see *salidas hoy* (departures today) and *salidas otros días* (departures other days). If you're not sure, ask fellow passengers by mentioning your destination and day: *Barcelona, mañana?* If you have to take a number, the *su turno* (your turn) board tells you the *número* (number) and *puesto* (desk to report to) currently being served. Since train-station ticket offices can get crowded, you may find it easier to go to a local travel agency or book online (www.renfe.es).

Train Reservations

For some long-distance trains, seat reservations *(reservas)* are required and included in the fare; these are optional for other trains. Those that require reservations are noted with an Ⓡ in the schedule. (If you're using a railpass, you must pay an extra *suplemento* to reserve.)

Is a reservation required?	¿Se requiere reserva? say reh-kee-**ehr**-ay reh-**sehr**-bah
I'd / We'd like to reserve...	Me / Nos gustaría reservar... may / nohs goo-stah-**ree**-ah reh-sehr-**bar**
...a seat.	...un asiento. oon ah-see-**ehn**-toh
...an aisle seat.	...un asiento de pasillo. oon ah-see-**ehn**-toh day pah-**see**-yoh
...a window seat.	...un asiento de ventana. oon ah-see-**ehn**-toh day behn-**tah**-nah
...two seats.	...dos asientos. dohs ah-see-**ehn**-tohs
...a couchette (sleeping berth).	...una litera. **oo**-nah lee-**teh**-rah
...an upper / middle / lower berth.	...una litera alta / media / baja. **oo**-nah lee-**teh**-rah **ahl**-tah / **meh**-dee-ah / **bah**-hah
...two couchettes.	...dos literas. dohs lee-**teh**-rahs
...a sleeper (with two beds).	...un coche cama (con dos camas). oon **koh**-chay **kah**-mah (kohn dohs **kah**-mahs)
...the entire train.	...todo el tren. **toh**-doh ehl trehn

For certain high-speed trains, the fare depends on demand. The peak time *(hora punta)* is most expensive, followed by *llano* ("flat") and *valle* ("valley," the quietest and cheapest time).

Discounts

Is there a cheaper option?	¿Hay una opción más barata? Ī **oo**-nah ohp-thee-**ohn** mahs bah-**rah**-tah
discount	descuento dehs-**kwehn**-toh
reduced fare	tarifa reducida tah-**ree**-fah reh-doo-**thee**-dah
refund	devolución deh-boh-loo-thee-**ohn**
Is there a discount for...?	¿Hay un descuento para...? Ī oon dehs-**kwehn**-toh **pah**-rah
...**children**	...niños **neen**-yohs
...**youths**	...jóvenes **hoh**-beh-nehs
...**seniors**	...jubilados hoo-bee-**lah**-dohs
...**families**	...familias fah-**mee**-lee-ahs
...**groups**	...grupos **groo**-pohs
...**advance purchase**	...reserva anticipada reh-**sehr**-bah ahn-tee-thee-**pah**-dah
...**weekends**	...fin de semana feen day seh-**mah**-nah
Are there any deals for this journey?	¿Hay alguna oferta para este viaje? Ī ahl-**goo**-nah oh-**fehr**-tah **pah**-rah **eh**-stay bee-**ah**-hay

At the Train Station

Where is...?	¿Dónde está...? **dohn**-day eh-**stah**
...**the train station**	...la estación de tren lah eh-stah-thee-**ohn** day trehn
train information	información de trenes een-for-mah-thee-**ohn** day **treh**-nehs
customer service	atención al cliente / información ah-tehn-thee-**ohn** ahl klee-**ehn**-tay / een-for-mah-thee-**ohn**
tickets	billetes bee-**yeh**-tehs

Key Phrases: Trains

train station	estación de tren eh-stah-thee-**ohn** day trehn
train	tren trehn
platform	andén ahn-**dehn**
track	vía **bee**-ah
What track does it leave from?	¿Desde qué andén sale? **dehs**-day kay ahn-**dehn sah**-lay
Is this the train to _____?	¿Es éste el tren a _____? ehs **eh**-stay ehl trehn ah _____
Which train to _____?	¿Cuál tren para _____? kwahl trehn **pah**-rah _____
Tell me when to get off?	¿Me dice cuándo bajar? may **dee**-thay **kwahn**-doh bah-**har**
transfer	transbordo trahns-**bor**-doh
Change here for _____?	¿Se hace transbordo aquí para _____? say ah-**thay** trahns-**bor**-doh ah-**kee pah**-rah _____

(time of) departure / arrival	(hora de) salida / llegada (**oh**-rah day) sah-**lee**-dah / yeh-**gah**-dah
On time?	¿Puntual? poon-too-**ahl**
Late?	¿Tarde? **tar**-day
How late?	¿Con cuánto retraso? kohn **kwahn**-toh reh-**trah**-soh
platform	andén ahn-**dehn**
track	vía **bee**-ah
What track does it leave from?	¿Desde qué andén sale? **dehs**-day kay ahn-**dehn sah**-lay
waiting room	sala de espera / área de espera **sah**-lah day eh-**spehr**-ah / **ah**-reh-ah day eh-**spehr**-ah

(VIP) lounge	sala (VIP) **sah**-lah (beep)
lockers	taquillas tah-**kee**-yahs
baggage check	consigna kohn-**seeg**-nah
tourist info office	oficina de turismo oh-fee-**thee**-nah day too-**rees**-moh
lost and found office	oficina de objetos perdidos oh-fee-**thee**-nah day ohb-**heh**-tohs pehr-**dee**-dohs
toilets	servicios / aseos sehr-**bee**-thee-ohs / ah-**seh**-ohs

Most trains in Spain (which run mainly on the plain) are operated by the national rail company, **RENFE** (**rehn**-fay). The generic word for railway is *ferrocarril*. Types of trains are named for the distance they travel. *Cercanías* make short runs into the suburbs; *regionales* go to adjoining provinces. To go farther, you'll take a long-distance train (*larga distancia* or *largo recorrido*)—many of these are speedy, including the *AVE (Alta Velocidad Española), Altaria, Avant,* and *Talgo.*

Train and Bus Schedules

European timetables use the 24-hour clock. It's like American time until noon. After that, subtract twelve and add p.m. For example, 13:00 is 1 p.m., and 19:00 is 7 p.m.

To ask for a schedule at an information window, say *Horario para _____, por favor* (Schedule for _____ [city], please). On train schedules or at stations, you'll see these words:

hora	time
destino	destination
tren	train number
vía / andén	track / platform
observaciones	remarks

The ***observaciones*** often list the type of train you're taking (for example, ***AVE***), with notes on its status, such as ***salida inmediata*** (departs immediately), ***con parada en*** _____ (with a stop in _____), ***con retraso*** (delayed), or ***suprimido*** (canceled).

Here are common scheduling terms:

a	to
andén	platform
aviso (cambios)	advisory (listing changes)
cada _____ min	every _____ minutes
clase	class
coche	car
con parada en _____	with a stop in _____
con retraso	late
dársena	bus stall or platform
de	from
destino	destination
diario	daily
días	days
días laborables	weekdays (Mon-Fri)
directo	direct
domingo	Sunday
excepto	except
fecha	date
festivo	holiday
funciona	operates
hasta	until
hora	time
hora de salida	departure time
horas	hours
llegada	arrival
minutos	minutes
no	not
no efectua parada en todas las estaciones	does not make every stop
parada	stop
plaza	seat / place
por	via
próxima salida	next departure

retraso	delay
sábado	Saturday
sale (v)	leaves
salida	departure
salidas inmediatas	immediate departures
sólo	only
suprimido (sup.)	canceled
también	too
tipo de tren	type of train
todos	every
va (v)	goes
vía	track number; also via (by way of)

On schedules, **LMXJVSD** stands for the days of the week in Spanish, starting with Monday (see page 35 for a list). A train that runs **LMXJV-D** doesn't run on Saturdays. Days of the week are sometimes listed by number: for example, **1-5, 6, 7** corresponds to "Monday-Friday, Saturday, Sunday."

All Aboard

To find the platforms, look for signs: **a los andenes** or **acceso a las vías**. While the terms **andén** (platform) and **vía** (track) can be used interchangeably, at larger stations one **andén** can have access to two different **vías** (one on each side). At some major train stations, you'll need to show your ticket to reach the platform (look for the sign **acceso con billete,** access with a ticket). You may also have to go through **control de equipajes** (airport-like baggage security check).

platform	andén ahn-**dehn**
track	vía **bee**-ah
number	número **noo**-mehr-oh
train car	vagón / coche bah-**gohn** / **koh**-chay
conductor	conductor kohn-dook-**tor**
Is this the train to _____?	¿Es éste el tren a _____? ehs **eh**-stay ehl trehn ah _____

Which train to _____?	¿Cuál tren para _____?
	kwahl trehn **pah**-rah _____
Which train car to _____?	¿Cuál vagón para _____?
	kwahl bah-**gohn pah**-rah _____
Where is...?	¿Dónde está.....? **dohn**-day eh-**stah**
Is this...?	¿Es éste...? ehs **eh**-stay
...my seat	...mi asiento mee ah-see-**ehn**-toh
...first / second class	...primera / segunda clase
	pree-**mehr**-ah / seh-**goon**-dah **klah**-say
...the dining car	...el coche comedor
	ehl **koh**-chay koh-meh-**dor**
...the sleeper car	...el coche cama
	ehl **koh**-chay **kah**-mah
...the toilet	...el servicio / aseo
	ehl sehr-**bee**-thee-oh / ah-**seh**-oh
front / middle / back	frente / centro / detrás
	frehn-tay / **thehn**-troh / deh-**trahs**
reserved / occupied / free	reservado / ocupado / libre
	reh-sehr-**bah**-doh / oh-koo-**pah**-doh / **lee**-bray
aisle / window	pasillo / ventana
	pah-**see**-yoh / behn-**tah**-nah
Is this (seat) free?	¿Está libre (el asiento)?
	eh-**stah lee**-bray (ehl ah-see-**ehn**-toh)
May I / May we...?	¿Puedo / Podemos...?
	pweh-doh / poh-**deh**-mohs
...sit here	...sentarme / sentarnos aquí
	sehn-**tar**-may / sehn-**tar**-nohs ah-**kee**
...open the window	...abrir la ventana
	ah-**breer** lah behn-**tah**-nah
...eat here	...comer aquí koh-**mehr** ah-**kee**
...eat your meal	...comer su comida
	koh-**mehr** soo koh-**mee**-dah

(I think) that's my seat.	(Yo creo) ése es mi asiento. (yoh **kray**-oh) **eh**-say ehs mee ah-see-**ehn**-toh
These are our seats.	Éstos son nuestros asientos. **eh**-stohs sohn **nweh**-strohs ah-see-**ehn**-tohs
Save my place?	¿Me guarda mi asiento? may **gwar**-dah mee ah-see-**ehn**-toh
Save our places?	¿Nos guarda nuestros asientos? nohs **gwar**-dah **nweh**-strohs ah-see-**ehn**-tohs
Where are you going?	¿A dónde va? ah **dohn**-day bah
I'm going / We're going to _____.	Voy / Vamos a _____. boy / **bah**-mohs ah _____
Does this train stop in _____?	¿Para el tren en _____? **pah**-rah ehl trehn ehn _____
When will it arrive (in _____)?	¿Cuándo llegará (en _____)? **kwahn**-doh yeh-gah-**rah** (ehn _____)
Where is a (handsome) conductor?	¿Dónde hay un conductor (guapo)? **dohn**-day ī oon kohn-dook-**tor** (**gwah**-poh)
Tell me when to get off?	¿Me dice cuándo bajar? may **dee**-thay **kwahn**-doh bah-**har**
I'm getting off.	Me bajo aquí. may **bah**-hoh ah-**kee**
How do I open the door?	¿Cómo abro la puerta? **koh**-moh **ah**-broh lah **pwehr**-tah

As you approach a station on the train, you'll hear an announcement such as *Dentro de algunos minutos, llegaremos a Madrid* (In a few minutes, we will arrive in Madrid).

Changing Trains

Change here for _____?	¿Se hace transbordo aquí para _____? say ah-**thay** trahns-**bor**-doh ah-**kee** **pah**-rah _____
Where does one change for _____?	¿Dónde hay que hacer el transbordo para _____? **dohn**-day ī kay ah-**thehr** ehl trahns-**bor**-doh **pah**-rah _____
At what time?	¿A qué hora? ah kay **oh**-rah
From what track does the connecting train leave?	¿De qué vía sale el tren de conexión? day kay **bee**-ah **sah**-lay ehl trehn day koh-nehk-see-**ohn**
How many minutes in _____ (to change trains)?	¿Cuántos minutos hay que esperar en _____ (para cambiar de tren)? **kwahn**-tohs mee-**noo**-tohs ī kay eh-spehr-**ar** ehn _____ (**pah**-rah kahm-bee-**ar** day trehn)

Strikes

If a strike is pending, hoteliers and travel agencies can tell you when it will go into effect and which trains will continue to run.

strike	huelga **wehl**-gah
Is there a strike now?	¿Hay huelga ahora? ī **wehl**-gah ah-**oh**-rah
Only for today?	¿Solo hoy? **soh**-loh oy
Tomorrow, too?	¿Mañana también? mahn-**yah**-nah tahm-bee-**ehn**
Are there some trains today?	¿Salen algunos trenes hoy? **sah**-lehn ahl-**goo**-nohs **treh**-nehs oy
I'm going to _____.	Voy a _____. boy ah _____

LONG-DISTANCE BUSES

In Spain, buses can connect many smaller towns better and cheaper than trains. In general, a city bus is called an *autobús,* while a bus that makes longer runs (or is used for bus tours) is called an *autocar.* Many big cities have at least one *intercambiador*—a mega-station serving both long-distance buses and public transit. Remember that many phrases that apply to train travel can be used for bus travel as well. For ticket-buying help, see page 42.

long-distance bus	autocar	ow-toh-**kar**
bus station	estación de autobuses	eh-stah-thee-**ohn** day ow-toh-**boo**-sehs
bus terminal	terminal de autobuses	tehr-mee-**nahl** day ow-toh-**boo**-sehs
stall / platform	dársena	**dar**-seh-nah

Buses are described with the same terms as trains *(cercanías, regional, largo recorrido)*—see page 41. *Interurbano* buses take you between towns in the region. On bus schedules, the fastest buses are labeled *pista* or *autopista* and take the expressway. The next fastest are *directa,* which are quicker than buses noted as *semidirecta* or *ruta.* Major intermediate stops may be noted in the schedule: *con parada en _____* (with a stop in _____). For more tips on interpreting schedules, see page 48.

CITY BUSES AND SUBWAYS

Ticket Talk

Most big cities offer deals on transportation, such as one-day tickets, cheaper fares for youths and seniors, or a discount for buying a batch of tickets (which you can share with friends). For more discount-related terms, see page 46.

Where can I buy a ticket?	¿Dónde puedo comprar un billete? **dohn**-day **pweh**-doh kohm-**prar** oon bee-**yeh**-tay

Key Phrases: City Buses and Subways

bus	autobús ow-toh-**boos**
subway	metro **meh**-troh
How do I get to _____?	¿Cómo llego a _____? **koh**-moh **yeh**-goh ah _____
Which stop for _____?	¿Qué parada para _____? kay pah-**rah**-dah **pah**-rah _____
Tell me when to get off?	¿Me dice cuándo bajar? may **dee**-thay **kwahn**-doh bah-**har**

I want to go to _____.	Quiero ir a _____. kee-**ehr**-oh eer ah _____
How much (is a ticket to _____)?	¿Cuánto cuesta (el billete para _____)? **kwahn**-toh **kweh**-stah (ehl bee-**yeh**-tay **pah**-rah _____)
single (trip)	(viaje) sencillo (bee-**ah**-hay) sehn-**thee**-yoh
short-ride ticket	billete sencillo bee-**yeh**-tay sehn-**thee**-yoh
day ticket	abono / billete para todo el día ah-**boh**-noh / bee-**yeh**-tay **pah**-rah **toh**-doh ehl **dee**-ah
Is this ticket valid (for _____)?	¿Es este billete válido (para _____)? ehs **eh**-stay bee-**yeh**-tay **bah**-lee-doh (**pah**-rah _____)
Is there a...?	¿Hay un...? ī oon
...day pass	...pase para todo el día **pah**-say **pah**-rah **toh**-doh ehl **dee**-ah
...discount if I buy more tickets	...descuento si compro más billetes dehs-**kwehn**-toh see **kohm**-proh mahs bee-**yeh**-tehs

Can I buy a ticket on board the bus?	¿Puedo comprar el billete a bordo el autobús?
	pweh-doh kohm-**prar** ehl bee-**yeh**-tay ah **bor**-doh ehl ow-toh-**boos**
Exact change only?	¿Cambio exacto?
	kahm-bee-oh ehk-**sahk**-toh
validate (here)	validar (aquí)
	bah-lee-**dar** (ah-**kee**)

In many cities, you are required to *validar* (validate) your ticket by sticking it into a validation machine as you enter the subway station, bus, or tram. If you have an all-day or multi-day ticket, validate it only the first time you use it.

Transit Terms

Big cities can have various types of public transit, including *metro* (subway) and *autobús* (bus). For basic ticket-buying terms, see page 42.

city bus	autobús ow-toh-**boos**
bus stop	parada de autobús
	pah-**rah**-dah day ow-toh-**boos**
bus map	plano del autobús
	plah-noh dehl ow-toh-**boos**
subway	metro **meh**-troh
subway station	estación de metro
	eh-stah-thee-**ohn** day **meh**-troh
subway map	plano del metro **plah**-noh dehl **meh**-troh
subway entrance	entrada al metro
	ehn-**trah**-dah ahl **meh**-troh
subway stop	parada de metro
	pah-**rah**-dah day **meh**-troh
exit	salida sah-**lee**-dah
line	línea **lee**-neh-ah
direction	dirección dee-rehk-thee-**ohn**

direct	directo dee-**rehk**-toh
connection	conexión koh-nehk-see-**ohn**
public transit network map	un plano de transporte público oon **plah**-noh day trahn-**spor**-tay **poo**-blee-koh
pickpocket	carterista kar-teh-**ree**-stah

After inserting your ticket into the turnstile and passing through, don't forget to reclaim your ticket *(no olvide retirar su billete)*. At the platform, there may be a sign overhead that tells you that the *próximo tren llegará en ____ min* (the next train arrives in ____ minutes).

Public Transit

How do I / we get to ____?	¿Cómo llego / llegamos a ____? **koh**-moh **yeh**-goh / yeh-**gah**-mohs ah ____
Which bus to ____?	¿Cuál autobús para ____? kwahl ow-toh-**boos** pah-rah ____
Does it stop at ____?	¿Tiene parada en ____? tee-**ehn**-ay pah-**rah**-dah ehn ____
Which bus stop for ____?	¿Dónde bajo para ____? **dohn**-day **bah**-hoh pah-rah ____
Which subway stop for ____?	¿Cuál parada de metro para ____? kwahl pah-**rah**-dah day **meh**-troh **pah**-rah ____
Which direction for____?	¿En qué dirección para ____? ehn kay dee-rehk-thee-**ohn pah**-rah ____
Is a transfer required?	¿Se requiere un transbordo? say reh-kee-**ehr**-ay oon trahns-**bor**-doh
When is the...?	¿Cuándo es el...? **kwahn**-doh ehs ehl
...first / next / last...	...primero / siguiente / último... pree-**mehr**-oh / seeg-ee-**ehn**-tay / **ool**-tee-moh
...bus / subway	...autobús / metro ow-toh-**boos** / **meh**-troh

How often does it run (per hour / day)?	¿Con qué frecuencia sale (por hora / día)? kohn kay freh-**kwehn**-thee-ah **sah**-lay (por **oh**-rah / **dee**-ah)
When does the next one leave?	¿Cuándo sale el siguiente? **kwahn**-doh **sah**-lay ehl seeg-ee-**ehn**-tay
Where does it leave from?	¿Desde dónde sale? **dehs**-day **dohn**-day **sah**-lay
Tell me when to get off?	¿Me dice cuándo bajar? may **dee**-thay **kwahn**-doh bah-**har**
I'm getting off.	Me bajo aquí. may **bah**-hoh ah-**kee**
How do I open the door?	¿Cómo abro la puerta? **koh**-moh **ah**-broh lah **pwehr**-tah

On some trains, an electronic board and a voice both announce the next station *(próxima estación)*. If you press the button to request a stop on a bus or tram, a sign lights up that says *parada solicitada* (stop requested). Upon arrival, you might have to press a button or pull a lever to open the door *(abrir la puerta)*—watch locals and imitate.

TAXIS

Taxis are generally affordable, efficient, and worth considering. They usually take up to four people. If you have trouble flagging down a taxi, ask for directions to a *parada de taxi* (taxi stand) or seek out a big hotel where they're waiting for guests. The simplest way to tell a cabbie where you want to go is by stating your destination followed by "please" *(El Prado, por favor)*. Tipping isn't expected, but it's polite to round up—if the fare is €19, round up to €20.

Getting a Taxi

Taxi!	¡Taxi! **tahk**-see
Can you call a taxi?	¿Puede llamarme un taxi? **pweh**-day yah-**mar**-may oon **tahk**-see
Where can I get a taxi?	¿Dónde puedo coger un taxi? **dohn**-day **pweh**-doh koh-**hehr** oon **tahk**-see

Key Phrases: Taxis

Taxi!	¡Taxi! **tahk**-see
taxi stand	parada de taxi pah-**rah**-dah day **tahk**-see
Are you free?	¿Está libre? eh-**stah** lee-bray
Occupied.	Ocupado. oh-koo-**pah**-doh
To ____, please.	A ____, por favor. ah ____ por fah-**bor**
The meter, please.	El taxímetro, por favor. ehl tahk-**see**-meh-troh por fah-**bor**
Stop here.	Pare aquí. **pah**-ray ah-**kee**
My change, please.	Mi cambio, por favor. mee **kahm**-bee-oh por fah-**bor**
Keep the change.	Quédese con el cambio. **kay**-deh-say kohn ehl **kahm**-bee-oh

Where is a taxi stand?	¿Dónde está una parada de taxi? **dohn**-day eh-**stah oo**-nah pah-**rah**-dah day **tahk**-see
Are you free?	¿Está libre? eh-**stah** lee-bray
Occupied.	Ocupado. oh-koo-**pah**-doh
To ____, please.	A ____, por favor. ah ____ por fah-**bor**
To this address.	A esta dirección. ah **eh**-stah dee-rehk-thee-**ohn**
Approximately how much does it cost to go...?	¿Cuánto cuesta más o menos para ir...? **kwahn**-toh **kweh**-stah mahs oh **meh**-nohs **pah**-rah eer
...to ____	...a ____ ah ____
...to the airport	...al aeropuerto ahl ah-eh-roh-**pwehr**-toh
...to the train station	...a la estación de tren ah lah eh-stah-thee-**ohn** day trehn

...to this address	...a esta dirección
	ah **eh**-stah dee-rehk-thee-**ohn**
Is there an extra supplement?	¿Hay un suplemento extra?
	ī oon soo-pleh-**mehn**-toh **ehk**-strah
Too much.	Demasiado. deh-mah-see-**ah**-doh
Can you take _____ people?	¿Puede llevar _____ personas?
	pweh-day yeh-**bar** _____ pehr-**soh**-nahs
Any extra fee?	¿Hay una tasa extra?
	ī **oo**-nah **tah**-sah **ehk**-strah
Do you have an hourly rate?	¿Tiene una tarifa por hora?
	tee-**ehn**-ay oo-nah tah-**ree**-fah por **oh**-rah
How much for a one-hour city tour?	¿Cuánto cuesta una excursión de una hora por la ciudad?
	kwahn-toh **kweh**-stah **oo**-nah ehk-skoor-see-**ohn** day **oo**-nah **oh**-rah por lah thee-oo-**dahd**

Before hopping in a taxi, it's smart to ask *¿Cuánto cuesta más o menos para ir a _____?* (Approximately how much does it cost to go to _____?).

Cabbie Conversation

The meter, please.	El taxímetro, por favor.
	ehl tahk-**see**-meh-troh por fah-**bor**
Where is the meter?	¿Dónde está el taxímetro?
	dohn-day eh-**stah** ehl tahk-**see**-meh-troh
I'm / We're in a hurry.	Tengo / Tenemos prisa.
	tehn-goh / teh-**neh**-mohs **pree**-sah
Slow down.	Más despacio. mahs deh-**spah**-thee-oh
If you don't slow down, I'll throw up.	Si no va más despacio, voy a vomitar.
	see noh bah mahs dehs-**pah**-thee-oh boy ah boh-mee-**tar**
(To the) left.	(A la) izquierda.
	(ah lah) eeth-kee-**ehr**-dah

(To the) right.	(A la) derecha. (ah lah) deh-**reh**-chah
Straight ahead.	Recto. **rehk**-toh
Please stop here...	Por favor pare aquí.... por fah-**bor** pah-ray ah-**kee**
...for a moment.	...un momento. oon moh-**mehn**-toh
...for ____ minutes.	...durante ____ minutos. doo-**rahn**-tay ____ mee-**noo**-tohs
Can you wait?	¿Puede esperar? **pweh**-day eh-spehr-**ar**
Crazy traffic, isn't it?	Un tráfico de locos, ¿no? oon **trah**-fee-koh day **loh**-kohs noh
You drive like a madman!	¡Usted conduce como un loco! oo-**stehd** kohn-**doo**-thay **koh**-moh oon **loh**-koh
You drive very well.	Usted conduce muy bien. oo-**stehd** kohn-**doo**-thay **moo**-ee bee-**ehn**
I can see it from here.	Lo veo desde aquí. loh **beh**-oh **dehs**-day ah-**kee**
Point it out?	¿Me lo señala? may loh sehn-**yah**-lah
Stop here.	Pare aquí. **pah**-ray ah-**kee**
Here is fine.	Aquí está bien. ah-**kee** eh-**stah** bee-**ehn**
At this corner.	En ésta esquina. ehn **eh**-stah eh-**skee**-nah
The next corner.	En la esquina siguiente. ehn lah eh-**skee**-nah seeg-ee-**ehn**-tay
My change, please.	Mi cambio, por favor. mee **kahm**-bee-oh por fah-**bor**
Keep the change.	Quédese con el cambio. **kay**-deh-say kohn ehl **kahm**-bee-oh
This ride is / was more fun than Disneyland.	Este recorrido es / fue más divertido que Disneylandia. **eh**-stay reh-koh-**ree**-doh ehs / fweh mahs dee-behr-**tee**-doh kay deez-neh-**lahn**-dee-ah

DRIVING

Renting Wheels

I'd like to rent a...	Me gustaría alquilar un / una... may goo-stah-**ree**-ah ahl-kee-**lar** oon / **oo**-nah
...car.	...coche. **koh**-chay
...station wagon.	...coche familiar. **koh**-chay fah-mee-lee-**ar**
...van.	...furgoneta. foor-goh-**neh**-tah
...convertible.	...coche descapotable. **koh**-chay dehs-kah-poh-**tah**-blay
...motorcycle.	...moto. **moh**-toh
...motor scooter.	...motocicleta. moh-toh-thee-**kleh**-tah
How much per...?	¿Cuánto es por...? **kwahn**-toh ehs por
...hour	...hora **oh**-rah
...(half) day	...(medio) día (**meh**-dee-oh) **dee**-ah
...week	...semana seh-**mah**-nah
car rental agency	oficina de alquiler de coches oh-fee-**thee**-nah day ahl-kee-**lehr** day **koh**-chehs
tax / insurance	IVA / seguro **ee**-bah / seh-**goo**-roh
Includes taxes and insurance?	¿Incluye el IVA y el seguro? een-**kloo**-yay ehl **ee**-bah ee ehl seh-**goo**-roh
Any extra fee?	¿Tienen alguna tasa extra? tee-**ehn**-ehn ahl-**goo**-nah **tah**-sah **ehk**-strah
Unlimited mileage?	¿Sin límite de kilómetros? seen **lee**-mee-tay day kee-**loh**-meh-trohs
manual / automatic (transmission)	manual / automático (transmisión) mah-noo-**ahl** / ow-toh-**mah**-tee-koh (trahns-mee-see-**ohn**)

Key Phrases: Driving

car	coche **koh**-chay
gas station	gasolinera gah-soh-lee-**neh**-rah
parking lot	aparcamiento ah-par-kah-mee-**ehn**-toh
Where can I park?	¿Dónde puedo aparcar? **dohn**-day **pweh**-doh ah-par-**kar**
downtown	centro ciudad **thehn**-troh thee-oo-**dahd**
straight ahead	recto / derecho **rehk**-toh / deh-**reh**-choh
left	izquierda eeth-kee-**ehr**-dah
right	derecha deh-**reh**-chah
I'm lost.	Estoy perdido[a]. **eh**-stoy pehr-**dee**-doh
How do I get to _____?	¿Cómo llego a _____? **koh**-moh **yeh**-goh ah _____

pick up / drop off	recoger / devolver reh-koh-**hehr** / deh-bohl-**behr**
Is there...?	¿Hay...? ī
...a discount	...un descuento oon dehs-**kwehn**-toh
...a deposit	...un depósito oon deh-**poh**-see-toh
...a helmet	...un casco oon **kah**-skoh
When must I bring it back?	¿Cuándo tengo que traerlo de vuelta? **kwahn**-doh **tehn**-goh kay trah-**ehr**-loh day **bwehl**-tah
Can I drop it off in another city / in _____?	¿Puedo devolverlo en otra ciudad / en _____? **pweh**-doh deh-bohl-**behr**-loh ehn **oh**-trah thee-oo-**dahd** / ehn _____
How do I get to the expressway / to _____?	¿Cómo voy a la autopista / a _____? **koh**-moh boy ah lah ow-toh-**pee**-stah / ah _____

Before leaving the car-rental office, get directions to your next destination—or at least to the expressway. For all the details on the dizzying variety of insurance options, see www.ricksteves.com/cdw. If you'd rather rent a bike, see page 202.

Getting to Know Your Rental Car

Before driving off, familiarize yourself with your rental car. Examine it to be sure that all damage is already noted on the rental agreement so you won't be held responsible for it later.

It's damaged here.	Está dañado aquí. eh-**stah** dahn-**yah**-doh ah-**kee**
Add it to the rental agreement, please.	Añádalo al contrato de alquiler, por favor. ahn-**yah**-dah-loh ahl kohn-**trah**-toh day ahl-kee-**lehr** por fah-**bor**
The scratch / dent was already here.	La raya / abolladura ya estaba antes. lah **rī**-yah / ah-boy-yah-**doo**-rah yah eh-**stah**-bah **ahn**-tehs
What kind of gas does it take?	¿Qué tipo de gasolina usa? kay **tee**-poh day gah-soh-**lee**-nah **oo**-sah
gas	gasolina gah-soh-**lee**-nah
diesel	diesel / gasóleo **dee**-sehl / gah-**soh**-lee-oh
How do I open the gas cap?	¿Cómo se abre el depósito de gas? **koh**-moh say **ah**-bray ehl deh-**poh**-see-toh day gahs
How does this work?	¿Cómo funciona? **koh**-moh foon-thee-**oh**-nah
key	llave **yah**-bay
headlights	los faros lohs **fah**-rohs
radio	la radio lah **rah**-dee-oh
windshield wipers	los llmpiaparabrisas lohs leem-pee-ah-pah-rah-**bree**-sahs

alarm / security system	la alarma / el sistema de seguridad
	lah ah-**lar**-mah / ehl see-**steh**-mah day seh-goo-ree-**dahd**
How do I turn off the security system?	¿Cómo apago el sistema de seguridad?
	koh-moh ah-**pah**-goh ehl see-**steh**-mah day seh-goo-ree-**dahd**
GPS	GPS *hay* pay **ehs**-ay
How do I change the language to English?	¿Cómo lo cambio al inglés?
	koh-moh loh **kahm**-bee-oh ahl een-**glays**

Sometimes you can rent a GPS device with your car. The language for the menus and instructions can be changed to English.

Traffic Troubles

traffic	tráfico **trah**-fee-koh
traffic jam	atasco ah-**tah**-skoh
rush hour	hora punta **oh**-rah **poon**-tah
delay	retraso reh-**trah**-soh
construction	obras **oh**-brahs
accident	accidente ahk-thee-**dehn**-tay
detour	desvío dehs-**bee**-oh
How long is the delay?	¿Cuánto retraso hay?
	kwahn-toh reh-**trah**-soh ī
Is there another way to go (to _____)?	¿Hay otra manera de ir (a _____)?
	ī **oh**-trah mah-**neh**-rah day eer (ah _____)

For more navigational words, see "Finding Your Way" on page 71.

Tolls

Expressways (*autovías*) come with tolls, but save huge amounts of time. You'll usually pick up a ticket as you enter a toll road and pay when you leave, but sometimes you'll pay up front for a fixed length of road.

toll road	carretera de peaje
	kah-reh-**teh**-rah day peh-**ah**-hay
toll	peaje peh-**ah**-hay
tollbooth	cabina de peaje
	kah-**bee**-nah day peh-**ah**-hay
toll ticket	el ticket del peaje
	ehl tee-**keht** dehl peh-**ah**-hay
cash / card	en efectivo / con tarjeta
	ehn eh-fehk-**tee**-boh / kohn tar-**heh**-tah
to pay	pagar pah-**gar**

At the Gas Station

Unleaded is *sin plomo* (which can be *regular* or *super*), and in parts of Spain, diesel is *gasóleo*. Gas prices are listed per liter, and there are about four liters in a gallon.

gas station	gasolinera gah-soh-lee-**neh**-rah
The nearest gas station?	¿La gasolinera más cercana?
	lah gah-soh-lee-**neh**-rah mahs
	thehr-**kah**-nah
Self-service?	¿Autoservicio? ow-toh-sehr-**bee**-thee-oh
Fill the tank.	Llene el depósito.
	yeh-nay ehl deh-**poh**-see-toh
I need...	Necesito... neh-theh-**see**-toh
...gas.	...gasolina. gah-soh-**lee**-nah
...unleaded.	...sin plomo. seen **ploh**-moh
...regular.	...normal. nor-**mahl**
...super.	...súper. **soo**-pehr
...diesel.	...diesel / gasóleo.
	dee-sehl / gah-**soh**-lee-oh

Parking

parking lot	aparcamiento ah-par-kah-**mee**-ehn-toh
parking garage	parking / garaje **par**-keeng / gah-**rah**-hay
a parking space	un sitio para aparcar oon **seet**-yoh **pah**-rah ah-par-**kar**
ticket machine	máquina de pago **mah**-kee-nah day **pah**-goh
parking meter	parquímetro par-**kee**-meh-troh
available / full	libre / completo lee-**bray** / kohm-**pleh**-toh
Where can I park?	¿Dónde puedo aparcar? **dohn**-day **pweh**-doh ah-par-**kar**
Is parking nearby?	¿Hay un parking cercano? Ī oon **par**-keeng thehr-**kah**-noh
Can I park here?	¿Puedo aparcar aquí? **pweh**-doh ah-par-**kar** ah-**kee**
Is it safe?	¿Es seguro? ehs seh-**goo**-roh
How long can I park here?	¿Durante cuánto tiempo puedo aparcar aquí? doo-**rahn**-tay **kwahn**-toh tee-**ehm**-poh **pweh**-doh ah-par-**kar** ah-**kee**
Is it free?	¿Es gratis? ehs **grah**-tees
Where do I pay?	¿Dónde puedo pagar? **dohn**-day **pweh**-doh pah-**gar**
How much per hour / day?	¿Cuánto cuesta por hora / día? **kwahn**-toh **kweh**-stah por **oh**-rah / **dee**-ah

Parking in Spain can be hazardous. Park legally, and get safe parking tips from your hotel. Leave nothing of value in your car.

At pay parking spaces, you'll pay in advance for the length of your stay. Find the ticket machine (*máquina de pago*) or parking meter (*parquímetro*), and pay for the amount of time you need. If the machine issues a ticket, you'll generally put it on your dashboard.

Garages are more expensive than street parking and often have extremely narrow spaces and tight corners; drive carefully. You'll usually receive a ticket when you enter the garage; take it with you and pay at the machine before returning to your car.

Car Trouble and Parts

accident	accidente	ahk-thee-**dehn**-tay
fender-bender	golpe con el coche	**gohl**-pay kohn ehl **koh**-chay
breakdown	averiado	ah-behr-ee-ah-**doh**
repair shop	taller	tī-**yehr**
strange noise	ruido extraño	roo-**ee**-doh ehk-**strahn**-yoh
electrical problem	problema eléctrico	proh-**bleh**-mah eh-**lehk**-tree-koh
warning light	piloto	pee-**loh**-toh
smoke	humo	**oo**-moh
My car won't start.	Mi coche no encenderá.	mee **koh**-chay noh ehn-thehn-deh-**rah**
My car is broken.	Mi coche está estropeado.	mee **koh**-chay eh-**stah** eh-stroh-peh-**ah**-doh
This doesn't work.	Esto no funciona.	**eh**-stoh noh foon-thee-**oh**-nah
Please check this.	Revise esto por favor.	reh-**bee**-say **eh**-stoh por fah-**bor**
oil	aceite	ah-**thay**-tay
(flat) tire	rueda (pinchada)	roo-**eh**-dah (peen-**chah**-dah)
air in the tires	aire en las ruedas	**ī**-ray ehn lahs roo-**eh**-dahs
radiator	radiador	rah-dee-ah-**dor**
(dead) battery	batería (descargada)	bah-teh-**ree**-ah (deh-skar-**gah**-dah)

sparkplug	bujía boo-**hee**-ah
fuse	fusible foo-**see**-blay
headlights	faros **fah**-rohs
taillights	luces de atrás **loo**-thehs day ah-**trahs**
turn signal	el intermitente ehl een-tehr-mee-**tehn**-tay
brakes	frenos **freh**-nohs
window	ventana behn-**tah**-nah
windshield	parabrisas pah-rah-**bree**-sahs
windshield wipers	limpiaparabrisas leem-pee-ah-pah-rah-**bree**-sahs
engine	motor moh-**tor**
fanbelt	correa del ventilador koh-**reh**-ah dehl behn-tee-lah-**dor**
starter	motor de arranque moh-**tor** day ah-**rahn**-kay
transmission (fluid)	(líquido de) transmisión (**lee**-kee-doh day) trahns-mee-see-**ohn**
key	llave **yah**-bay
alarm	alarma ah-**lar**-mah
It's overheating.	Está sobrecalentando. eh-**stah** soh-breh-kah-lehn-**tahn**-doh
It's a lemon (swindle).	Es un timo. ehs oon **tee**-moh
I need...	Necesito... neh-theh-**see**-toh
...a tow truck.	...una grúa. **oo**-nah **groo**-ah
...a mechanic.	...un mecánico. oon meh-**kah**-nee-koh
...a stiff drink.	...un trago. oon **trah**-goh

For help with repair, see "Repairs" on page 262 of the Services chapter.

The Police

In any country, the flashing lights of a patrol car are a sure sign that someone's in trouble. If it's you, try this handy phrase: ***Lo siento, soy*** *un turista* (Sorry, I'm a tourist). Or, for the adventurous: *Si no le gusta como conduzco, quítese de la acera* (If you don't like how I drive, stay off the sidewalk). If you're in serious need of assistance, turn to the Help! chapter on page 249.

police officer	un policía oon poh-lee-**thee**-ah
driver's license	carnet de conducir kar-**neht** day kohn-doo-**theer**
international driving permit	permiso de conducir internacional pehr-**mee**-soh day kohn-doo-**theer** een-tehr-nah-thee-oh-**nahl**
What seems to be the problem?	¿Cuál puede ser el problema? kwahl **pweh**-day sehr ehl proh-**bleh**-mah
restricted zone	zona restringida **thoh**-nah reh-streen-**hee**-dah
pedestrian-only	zona peatonal **thoh**-nah pee-ah-toh-**nahl**
speeding	exceso de velocidad ehk-**theh**-soh day beh-loh-thee-**dahd**
I didn't know the speed limit.	No sabía el límite de velocidad. noh sah-**bee**-ah ehl **lee**-mee-tay day beh-loh-thee-**dahd**
parking ticket	multa de parking **mool**-tah day **par**-keeng
I didn't know where to park.	No sé dónde aparcar. noh say **dohn**-day ah-par-**kar**
I am very sorry.	Lo siento mucho. loh see-**ehn**-toh **moo**-choh
Can I buy your hat?	¿Puedo comprar su sombrero? **pweh**-doh kohm-**prar** soo sohm-**brehr**-oh

FINDING YOUR WAY

Whether you're driving, walking, or biking, these phrases will help you get around.

Route-Finding Phrases

I'm going / We're going to _____.	Voy / Vamos a _____. boy / **bah**-mohs ah _____
Do you have a...?	¿Tiene un...? tee-**ehn**-ay oon
...city map	...mapa de la ciudad **mah**-pah day lah thee-oo-**dahd**
...road map	...mapa de carretera **mah**-pah day kah-reh-**teh**-rah
How many minutes / hours...?	¿Cuántos minutos / horas...? **kwahn**-tohs mee-**noo**-tohs / **oh**-rahs
...on foot	...a pie ah pee-**ay**
...by bicycle	...en bicicleta ehn bee-thee-**kleh**-tah
...by car	...en coche ehn **koh**-chay
How many kilometers to _____?	¿Cuántos kilómetros a _____? **kwahn**-tohs kee-**loh**-meh-trohs ah _____
What's the... route to Madrid?	¿Cuál es la ruta... a Madrid? kwahl ehs lah **roo**-tah... ah mah-**dreed**
...most scenic	...más panorámica mahs pah-noh-**rah**-mee-kah
...fastest	...más rápida mahs **rah**-pee-dah
...easiest	...más fácil mahs **fah**-theel
...most interesting	...más interesante mahs een-teh-reh-**sahn**-tay
Point it out?	¿Señálelo? sehn-**yah**-leh-loh
Where is this address?	¿Dónde se encuentra esta dirección? **dohn**-day say ehn-**kwehn**-trah **eh**-stah dee-rehk-thee-**ohn**

Directions

In smaller towns, following signs to *centro ciudad* will land you in the heart of things.

downtown	centro ciudad **thehn**-troh thee-oo-**dahd**
straight ahead	recto / derecho **rehk**-toh / deh-**reh**-choh
(to the) left / right	(a la) izquierda / derecha (ah lah) eeth-kee-**ehr**-dah / deh-**reh**-chah
first	primero pree-**mehr**-oh
next	siguiente seeg-ee-**ehn**-tay
intersection	intersección een-tehr-sehk-thee-**ohn**
corner	esquina eh-**skee**-nah
block	cuadra **kwah**-drah
roundabout	glorieta gloh-ree-**eh**-tah
stoplight	semáforo seh-**mah**-foh-roh
(main) square	plaza (principal) **plah**-thah (preen-thee-**pahl**)
street	calle **kah**-yay
avenue	avenida ah-beh-**nee**-dah
boulevard	bulevar boo-leh-**bar**
curve	curva **koor**-bah
bridge	puente **pwehn**-tay
tunnel	túnel **too**-nehl
road	carretera kah-reh-**teh**-rah
ring road	circunvalación theer-koon-bah-lah-thee-**ohn**
expressway	autopista / autovía ow-toh-**pee**-stah / ow-toh-**bee**-ah
north	norte **nor**-tay
south	sur soor
east	este **eh**-stay
west	oeste oh-**eh**-stay

| shortcut | atajo ah-**tah**-hoh |
| traffic jam | atasco ah-**tah**-skoh |

Lost Your Way

I'm lost.	Estoy perdido[a].
	eh-stoy pehr-**dee**-doh
We're lost.	Estamos perdidos[as].
	eh-**stah**-mohs pehr-**dee**-dohs
Excuse me, can you help?	¿Perdone, me puede ayudar?
	pehr-**doh**-nay may **pweh**-day ī-yoo-**dar**
Where am I?	¿Dónde estoy? **dohn**-day **eh**-stoy
Where is _____?	¿Dónde está _____?
	dohn-day eh-**stah** _____
How do I / we get to _____?	¿Cómo llego / llegamos a _____?
	koh-moh **yeh**-goh / yeh-**gah**-mohs ah _____
Can you show me the way?	¿Me puede indicar el camino?
	may **pweh**-day een-dee-**kar** ehl kah-**mee**-noh

Reading Road Signs

Carretera de peaje	Toll road
Ceda el paso	Yield
Centro ciudad	To the center of town
Construcción / Obras	Construction
Cuidado	Caution
Despacio	Slow
Desvío	Detour
Dirección única	One-way street
Entrada	Entrance
Estacionamiento prohibido	No parking
No adelantar	No passing
No se permite	Not allowed
Obras	Workers ahead

Parquímetro	Parking meter
Peaje	Toll
Peatónes	Pedestrians
Próxima salida	Next exit
Salida	Exit
Sin salida	Dead end
Stop	Stop
Todas direcciones (follow when leaving a town)	All directions

For a list of other signs you might see, turn to page 19 in the Spanish Basics chapter.

STOP AND LEARN THESE ROAD SIGNS

Speed Limit (km/hr)

Yield

No Passing

End of No Passing Zone

One Way

Intersection

Main Road

Expressway

Danger

No Entry

Cars Prohibited

All Vehicles Prohibited

No Through Road

Restrictions No Longer Apply

Yield to Oncoming Traffic

No Stopping

Parking

No Parking

Customs

Peace

One Way

Danger

SLEEPING

This chapter covers making reservations, hotel stays (including checking in, typical hotel words, making requests, and dealing with difficulties), specific concerns (such as families and mobility issues), and hostels.

RESERVATIONS

Making a Reservation

reservation	reserva reh-**sehr**-bah
Do you have...?	¿Tiene...? tee-**ehn**-ay
I'd like to reserve...	Me gustaría reservar... may goo-stah-**ree**-ah reh-sehr-**bar**
...a room for...	...una habitación para... **oo**-nah ah-bee-tah-thee-**ohn pah**-rah
...one person / two people	...una persona / dos personas **oo**-nah pehr-**soh**-nah / dohs pehr-**soh**-nahs
...today / tomorrow	...hoy / mañana oy / mahn-**yah**-nah
...one night	...una noche **oo**-nah **noh**-chay
two / three nights	dos / tres noches dohs / trehs **noh**-chehs
June 21	el veintiuno de junio ehl bayn-tee-**oo**-noh day **hoo**-nee-yoh
How much is it?	¿Cuánto cuesta? **kwahn**-toh **kweh**-stah
Anything cheaper?	¿Nada más barato? **nah**-dah mahs bah-**rah**-toh
I'll take it.	La quiero. lah kee-**ehr**-oh
My name is ____.	Me llamo ____. may **yah**-moh ____
Do you need a deposit?	¿Necesita un depósito? neh-theh-**see**-tah oon deh-**poh**-see-toh
Do you accept credit cards?	¿Se aceptan tarjetas de crédito? say ah-**thehp**-tahn tar-**heh**-tahs day **kray**-dee-toh

Key Phrases: Sleeping

Do you have a room?	¿Tiene una habitación? tee-**ehn**-ay **oo**-nah ah-bee-tah-thee-**ohn**
for one person / two people	para una persona / dos personas **pah**-rah **oo**-nah pehr-**soh**-nah / dohs pehr-**soh**-nahs
today / tomorrow	hoy / mañana **oy** / mahn-**yah**-nah
How much is it?	¿Cuánto cuesta? **kwahn**-toh **kweh**-stah
hotel	hotel oh-**tehl**
inexpensive hotel	pensión pehn-see-**ohn**
vacancy / no vacancy	libre / completo **lee**-bray / kohm-**pleh**-toh

SLEEPING Reservations

Can I reserve with a credit card and pay in cash?	¿Puedo reservar con una tarjeta de crédito y pagar en efectivo? **pweh**-doh reh-sehr-**bar** kohn **oo**-nah tar-**heh**-tah day **kray**-dee-toh ee pah-**gar** ehn eh-fehk-**tee**-boh

Spanish hotels come with a handy government-regulated classification system. Look for a blue-and-white plaque by the hotel door indicating the category:

Parador: Government-run hotels, often in refurbished castles or palaces

Hotel (H): Comfortable and expensive accommodations (rated with stars)

Hotel-Residencia (HR) / Hostal-Residencia (HsR): Hotels without restaurants

Hostal (Hs): Less expensive than hotels, but still rated by stars. Don't confuse *hostales* with basic hostels

Pensión (P) / Casa de Huéspedes (CH) / Fonda (F): Cheaper, usually family-run places

Albergue: Basic hostel

Casa Particular / Habitación ("Room") / Camas ("Beds"): Private homes renting budget rooms

Casa Rural: Country house renting rooms, ranging from rustic to fancy

Getting Specific

I'd like a...	Me gustaría una... may goo-stah-**ree**-ah **oo**-nah
...single room.	...habitación individual. ah-bee-tah-thee-**ohn** een-dee-bee-doo-**ahl**
...double room.	...habitación doble. ah-bee-tah-thee-**ohn doh**-blay
...triple room.	...habitación triple. ah-bee-tah-thee-**ohn** tree-play
...room for _____ people.	...habitación para _____ personas. ah-bee-tah-thee-**ohn pah**-rah _____ pehr-**soh**-nahs
with / without / and	con / sin / y kohn / seen / ee
double bed	cama de matrimonio **kah**-mah day mah-tree-**moh**-nee-oh
twin beds...	dos camas... dohs **kah**-mahs
...together / separate	...juntas / separadas **hoon**-tahs / seh-pah-**rah**-dahs
single bed	cama individual **kah**-mah een-dee-bee-doo-**ahl**
bed without a footboard	cama sin un piecero **kah**-mah seen oon pee-eh-**theh**-roh
private bathroom	baño privado **bahn**-yoh pree-**vah**-doh
toilet	váter **bah**-tehr
shower	ducha **doo**-chah
bathtub	bañera bahn-**yeh**-rah

with only a sink	sólo con lavabo **soh**-loh kohn lah-**bah**-boh
shower outside the room	ducha fuera de la habitación **doo**-chah **fwehr**-ah day lah ah-bee-tah-thee-**ohn**
balcony	balcón bahl-**kohn**
view	vista **bee**-stah
cheap	económico ee-koh-**noh**-mee-koh
quiet	tranquilo trahn-**kee**-loh
romantic	romántico roh-**mahn**-tee-koh
on the ground floor	en la planta baja ehn lah **plahn**-tah **bah**-hah
Do you have...?	¿Hay...? Ī
...an elevator	...un ascensor oon ah-thehn-**sor**
...air-conditioning	...aire acondicionado **Ī**-ray ah-kohn-dee-thee-oh-**nah**-doh
...Internet access	...acceso a Internet ahk-**seh**-soh ah **een**-tehr-neht
...Wi-Fi (in the room)	...Wi-Fi (en la habitación) **wee**-fee (ehn lah ah-bee-tah-thee-**ohn**)
...parking	...aparcamiento ah-par-kah-mee-**ehn**-toh
...a garage	...un parking oon **par**-keeng
What is your...?	¿Cuál es su...? kwahl ehs soo
...email address	...email "email"
...cancellation policy	...norma de cancelación **nor**-mah day kahn-theh-lah-thee-**ohn**

In Spain, a true double or queen-size bed is relatively rare. More often, a "double bed" is two twin beds in separate frames, pushed together. Taller guests may want to request a *cama sin un piecero* (bed without a footboard).

What Your Hotelier Wants to Know

If you'd like to reserve by email, your hotelier needs to know the following information: number and type of rooms (i.e., single or double); number of nights; date of arrival (written day/month/year); date of departure; and any special needs (bathroom in the room, cheapest room, twin beds vs. one big bed, crib, air-conditioning, quiet, view, ground floor, no stairs, and so on). Here's a sample email I'd send to make a reservation.

> **From:** rick@ricksteves.com
> **Sent:** Today
> **To:** info@hotelcentral.com
> **Subject:** Reservation request for 19-22 July
>
> Dear Hotel Central,
>
> I would like to reserve a double room for 2 people for 3 nights, arriving 19 July and departing 22 July. If possible, I would like a quiet room with a bathroom inside the room.
>
> Please let me know if you have a room available and the price.
>
> Thank you!
> Rick Steves

The hotel will reply with its room availability and rates for your dates. This is not a confirmation—you must email back to say that you want the room at the given rate, and you'll likely be asked for your credit-card number for a deposit.

Nailing Down the Price

price	precio **preh**-thee-oh
Can I see...?	¿Puedo ver...? **pweh**-doh behr
...the official price list	...la lista oficial de tarifas lah **lee**-stah oh-fee-thee-**ahl** day tah-**ree**-fahs
How much is...?	¿Cuánto cuesta...? **kwahn**-toh **kweh**-stah
...a room for _____ people	...una habitación para _____ personas **oo**-nah ah-bee-tah-thee-**ohn pah**-rah _____ pehr-**soh**-nahs
...your cheapest room	...su habitación más barata soo ah-bee-tah-thee-**ohn** mahs bah-**rah**-tah
Is breakfast included?	¿Está incluido el desayuno? eh-**stah** een-kloo-**ee**-doh ehl deh-sah-**yoo**-noh
Complete price?	¿El precio completo? ehl **preh**-thee-oh kohm-**pleh**-toh
Is it cheaper if...?	¿Es más económico si...? ehs mahs eh-koh-**noh**-mee-koh see
...I stay three nights	...me quedo tres noches may **keh**-doh trehs **noh**-chehs
...I pay cash	...pago en efectivo **pah**-goh ehn eh-fehk-**tee**-boh

Many hotels are willing to lower the price if you stay for longer periods and/or pay in cash. Rates can vary by season: High season (*temporada alta*) is more expensive than low season (*temporada baja*). At some hotels in resort towns, you're required to pay for half-pension (*media pensión*), which covers lunch or dinner at their restaurant.

Arrival and Departure

arrival (date)	llegada yeh-**gah**-dah
departure (date)	salida sah-**lee**-dah
I'll arrive / We'll arrive...	Llego / Llegamos... **yeh**-goh / yeh-**gah**-mohs
I'll depart / We'll depart...	Salgo / Salimos... **sahl**-goh / sah-**lee**-mohs
...August 16.	...el dieciséis de agosto. ehl dee-eh-thee-**says** day ah-**goh**-stoh
...in the morning / afternoon / evening.	...por la mañana / tarde / noche. por lah mahn-**yah**-nah / **tar**-day / **noh**-chay
...Friday before 6 p.m.	...viernes antes de las seis de la tarde. bee-**ehr**-nehs **ahn**-tehs day lahs says day lah **tar**-day
I'll stay...	Me quedaré... may keh-dah-**ray**
We'll stay...	Nos quedaremos... nohs keh-dah-**reh**-mohs
...two nights.	...dos noches. dohs **noh**-chehs
We arrive Monday, depart Wednesday.	Llegamos el lunes, salimos el miércoles. yeh-**gah**-mohs ehl **loo**-nehs sah-**lee**-mohs ehl mee-**ehr**-koh-lehs

For help with saying dates in Spanish, see "Time and Dates," starting on page 31.

Confirm, Change, or Cancel

It's smart to call a day or two in advance to confirm your reservation.

I have a reservation.	Tengo una reserva hecha. **tehn**-goh **oo**-nah reh-**sehr**-bah **eh**-chah
My name is _____.	Me llamo _____. may **yah**-moh _____
I'd like to... my reservation.	Me gustaría... la reserva. may goo-stah-**ree**-ah... lah ray-**sehr**-bah

...confirm	...confirmar kohn-feer-**mar**
...change	...cambiar kahm-bee-**ar**
...cancel	...cancelar kahn-theh-**lar**
The reservation is for...	La reserva es para... lah reh-**sehr**-bah ehs **pah**-rah
...today / tomorrow.	...hoy / mañana. oy / mahn-**yah**-nah
...June 13.	...el trece de junio. ehl **treh**-thay day **hoo**-nee-oh
Did you find the reservation?	¿Encontró la reserva? ehn-kohn-**troh** lah reh-**sehr**-bah
Is everything OK?	¿Está todo bien? eh-**stah** **toh**-doh bee-**ehn**
See you then.	Hasta entonces. **ah**-stah ehn-**tohn**-thehs
I'm sorry that I need to cancel.	Siento tener que cancelar. see-**ehn**-toh teh-**nehr** kay kahn-theh-**lar**
Is there a penalty (for canceling the reservation)?	¿Hay una penalización (por cancelar la reserva)? ī **oo**-nah peh-nah-lee-thah-thee-**ohn** (por kahn-theh-**lar** lah reh-**sehr**-bah)

Depending on how far ahead you cancel a reservation—and on the hotel's cancellation policy—you might pay a penalty.

AT THE HOTEL

Checking In

My name is ____.	Me llamo ____. may **yah**-moh ____
I have a reservation.	Tengo una reserva hecha. **tehn**-goh **oo**-nah reh-**sehr**-bah **eh**-chah
one night	una noche **oo**-nah **noh**-chay
two / three nights	dos / tres noches dohs / trehs **noh**-chehs

Where is...?	¿Dónde está...? **dohn**-day eh-**stah**
...my room	...mi habitación mee ah-bee-tah-thee-**ohn**
...the elevator	...el ascensor ehl ah-thehn-**sor**
...the breakfast room	...el salón del desayuno ehl sah-**lohn** dehl deh-sah-**yoo**-noh
Is breakfast included?	¿Está incluido el desayuno? eh-**stah** een-kloo-**ee**-doh ehl deh-sah-**yoo**-noh
When does breakfast start and end?	¿Cuál es el horario del desayuno? kwahl ehs ehl oh-**rah**-ree-oh dehl deh-sah-**yoo**-noh
key	llave **yah**-bay
Two keys, please.	Dos llaves, por favor. dohs **yah**-behs por fah-**bor**

Choosing a Room

Can I see a...?	¿Puedo ver una...? **pweh**-doh behr **oo**-nah
...room	...habitación ah-bee-tah-thee-**ohn**
...different room	...habitación diferente ah-bee-tah-thee-**ohn** dee-feh-**rehn**-tay
Do you have something...?	¿Tiene algo...? tee-**ehn**-ay **ahl**-goh
...larger / smaller	...más grande / más pequeña mahs **grahn**-day / mahs peh-**kehn**-yah
...better / cheaper	...mejor / más económica meh-**hor** / mahs eh-koh-**noh**-mee-kah
...brighter	...con más claridad kohn mahs klah-ree-**dahd**
...quieter	...más tranquila mahs trahn-**kee**-lah
...in the back	...en la parte de atrás ehn lah **par**-tay day ah-**trahs**

...with a view	...con vista kohn **bee**-stah
...on a lower floor / higher floor	...en un piso más bajo / piso más alto ehn oon **pee**-soh mahs **bah**-hoh / **pee**-soh mahs **ahl**-toh
No, thank you.	No, gracias. noh **grah**-thee-ahs
What a charming room!	¡Qué bonita habitación! kay boh-**nee**-tah ah-bee-tah-thee-**ohn**
I'll take it.	Me la quedo. may lah **keh**-doh

Be aware that a room *con vista* (with a view) can also come with more noise. If a *habitación tranquila* is important to you, say so.

Hotel Words

cancellation policy	norma de cancelación **nor**-mah day kahn-theh-lah-thee-**ohn**
check-in time	la hora del check-in lah **oh**-rah dehl **chehk**-een
check-out time	la hora del check-out lah **oh**-rah dehl "check-out"
elevator	ascensor ah-thehn-**sor**
emergency exit	salida de emergencia sah-**lee**-dah day eh-mehr-**hehn**-thee-ah
fire escape	escalera de incendios eh-skah-**lehr**-ah day een-**thehn**-dee-ohs
floor...	piso... **pee**-soh
...lower / higher	...más bajo / más alto mahs **bah**-hoh / mahs **ahl**-toh
ground floor	planta baja **plahn**-tah **bah**-hah
Internet access	acceso a Internet ahk-**seh**-soh ah **een**-tehr-neht
laundry	lavandería lah-vahn-deh-**ree**-ah
parking	parking / garaje **par**-keeng / gah-**rah**-hay

price list	lista oficial de precios **lee**-stah oh-fee-thee-**ahl** day **preh**-thee-ohs
reservation	reserva reh-**sehr**-bah
room...	habitación... ah-bee-tah-thee-**ohn**
...single	...individual een-dee-bee-doo-**ahl**
...double	...doble **doh**-blay
...triple	...triple **tree**-play
...family	...familiar fah-mee-lee-**ar**
stairs	escaleras eh-skah-**lehr**-ahs
suite	suite **swee**-tay
swimming pool	piscina pee-**thee**-nah
view	vista **bee**-stah
Wi-Fi	Wi-Fi **wee**-fee

In Your Room

air-conditioner	aire acondicionado **ī**-ray ah-kohn-dee-thee-oh-**nah**-doh
alarm clock	despertador dehs-pehr-tah-**dor**
balcony	balcón bahl-**kohn**
bathroom	baño **bahn**-yoh
bathtub	bañera bahn-**yeh**-rah
bed	cama **kah**-mah
bedspread	cubrecama koo-breh-**kah**-mah
blanket	manta **mahn**-tah
blinds	persianas pehr-see-ah-**nahs**
city map	plano de la ciudad **plah**-noh day lah thee-oo-**dahd**
chair	silla **see**-yah
closet	armario ar-**mah**-ree-oh
corkscrew	sacacorchos sah-kah-**kor**-chohs

crib	cuna **koo**-nah
curtains	cortinas kor-**tee**-nahs
door	puerta **pwehr**-tah
double bed	cama de matrimonio **kah**-mah day mah-tree-**moh**-nee-oh
drain	desagüe deh-sah-**gway**
electrical adapter	adaptador eléctrico ah-dahp-tah-**dor** eh-**lehk**-tree-koh
electrical outlet	enchufe ehn-**choo**-fay
faucet	grifo **gree**-foh
hair dryer	secador de pelo seh-kah-**dor** day **peh**-loh
hanger	percha **pehr**-chah
key	llave **yah**-bay
kitchenette	cocina koh-**thee**-nah
lamp	lámpara **lahm**-pah-rah
lightbulb	bombilla bohm-**bee**-yah
lock	cerradura thehr-rah-**doo**-rah
mirror	espejo ehs-**peh**-hoh
pillow	almohada ahl-moh-**ah**-dah
radio	radio **rah**-dee-oh
remote control...	mando a distancia... **mahn**-doh ah dees-**tahn**-thee-ah
...for TV	...para la tele **pah**-rah lah **teh**-lay
...for air-conditioner	...para el aire acondicionado **pah**-rah ehl **ī**-ray ah-kohn-dee-thee-oh-**nah**-doh
safe (n)	caja fuerte **kah**-hah **fwehr**-tay
scissors	tijeras tee-**heh**-rahs
shampoo	champú chahm-**poo**
sheets	sábanas **sah**-bah-nahs
shower	ducha **doo**-chah

shutters	contraventana	kohn-trah-behn-**tah**-nah
single bed	cama individual	
	kah-mah een-dee-bee-doo-**ahl**	
sink	lavabo	lah-**bah**-boh
sink stopper	tapón	tah-**pohn**
soap	jabón	hah-**bohn**
telephone	teléfono	teh-**lay**-foh-noh
television	televisión	teh-leh-bee-thee-**ohn**
toilet	váter	**bah**-tehr
toilet paper	papel higiénico	
	pah-**pehl** ee-hee-**ay**-nee-koh	
towel (hand)	toalla de manos	
	toh-**ī**-yah day **mah**-nohs	
towel (bath)	toalla de baño	toh-**ī**-yah day **bahn**-yoh
twin beds	dos camas	dohs **kah**-mahs
wake-up call	llamar para despertarme	
	yah-**mar pah**-rah deh-spehr-**tar**-may	
washcloth	toalla pequeña	toh-**ī**-yah peh-**kehn**-yah
water (hot / cold)	agua (caliente / fría)	
	ah-gwah (kah-lee-**ehn**-tay / **free**-ah)	
window	ventana	behn-**tah**-nah
window screen	mosquitero	moh-skee-**tehr**-oh

If you don't see remote controls in the room (for the TV or air-conditioner), ask for them at the front desk. A comfortable setting for the air-conditioner is about 20 degrees Celsius. On Spanish faucets, a **C** stands for *caliente* (hot)—the opposite of cold.

Hotel Hassles

Combine these phrases with the words in the previous table to make simple and clear statements such as: *El váter no funciona* (The toilet doesn't work).

There is a problem in my room.	Hay un problema con la habitación. Ī oon proh-**bleh**-mah kohn lah ah-bee-tah-thee-**ohn**
Come with me.	Venga conmigo. **behn**-gah kohn-**mee**-goh
The room is...	La habitación está... lah ah-bee-tah-thee-**ohn** eh-**stah**
It's...	Está... eh-**stah**
...**dirty.**	...sucia. **soo**-thee-ah
...**musty.**	...con olor a cerrado. kohn oh-**lor** ah thehr-**ah**-doh
...**smoky.**	...con olor a tabaco. kohn oh-**lor** ah tah-**bah**-koh
...**stinky.**	...con malos olores. kohn **mah**-lohs oh-**lor**-ehs
The room is moldy.	La habitación tiene moho. lah ah-bee-tah-thee-**ohn** tee-**ehn**-ay **moh**-oh
It's noisy.	Es ruidosa. ehs roo-ee-**doh**-sah
It's very hot / cold in the room.	Hace mucho calor / frío en la habitación. **ah**-thay **moo**-choh kah-**lor** / **free**-oh ehn lah ah-bee-tah-thee-**ohn**
How can I make the room cooler / warmer?	¿Cómo puedo refrescar / calentar la habitación? **koh**-moh **pweh**-doh reh-freh-**skar** / kah-lehn-**tar** lah ah-bee-tah-thee-**ohn**
There's no (hot) water.	No hay agua (caliente). noh ī **ah**-gwah (kah-lee-**ehn**-tay)
I can't open / shut / lock...	No puedo abrir / cerrar / cerrar con llave... noh **pweh**-doh ah-**breer** / theh-**rar** / theh-**rar** kohn **yah**-bay
...**the door / the window.**	...la puerta / la ventana. lah **pwehr**-tah / lah behn-**tah**-nah
How does this work?	¿Cómo funciona esto? **koh**-moh foon-thee-**oh**-nah **eh**-stoh

This doesn't work.	Esto no funciona. **eh**-stoh noh foon-thee-**oh**-nah
When will you fix it?	¿Cuándo lo arreglarán? **kwahn**-doh loh ah-reh-glah-**rahn**
The bed is too soft / hard.	La cama es demasiado blanda / dura. lah **kah**-mah ehs deh-mah-see-**ah**-doh **blahn**-dah / **doo**-rah
I can't sleep.	No puedo dormir. noh **pweh**-doh dor-**meer**
ants	hormigas or-**mee**-gahs
bedbugs	chinches **cheen**-chehs
cockroaches	cucarachas koo-kah-**rah**-chahs
mice	ratones rah-**toh**-nehs
mosquitoes	mosquitos moh-**skee**-tohs
I'm covered with bug bites.	Estoy lleno(a) de picaduras. **eh**-stoy **yeh**-noh day pee-kah-**doo**-rahs
My... was stolen.	Me han robado mi... may ahn roh-**bah**-doh mee
...money	...dinero dee-**nehr**-oh
...computer	...ordenador or-deh-nah-**dor**
...camera	...cámara **kah**-mah-rah
I need to speak to the manager.	Necesito hablar con el encargado. neh-theh-**see**-toh ah-**blar** kohn ehl ehn-kar-**gah**-doh
I want to make a complaint.	Quiero poner una reclamación. kee-**ehr**-oh poh-**nehr oo**-nah reh-klah-mah-thee-**ohn**
Complaint book, please.	Libro de reclamaciones, por favor. **lee**-broh day reh-klah-mah-thee-**oh**-nehs por fah-**bor**

Keep your valuables with you, out of sight in your room, or in a room safe (if available). For help on dealing with theft or loss, including a list of items, see page 251.

Hotels are legally required to keep an official complaint book *(libro de reclamaciones).* Asking for the book can help bring a quick resolution to your problem.

Hotel Help

Use the "In Your Room" words (on page 88) to fill in the blanks.

I'd like...	Me gustaría... may goo-stah-**ree**-ah
Do you have...?	¿Tiene...? tee-**ehn**-ay
a / another	un / otro oon / **oh**-troh
extra	extra **ehk**-strah
different	diferente dee-feh-**rehn**-tay
Please change...	Cambien... por favor. **kahm**-bee-ehn... por fah-**bor**
Please don't change...	No cambien... por favor. noh **kahm**-bee-ehn... por fah-**bor**
...the towels / sheets.	...las toallas / sábanas lahs toh-**ī**-yahs / **sah**-bah-nahs
What is the charge to...?	¿Cúanto cobran por...? **kwahn**-toh **koh**-brahn por
...use the telephone	...usar el teléfono oo-**sar** ehl teh-**lay**-foh-noh
...use the Internet	...usar el Internet oo-**sar** ehl **een**-tehr-neht
Do you have Wi-Fi...?	¿Tienen Wi-Fi...? tee-**ehn**-ehn **wee**-fee
...in the room / lobby	...en la habitación / en la recepción ehn lah ah-bee-tah-thee-**ohn** / ehn lah reh-thehp-thee-**ohn**
What is the network name / password?	¿Cúal es el nombre de la red / la clave? kwahl ehs ehl **nohm**-bray day lah rehd / lah **klah**-bay
Is a... nearby?	¿Hay un / una... cerca? ī oon / **oo**-nah... **thehr**-kah

At the Hotel

...full-service laundry	...lavandería lah-vahn-deh-**ree**-ah
...self-service laundry	...lavandería de autoservicio lah-vahn-deh-**ree**-ah day ow-toh-sehr-**bee**-thee-oh
...pharmacy	...farmacia far-mah-**thee**-ah
...Internet café	...ciber café thee-**behr** kah-**fay**
...grocery store	...supermercado soo-pehr-mehr-**kah**-doh
...restaurant	...restaurante reh-stoh-**rahn**-tay
Where do you go to eat lunch / to eat dinner / to drink coffee?	¿Dónde se puede comer / cenar / tomar un café? **dohn**-day say **pweh**-day koh-**mehr** / theh-**nar** / toh-**mar** oon kah-**fay**
Will you call a taxi for me?	¿Me llamaría un taxi? may yah-mah-**ree**-ah oon **tahk**-see
Where can I park?	¿Dónde se puede aparcar? **dohn**-day say **pweh**-day ah-par-**kar**
What time do you lock up?	¿A qué hora cierran la puerta? ah kay **oh**-rah thee-**ehr**-ahn lah **pwehr**-tah
Wake me at 7:00, please.	Despiérteme a las siete, por favor. deh-spee-**ehr**-teh-may ah lahs see-**eh**-tay por fah-**bor**
I'd like to stay another night.	Me gustaría quedarme otra noche. may goo-stah-**ree**-ah keh-**dar**-may **oh**-trah **noh**-chay
Will you call my next hotel...?	¿Podría llamar a mi próximo hotel...? poh-**dree**-ah yah-**mar** ah mee **prohk**-see-moh oh-**tehl**
...for tonight	...para esta noche **pah**-rah **eh**-stah **noh**-chay

...to make / to confirm a reservation	...para hacer / confirmar una reserva pah-rah ah-**thehr** / kohn-feer-**mar** **oo**-nah reh-**sehr**-bah
Will you please call another hotel for me? (if hotel is booked)	¿Llamaría a otro hotel por mí? yah-mah-**ree**-ah ah **oh**-troh oh-**tehl** por mee
I will pay for the call.	Pagaré por la llamada. pah-gah-**ray** por lah yah-**mah**-dah

Checking Out

When is check-out time?	¿Cuándo es la hora del check-out? **kwahn**-doh ehs lah **oh**-rah dehl "check-out"
Can I check out later?	¿Podría hacer el check-out más tarde? poh-**dree**-ah ah-**thehr** ehl "check-out" mahs **tar**-day
I'll leave...	Me iré... may ee-**ray**
We'll leave...	Nos iremos... nohs ee-**reh**-mohs
...today / tomorrow.	...hoy / mañana. oy / mahn-**yah**-nah
...very early.	...muy temprano. **moo**-ee tehm-**prah**-noh
Can I pay now?	¿Puedo pagar ahora? **pweh**-doh pah-**gar** ah-**oh**-rah
The bill, please.	La cuenta, por favor. lah **kwehn**-tah por fah-**bor**
I think this is too high.	Creo que me están cobrando demasiado. **kreh**-oh kay may eh-**stahn** koh-**brahn**-doh deh-mah-see-**ah**-doh
Can you explain / itemize the bill?	¿Podría explicarme / detallarme la cuenta? poh-**dree**-ah ehk-splee-**kar**-may / deh-tah-**yar**-may lah **kwehn**-tah

Do you accept credit cards?	¿Se aceptan tarjetas de crédito? say ah-**thehp**-tahn tar-**heh**-tahs day **kray**-dee-toh
Is it cheaper if I pay cash?	¿Es más barato si pago en efectivo? ehs mahs bah-**rah**-toh see **pah**-goh ehn eh-fehk-**tee**-boh
Everything was great.	Todo estuvo muy bien. **toh**-doh eh-**stoo**-boh **moo**-ee bee-**ehn**
I slept like a log.	He dormido como un tronco. ay dor-**mee**-doh **koh**-moh oon **trohn**-koh
Can I / Can we...?	¿Puedo / Podemos...? **pweh**-doh / poh-**deh**-mohs
...leave baggage here until _____ o'clock	...guardar el equipaje aquí hasta las _____ gwar-**dar** ehl eh-kee-**pah**-hay ah-**kee ah**-stah lahs _____
A tip for you.	Una propina para usted. **oo**-nah proh-**pee**-nah **pah**-rah oo-**stehd**

SPECIAL CONCERNS

Families

Do you have...?	¿Tiene...? tee-**ehn**-ay
...a family room	...una habitación familiar **oo**-nah ah-bee-tah-thee-**ohn** fah-mee-lee-**ar**
...a family discount	...un descuento familiar oon dehs-**kwehn**-toh fah-mee-lee-**ar**
...a discount for children	...un descuento para niños oon dehs-**kwehn**-toh **pah**-rah **neen**-yohs
I have / We have...	Tengo / Tenemos... **tehn**-goh / teh-**neh**-mohs
...one child.	...un niño. oon **neen**-yoh

...two children.	...dos niños. dohs **neen**-yohs
_____ **months old**	de _____ meses day _____ **meh**-sehs
_____ **years old**	de _____ años day _____ **ahn**-yohs
Do you accept children?	¿Se permiten niños? say pehr-**mee**-tehn **neen**-yohs
Is there an age limit?	¿Hay un límite de edad? ī oon **lee**-mee-tay day eh-**dahd**
I'd / We'd like...	Me / Nos gustaría... may / nohs goo-stah-**ree**-ah
...a crib.	...una cuna. **oo**-nah **koo**-nah
...an extra bed.	...una cama extra. **oo**-nah **kah**-mah **ehk**-strah
...bunk beds.	...una litera. **oo**-nah lee-**teh**-rah
...babysitting service.	...servicio de canguro. sehr-**bee**-thee-oh day kahn-**goo**-roh
Is... nearby?	¿Hay... cerca? ī... **thehr**-kah
...a park	...un parque oon **par**-kay
...a playground	...un área para jugar oon **ah**-reh-ah **pah**-rah hoo-**gar**
...a swimming pool	...una piscina **oo**-nah pee-**thee**-nah

Mobility Issues

For related phrases, see page 291 in the Personal Care and Health chapter.

Do you have...?	¿Tiene...? tee-**ehn**-ay
...an elevator	...un ascensor oon ah-thehn-**sor**
...a ground-floor room	...una habitación en la planta baja **oo**-nah ah-bee-tah-thee-**ohn** ehn lah **plahn**-tah **bah**-hah
...a wheelchair-accessible room	...acceso para silla de ruedas ahk-**seh**-soh **pah**-rah **see**-yah day roo-**eh**-dahs

AT THE HOSTEL

Europe's cheapest beds are in hostels, open to travelers of any age. Official hostels (affiliated with Hostelling International) are usually big and institutional. Independent hostels are more casual, with fewer rules.

hostel	albergue ahl-**behr**-gay
dorm bed	litera lee-**teh**-rah
How many beds per room?	¿Cúantas camas hay en una habitación? **kwahn**-tahs **kah**-mahs ī ehn **oo**-nah ah-bee-tah-thee-**ohn**
dorm for women only	dormitorio sólo para mujeres dor-mee-**toh**-ree-oh **soh**-loh **pah**-rah moo-**hehr**-ehs
co-ed dorm	dormitorio mixto dor-mee-**toh**-ree-oh **meek**-stoh
double room	habitación doble ah-bee-tah-thee-**ohn doh**-blay
family room	habitación familiar ah-bee-tah-thee-**ohn** fah-mee-lee-**ar**
Is breakfast included?	¿El desayuno está incluido? ehl deh-sah-**yoo**-noh eh-**stah** een-kloo-**ee**-doh
curfew	toque de queda **toh**-kay day **keh**-dah
lockout	cerrado por limpieza thehr-**ah**-doh por leem-pee-**eh**-thah
membership card	carné de alberguista kar-**nay** day ahl-behrg-**ee**-stah

EATING

Dig into this chapter's phrases for dining at restaurants, special concerns (including dietary restrictions, children, and being in a hurry), types of food and drink, and shopping for your picnic. The next chapter is a Menu Decoder.

The Spanish eating schedule frustrates many visitors. Restaurants serve meals late. Lunch (*almuerzo* or *comida*), eaten later than in the US (1:00–4:00 p.m.), is the largest meal of the day. Because most Spaniards work until 7:30 p.m., a light supper *(cena)* is usually served around 9:00 or 10:00 p.m. Generally, no good restaurant serves meals at American hours (and many restaurants close during August). But to eat early, well, and within even the tightest budget any time of year, you can duck into a bar, where you can stab toothpicks into munchies (see "Tapas" on page 143).

RESTAURANTS

Types of Restaurants

Contrary to what many Americans assume, Spanish cuisine is nothing like Mexican cuisine. Spanish food—usually not spicy, often fried, and heavy on seafood—was influenced by 700 years of Muslim rule. The Moors, who were great horticulturists, introduced new herbs, spices, fruits, and vegetables. The Moorish legacy is well represented by one of Spain's best-known dishes, *paella,* combining saffron (an Eastern flavor) with rice and various types of seafood and sausage. Spain's most significant contribution to our global culinary culture is *tapas*—tasty appetizers that can add up to a full meal.

Spain offers many types of eateries to try:

Restaurante: Any eating establishment with a written menu and table service

Fonda / Hostería / Venta / Posada: Inns, of varying formality, serving hearty, regional Spanish food

Casa de comidas: "House of eating," a traditional eatery

Cafetería: Coffee shop with counter or table service (not like self-service cafeterias in the US)

Merendero / Chiringuito: Seafood stall or restaurant on the beach
Pastelería / Confitería: Pastry shop
Taberna / Tasca / Bar: Bars serving snacks and drinks
Cervecería: Beer bar
Bodega / Vinoteca: Wine bar (cellar)
Mesón: Long, skinny, cave-like bar (Madrid)
Carmen: Restaurant in a stately home (Granada)

Finding a Restaurant

Where's a good... **restaurant nearby?**	¿Dónde hay un buen... restaurante cerca? **dohn**-day ī oon bwehn... reh-stoh-**rahn**-tay **thehr**-kah
...cheap	...barato bah-**rah**-toh
...local-style	...regional reh-hee-oh-**nahl**
...untouristy	...que no sea un sitio de turistas kay noh **seh**-ah oon **seet**-yoh day too-**ree**-stahs
...romantic	...romántico roh-**mahn**-tee-koh
...vegetarian	...vegetariano beh-heh-tah-ree-**ah**-noh
...fast	...rápido **rah**-pee-doh
...fast food	...de comida rápida day koh-**mee**-dah **rah**-pee-dah
...self-service buffet	...con buffet de autoservicio kohn boo-**fay** day ow-toh-sehr-**bee**-thee-oh
...Asian	...asiático ah-see-**ah**-tee-koh
with a salad bar	con una barra de ensaladas kohn **oo**-nah **bah**-rah day ehn-sah-**lah**-dahs
with candles	con velas kohn **beh**-lahs
popular with locals	con gente de aquí kohn **hehn**-tay day ah-**kee**
moderate price	precio moderado **preh**-thee-oh moh-deh-**rah**-doh

a splurge	una extravagancia
	oo-nah ehk-strah-bah-**gahn**-thee-ah
Is it better than McDonald's?	¿Es mejor que McDonald?
	ehs meh-**hor** kay meek-**doh**-nahld

This is the sequence of a typical restaurant experience: To get your server's attention, simply say *Por favor*. The waiter will give you a menu *(la carta)*, then ask if he can help you *(¿Cómo puedo servirles?* or simply *Dígame*—Talk to me). Next he'll ask what you'd like to drink or eat *(¿Qué quiere beber / comer?)*, and later, he'll ask if you're finished *(¿Han acabado?)*. Ask for the bill by saying *La cuenta, por favor*.

Getting a Table

I'd / We'd like...	Me / Nos gustaría...
	may / nohs goo-stah-**ree**-ah
...a table...	...una mesa... **oo**-nah **meh**-sah
...for one / two.	...para uno / dos.
	pah-rah **oo**-noh / dohs
...inside / outside.	...dentro / fuera.
	dehn-troh / **fweh**-rah
...by the window.	...cerca de la ventana.
	thehr-kah day lah behn-**tah**-nah
...with a view.	...con vista. kohn **bee**-stah
quiet	tranquila trahn-**kee**-lah
Is this table free?	¿Está libre esta mesa?
	eh-**stah lee**-bray **eh**-stah **meh**-sah
Can I sit here?	¿Puedo sentarme aquí?
	pweh-doh sehn-**tar**-may ah-**kee**
Can we sit here?	¿Podemos sentarnos aquí?
	poh-**deh**-mohs sehn-**tar**-nohs ah-**kee**
How long is the wait?	¿Cuánto tiempo hay que esperar?
	kwahn-toh tee-**ehm**-poh ī kay
	eh-spehr-**ar**

Key Phrases: Restaurants

Where's a good restaurant nearby?	¿Dónde hay un buen restaurante cerca? **dohn**-day ī oon bwehn reh-stoh-**rahn**-tay **thehr**-kah
I'd / We'd like...	Me / Nos gustaría... may / nohs goo-stah-**ree**-ah
...a table for one / two.	...una mesa para uno / dos. **oo**-nah **meh**-sah **pah**-rah **oo**-noh / dohs
Is this table free?	¿Está libre esta mesa? eh-**stah** lee-bray **eh**-stah **meh**-sah
How long is the wait?	¿Cuánto tiempo hay que esperar? **kwahn**-toh tee-**ehm**-poh ī kay eh-spehr-**ar**
The menu (in English), please.	La carta (en inglés), por favor. lah **kar**-tah (ehn een-**glays**) por fah-**bor**
The bill, please.	La cuenta, por favor. lah **kwehn**-tah por fah-**bor**
Do you accept credit cards?	¿Se aceptan tarjetas de crédito? say ah-**thehp**-tahn tar-**heh**-tahs day **kray**-dee-toh

How many minutes?	¿Cuántos minutos? **kwahn**-tohs mee-**noo**-tohs
Where are the toilets?	¿Dónde están los servicios? **dohn**-day eh-**stahn** lohs sehr-**bee**-thee-ohs

Reservations

reservation	reserva reh-**sehr**-bah
Are reservations recommended?	¿Se debe reservar? say **deh**-bay reh-sehr-**bar**

I'd like to make a reservation...	Me gustaría hacer una reserva... may goo-stah-**ree**-ah ah-**thehr** oo-nah reh-**sehr**-bah
...for one person.	...para una persona. **pah**-rah oo-nah pehr-**soh**-nah
...for two people.	...para dos personas. **pah**-rah dohs pehr-**soh**-nahs
...for today / tomorrow.	...para hoy / mañana. **pah**-rah oy / mahn-**yah**-nah
...for lunch / dinner.	...para almorzar / cenar. **pah**-rah ahl-mor-**thar** / theh-**nar**
...at _____ o'clock.	...a las _____. ah lahs _____
My name is _____.	Me llamo _____. may **yah**-moh
I have a reservation for _____ people.	Tengo una reserva para _____ personas. **tehn**-goh oo-nah reh-**sehr**-bah **pah**-rah _____ per-**soh**-nahs

The Menu

Here's the typical lingo you may see on menus. Some also list *sugerencias* (suggestions).

menu	la carta lah **kar**-tah
The menu (in English), please.	La carta (en inglés), por favor. lah **kar**-tah (ehn een-**glays**) por fah-**bor**
special of the day	especial del día eh-speh-thee-**ahl** dehl **dee**-ah
specialty of the house	especialidad de la casa eh-speh-thee-ah-lee-**dahd** day lah **kah**-sah
menu of the day	menú del día meh-**noo** dehl **dee**-ah
children's menu	menú para niños meh-**noo** **pah**-rah **neen**-yohs
combination plate	plato combinado / tabla **plah**-toh kohm-bee-**nah**-doh / **tah**-blah

A Sample Menu of the Day

Choose a first course, second course, dessert, and beverage.

Mesón Pedro
Plaza Mayor, Salamanca

MENÚ DEL DÍA €12

PRIMEROS (FIRST COURSE)
- ENSALADA MIXTA (MIXED SALAD)
- GAZPACHO
- ESCALIVADA (ROASTED EGGPLANT + PEPPERS)
- GAMBAS A LA PLANCHA (GRILLED SHRIMP)

SEGUNDOS (SECOND COURSE)
- COCHINILLO ASADO (ROAST SUCKLING PIG)
- PAELLA VALENCIANA
- PATO CON HIGOS (DUCK W/ FIGS)

POSTRE (DESSERT)
    FLAN o HELADO (CUSTARD OR ICE CREAM)

+ PAN, VINO o AGUA (BREAD, WINE OR WATER)

I.V.A. INCLUIDO (TAX INCLUDED)

¡Gracias y Buen Provecho!

breakfast	desayuno deh-sah-**yoo**-noh
lunch	almuerzo / comida ahlm-**wehr**-thoh / koh-**mee**-dah
dinner	cena **theh**-nah
dishes	platos **plah**-tohs
warm / cold plates	platos calientes / fríos **plah**-tohs kah-lee-**ehn**-tehs / **free**-ohs
appetizers	aperitivos ah-peh-ree-**tee**-bohs
sandwiches	bocadillos boh-kah-**dee**-yohs
bread	pan pahn
salad	ensalada ehn-sah-**lah**-dah
soup	sopa **soh**-pah
first course	primer plato pree-**mehr plah**-toh
main course	segundo plato seh-**goon**-doh **plah**-toh
meat	carne **kar**-nay
poultry	aves **ah**-behs
fish	pescado peh-**skah**-doh
seafood	marisco mah-**ree**-skoh
egg dishes	tortillas tor-**tee**-yahs
side dishes	a parte ah **par**-tay
vegetables	verduras behr-**doo**-rahs
cheese	queso **keh**-soh
dessert	postres **poh**-strays
bar snacks	tapas **tah**-pahs
drink menu	carta de bebidas **kar**-tah day beh-**bee**-dahs
beverages	bebidas beh-**bee**-dahs
beer	cerveza thehr-**beh**-thah
wine	vino **bee**-noh
cover charge	precio de entrada **preh**-thee-oh day ehn-**trah**-dah
service (not) included	servicio (no) incluido sehr-**bee**-thee-oh (noh) een-kloo-**ee**-doh

hot / cold	caliente / frío kah-lee-**ehn**-tay / **free**-oh
comes with	se sirve con seh **seer**-bay kohn
choice of	a elegir entre ah eh-leh-**heer ehn**-tray

For a budget meal in a restaurant, try a **plato combinado** (a combination plate that includes portions of one or two main dishes, vegetables, and bread). For a heartier three-course meal, order the **menú del día** (menu of the day): You'll typically choose from a few options for the first course (**primeros** or **1° plato**), then a second course (**segundos** or **2° plato**), followed by dessert **(postre)**. **Vino** (wine) or **caña** (a small beer) may be included, along with **pan** (bread).

Ordering

Remember, to summon your server, say **Por favor.** If you have allergies or dietary restrictions, see page 114.

waiter	camarero kah-mah-**reh**-roh
waitress	camarera kah-mah-**reh**-rah
I'm / We're ready to order.	Me / Nos gustaría pedir. may / nohs goo-stah-**ree**-ah peh-**deer**
I need / We need more time.	Necesito / Necesitamos más tiempo. neh-theh-**see**-toh / neh-theh-see-**tah**-mohs mahs tee-**ehm**-poh
I'd / We'd like...	Me / Nos gustaría... may / nohs goo-stah-**ree**-ah
...just a drink.	...sólo una bebida. **soh**-loh **oo**-nah beh-**bee**-dah
...to see the menu.	...ver la carta. behr lah **kar**-tah
...to eat.	...comer. koh-**mehr**
Do you have...?	¿Tiene...? tee-**ehn**-ay
...an English menu	...una carta en inglés **oo**-nah **kar**-tah ehn een-**glays**
...a menu of the day	...un menú del día oon meh-**noo** dehl **dee**-ah

...half portions	...media raciones **meh**-dee-ah rah-thee-**oh**-nehs
What do you recommend?	¿Qué recomienda? kay reh-koh-mee-**ehn**-dah
What's your favorite dish?	¿Cuál es su plato favorito? kwahl ehs soo **plah**-toh fah-boh-**ree**-toh
What is better? (point to menu items)	¿Cuál es mejor? kwahl ehs may-**hor**
What is...?	¿Qué es...? kay ehs
Is it...?	¿Es esto...? ehs **eh**-stoh
...good	...bueno **bweh**-noh
...affordable	...asequible ah-seh-**kee**-blay
...expensive	...caro **kah**-roh
...local	...típico **tee**-pee-koh
...fresh	...fresco **freh**-skoh
...fast	...lo más rápido loh mahs **rah**-pee-doh
...spicy (hot)	...picante pee-**kahn**-tay
Is it filling?	¿Llena mucho? **yeh**-nah **moo**-choh
Make me happy.	Hágame feliz. **ah**-gah-may feh-**leeth**
Around _____ euros.	Unos _____ euros. **oo**-nohs _____ **yoo**-rohs
What is that? (pointing)	¿Qué es esto? kay ehs **eh**-stoh
How much is it?	¿Cuánto cuesta? **kwahn**-toh **kweh**-stah
Nothing with eyeballs.	Nada con ojos. **nah**-dah kohn **oh**-hohs
Can I substitute (something) for the _____?	¿Puedo sustituir (algo) por el _____? **pweh**-doh soo-stee-too-**eer** (**ahl**-goh) por ehl _____
Can I / we get it "to go"?	¿Me / Nos lo empaqueta para llevar? may / nohs loh ehm-pah-**keh**-tah **pah**-rah yeh-**bar**

When going to a good restaurant that has an approachable staff, I like to say **Hágame feliz** (Make me happy), and set a price limit.

Tableware and Condiments

I need / We need a...	Necesito / Necesitamos un / una... neh-theh-**see**-toh / neh-theh-see-**tah**-mohs oon / **oo**-nah
...napkin.	...servilleta. sehr-bee-**yeh**-tah
...knife.	...cuchillo. koo-**chee**-yoh
...fork.	...tenedor. teh-neh-**dor**
...spoon.	...cuchara. koo-**chah**-rah
...cup.	...taza. **tah**-thah
...glass.	...vaso. **bah**-soh
Please, another...	Por favor, otro... por fah-**bor oh**-troh
...table setting.	...servicio. sehr-**bee**-thee-oh
...plate.	...plato. **plah**-toh
silverware	cubiertos koo-bee-**ehr**-tohs
carafe	garrafa gah-**rah**-fah
water	agua **ah**-gwah
bread	pan pahn
butter	mantequilla mahn-teh-**kee**-yah
margarine	margarina mar-gah-**ree**-nah
salt / pepper	sal / pimiento sahl / pee-mee-**ehn**-toh
sugar	azúcar ah-**thoo**-kar
artificial sweetener	edulcorante eh-dool-koh-**rahn**-tay
honey	miel mee-**ehl**
mustard	mostaza moh-**stah**-thah
mayonnaise	mayonesa mī-yoh-**neh**-sah
toothpick	palillo pah-**lee**-yoh

The Food Arrives

After serving the meal, your server might wish you a cheery *¡Qué aproveche!* (Bon appétit).

Looks delicious!	¡Parece delicioso! pah-**reh**-thay deh-lee-thee-**oh**-soh
Is this included with the meal?	¿Está esto incluido con la comida? eh-**stah** **eh**-stoh een-kloo-**ee**-doh kohn lah koh-**mee**-dah
I did not order / We did not order this.	No pedí / No pedimos esto. noh peh-**dee** / noh peh-**dee**-mohs **eh**-stoh
Can you heat this up?	¿Me puede calentar esto? may **pweh**-day kah-lehn-**tar eh**-stoh
A little.	Un poco. oon **poh**-koh
More. / Another.	Más. / Otro. mahs / **oh**-troh
One more, please.	Uno más, por favor. **oo**-noh mahs por fah-**bor**
The same.	El mismo. ehl **mees**-moh
Enough.	Suficiente. soo-fee-thee-**ehn**-tay
Finished.	Terminado. tehr-mee-**nah**-doh
I'm full.	Estoy lleno[a]. **eh**-stoy **yeh**-noh
I'm stuffed! (I put on my boots!)	¡Me he puesto las botas! may ay **pweh**-stoh lahs **boh**-tahs
Thank you.	Gracias. **grah**-thee-ahs

Complaints

This is...	Esto está... **eh**-stoh eh-**stah**
...dirty.	...sucio. **soo**-thee-oh
...greasy.	...grasiento. grah-see-**ehn**-toh
...salty.	...salado. sah-**lah**-doh
...undercooked.	...crudo. **kroo**-doh

...overcooked.	...demasiado hecho. deh-mah-see-**ah**-doh **eh**-choh
...cold.	...frío. **free**-oh
...disgusting.	...asqueroso. ah-skeh-**roh**-soh
This is inedible.	Esto no está comestible. **eh**-stoh noh eh-**stah** koh-meh-**stee**-blay
Do any of your customers return?	¿Vuelven sus clientes? **bwehl**-behn soos klee-**ehn**-tehs
Yuck!	¡Que asco! kay **ah**-skoh

Compliments to the Chef

Yummy!	¡Que rico! kay **ree**-koh
Delicious!	¡Delicioso! deh-lee-thee-**oh**-soh
Very tasty!	¡Muy sabroso! **moo**-ee sah-**broh**-soh
I love Spanish food.	Me encanta la comida española. may ehn-**kahn**-tah lah koh-**mee**-dah eh-spahn-**yoh**-lah
My compliments to the chef!	Felicitaciones al cocinero! feh-lee-thee-tah-thee-**oh**-nehs ahl koh-thee-**neh**-roh

Paying

bill	la cuenta lah **kwehn**-tah
The bill, please.	La cuenta, por favor. lah **kwehn**-tah por fah-**bor**
Together.	Junto. **hoon**-toh
Separate checks.	En cheques separados. ehn **cheh**-kehs seh-pah-**rah**-dohs
Do you accept credit cards?	¿Se aceptan tarjetas de crédito? say ah-**thehp**-tahn tar-**heh**-tahs day **kray**-dee-toh

This is not correct.	Esto no es correcto. **eh**-stoh noh ehs koh-**rehk**-toh
Can you explain this?	¿Podría explicarme esto? poh-**dree**-ah ehk-splee-**kar**-may **eh**-stoh
Can you itemize the bill?	¿Podría detallarme la cuenta? poh-**dree**-ah deh-tah-**yar**-may lah **kwehn**-tah
What if I wash the dishes?	¿Qué le parece si lavo platos? kay lay pah-**reh**-thay see **lah**-boh **plah**-tohs
Could I have a receipt, please?	¿Podría darme un recibo, por favor? poh-**dree**-ah **dar**-may oon reh-**thee**-boh por fah-**bor**

It's rare for Spaniards to request separate checks; usually they just split the bill evenly, or take turns treating each other.

Tipping

If you're ordering food at a counter or tapas from a bar, a tip isn't expected, though you could round up a few small coins when you pay. At restaurants with table service, if the menu says *servicio incluido*, it means just that. If you want, you can add up to five percent for great service, though many Spaniards don't. If service is not included (*servicio no incluido*), you could tip up to 10 percent. When you're uncertain whether to tip, ask another customer if it's expected (*¿Se espera una propina?*).

tip	propina proh-**pee**-nah
service (not) included	servicio (no) incluido sehr-**bee**-thee-oh (noh) een-kloo-**ee**-doh
Is tipping expected?	¿Se espera una propina? say eh-**spehr**-ah **oo**-nah proh-**pee**-nah
What percent?	¿Qué porcentaje? kay por-thehn-**tah**-hay
Keep the change.	Quédese con el cambio. **kay**-deh-say kohn ehl **kahm**-bee-oh

Change, please.	El cambio, por favor.
	ehl **kahm**-bee-oh por fah-**bor**
This is for you.	Esto es para usted.
	eh-stoh ehs **pah**-rah oo-**stehd**

SPECIAL CONCERNS

In a Hurry

Europeans take their time at meals, so don't expect speedy service. However, if you're in a rush, let your server know.

I'm / We're in a hurry.	Tengo / Tenemos prisa.
	tehn-goh / teh-**neh**-mohs **pree**-sah
I'm sorry.	Lo siento. loh see-**ehn**-toh
I need to be served quickly.	Necesito que me sirvan en seguida.
	neh-theh-**see**-toh kay may **seer**-bahn
	ehn sehg-**ee**-dah
We need to be served quickly.	Necesitamos que nos sirvan en seguida.
	neh-theh-see-**tah**-mohs kay nohs **seer**-
	bahn ehn sehg-**ee**-dah
I must / We must...	Tengo / Tenemos que...
	tehn-goh / teh-**neh**-mohs kay
...leave in 30 minutes / one hour.	...salir en treinta minutos / una hora.
	sah-**leer** ehn **trayn**-tah mee-**noo**-tohs /
	oo-nah **oh**-rah
When will the food be ready?	¿Cuándo estará lista la comida?
	kwahn-doh eh-stah-**rah lee**-stah lah
	koh-**mee**-dah
Please bring the bill.	Por favor, traiga la cuenta.
	por fah-**bor trī**-gah lah **kwehn**-tah

To speed things up, ask for your bill when the waiter brings your food. You could explain *Lo siento. Tengo prisa.* (I'm sorry. I'm in a hurry.)

Allergies and Other Dietary Restrictions

If the food you're unable to eat doesn't appear in this list, look for it in the Menu Decoder (next chapter). You'll find vegetarian phrases in the next section.

I'm allergic to...	Soy alérgico[a] a... soy ah-**lehr**-hee-koh ah
I cannot eat...	No puedo comer... noh **pweh**-doh koh-**mehr**
He / She cannot eat...	Él / Ella no puede comer... ehl / **ay**-yah noh **pweh**-day koh-**mehr**
He / She has a life-threatening allergy to...	Él / Ella tiene una alergia peligrosa a... ehl / **ay**-yah tee-**ehn**-ay oo-nah ah-lehr-**hee**-ah peh-lee-**groh**-sah ah
No...	Sin... seen
...dairy products.	...productos lácteos. proh-**dook**-tohs **lahk**-teh-ohs
...nuts.	...frutos secos. **froo**-tohs **seh**-kohs
...peanuts.	...cacahuetes. kah-kah-**weh**-tehs
...walnuts.	...nueces. **nweh**-thehs
...wheat / gluten.	...de trigo / gluten. day **tree**-goh / **gloo**-tehn
...shellfish.	...moluscos. moh-**loo**-skohs
...salt / sugar.	...sal / azúcar. sahl / ah-**thoo**-kar
I am diabetic.	Soy diabético[a]. soy dee-ah-**bay**-tee-koh
He / She is lactose intolerant.	Él / Ella es intolerante a la lactosa. ehl / **ay**-yah ehs een-toh-leh-**rahn**-tay ah lah lahk-**toh**-sah
I'd / We'd like a meal that's...	Me / Nos gustaría una comida... may / nohs goo-stah-**ree**-ah oo-nah koh-**mee**-dah
...kosher.	...kosher. **koh**-shehr

...halal.	...comida según la ley musulmana. koh-**mee**-dah seh-**goon** lah lay moo-sool-**mah**-nah
...low-fat.	...con poca grasa. kohn **poh**-kah **grah**-sah
Low cholesterol.	Bajo en colesterol. **bah**-hoh ehn koh-leh-steh-**rohl**
No caffeine.	Sin cafeína. seen kah-fay-**ee**-nah
No alcohol.	Sin alcohol. seen ahl-**kohl**
Organic.	Orgánica. or-**gah**-nee-kah
I eat only insects.	Sólo como insectos. **soh**-loh **koh**-moh een-**sehk**-tohs

Vegetarian Phrases

Many Spaniards think "vegetarian" means "no red meat" or "not much meat." If you're a strict vegetarian, tell your server what you don't eat: Write it out on a card and keep it handy. And it can be helpful to clarify what you do eat.

I'm a...	Soy... soy
...vegetarian.	...vegetariano[a]. beh-heh-tah-ree-**ah**-noh
...strict vegetarian.	...vegetariano[a] estricto[a]. beh-heh-tah-ree-**ah**-noh eh-**streek**-toh
...vegan.	...vegano[a]. **beh**-gah-noh
Is any meat or animal fat used in this?	¿Se ha usado carne o grasa animal en esto? say ah oo-**sah**-doh **kar**-nay oh **grah**-sah ah-nee-**mahl** ehn **eh**-stoh
What is vegetarian? (pointing to menu)	¿Qué comidas son vegetarianas? kay koh-**mee**-dahs sohn beh-heh-tah-ree-**ah**-nahs

I don't eat...	Yo no como... yoh noh **koh**-moh
I'd like this without...	Me gustaría esto sin... may goo-stah-**ree**-ah **eh**-stoh seen
...meat.	...carne. **kar**-nay
...eggs.	...huevos. **weh**-bohs
...animal products.	...ningún producto animal. neen-**goon** proh-**dook**-toh ah-nee-**mahl**
I eat...	Yo como... yoh **koh**-moh
Do you have...?	¿Tiene...? tee-**ehn**-ay
...anything with tofu	...alguna comida con tofu ahl-**goo**-nah koh-**mee**-dah kohn **toh**-foo
...veggie burgers	...hamburguesas vegetarianas ahm-boor-**geh**-sahs beh-heh-tah-ree-**ah**-nahs

Children

Do you have a children's menu?	¿Tiene un menú para niños? tee-**ehn**-ay oon meh-**noo pah**-rah **neen**-yohs
children's portions	raciones para niños rah-thee-**oh**-nehs **pah**-rah **neen**-yohs
half portions	media raciones **meh**-dee-ah rah-thee-**oh**-nehs
a high chair	una trona **oo**-nah **troh**-nah
a booster seat	una silla elevadora **oo**-nah **see**-yah eh-leh-bah-**doh**-rah
noodles	fideos fee-**deh**-ohs
rice	arroz ah-**rohth**
with butter	con mantequilla kohn mahn-teh-**kee**-yah
without sauce	sin salsa seen **sahl**-sah
sauce / dressing on the side	salsa / aliño a parte **sahl**-sah / ah-**leen**-yoh ah **par**-tay

pizza...	pizza... "pizza"
...cheese only	...sólo queso **soh**-loh **keh**-soh
...pepperoni	...salchichón sahl-chee-**chohn**
cheese sandwich...	sandwich de queso... **sahnd**-weech day **keh**-soh
...toasted	...tostada toh-**stah**-dah
...grilled	...a la parrilla ah lah pah-**ree**-yah
hot dog	perrito caliente pehr-**ree**-toh kah-lee-**ehn**-tay
hamburger	hamburguesa ahm-boor-**geh**-sah
French fries	patatas fritas pah-**tah**-tahs **free**-tahs
ketchup	ketchup "ketchup"
milk	leche **leh**-chay
straw	pajita pah-**hee**-tah
More napkins, please.	Más servilletas, por favor. mahs sehr-bee-**yeh**-tahs por fah-**bor**

WHAT'S COOKING?

Breakfast

Start your day with Spanish flair at a corner bar or at a colorful café near the town market hall. Ask for the ***desayuno*** (breakfast special, usually available until noon), which can include coffee, a roll (or sandwich), and juice for one price.

I'd / We'd like...	Me / Nos gustaría... may / nohs goo-stah-**ree**-ah
breakfast	desayuno deh-sah-**yoo**-noh
bread (white)	pan (de molde) pahn (day **mohl**-day)
baguette-style bread	pan de barra pahn day **bah**-rah
roll	panecillo pah-neh-**thee**-yoh
sweet roll	bollo boh-**yoh**

Key Phrases: What's Cooking?

food	comida	koh-**mee**-dah
breakfast	desayuno	deh-sah-**yoo**-noh
lunch	almuerzo / comida	ahlm-**wehr**-thoh / koh-**mee**-dah
dinner	cena	**theh**-nah
bread	pan	pahn
cheese	queso	**keh**-soh
soup	sopa	**soh**-pah
salad	ensalada	ehn-sah-**lah**-dah
fish	pescado	peh-**skah**-doh
chicken	pollo	**poh**-yoh
meat	carne	**kar**-nay
vegetables	verduras	behr-**doo**-rahs
fruit	fruta	**froo**-tah
dessert	postre	**poh**-stray

toasted bread...	tostada...	toh-**stah**-dah
...with olive oil (and tomato)	... con aceite (y tomate)	kohn ah-**thay**-tay (ee toh-**mah**-tay)
baguette sandwich...	bocadillo...	boh-kah-**dee**-yoh
...with ham / cheese / both	...con jamón / queso / mixto	kohn hah-**mohn** / **keh**-soh / **meek**-stoh
...with ham, cheese, and over-easy egg	...mixto con huevo	**meek**-stoh kohn **weh**-boh
potato omelet	tortilla española	tor-**tee**-yah eh-spahn-**yoh**-lah
butter	mantequilla	mahn-teh-**kee**-yah
jelly	mermelada	mehr-meh-**lah**-dah

honey	miel mee-**ehl**
fruit cup	macedonia mah-theh-**doh**-nee-ah
milk	leche **leh**-chay
coffee / tea	café / té kah-**fay** / tay
fruit juice	zumo de fruta **thoo**-moh day **froo**-tah
orange juice	zumo de naranja **thoo**-moh day nah-**rahn**-hah
hot chocolate	chocolate caliente choh-koh-**lah**-tay kah-lee-**ehn**-tay

The traditional Spanish breakfast is ***churros con chocolate***—greasy fritters or doughnuts dipped in a thick, warm chocolate drink. Try these at least once.

For a substantial breakfast, get a ***tortilla española***—an inexpensive potato omelet cooked fresh each morning and served in slices.

Pastries

pastries	bollos **boh**-yohs
cream puff	bamba de nata **bahm**-bah day **nah**-tah
filled with...	relleno de... reh-**yeh**-noh day
...jam	...mermelada mehr-meh-**lah**-dah

...strawberry /
   apricot / cherry
	...fresa / albaricoque / cereza
	   freh-sah / ahl-bah-ree-**koh**-kay /
	   theh-**reh**-thah

...apple	...manzana mahn-**thah**-nah
...chocolate	...chocolate choh-koh-**lah**-tay
...custard or crème	...crema **kreh**-mah
...nut / almond	...fruto seco / almendra **froo**-toh **seh**-koh / ahl-**mehn**-drah
...raisins	...pasas **pah**-sahs
What is fresh now?	¿Qué tiene recién hecho? kay tee-**ehn**-ay reh-thee-**ehn** eh-**choh**

Pastry Specialties

caracola kah-rah-**koh**-lah
conch-shaped twist (like a cinnamon roll)

croissant (a la plancha) krwah-**sahn** (ah lah **plahn**-chah)
our familiar croissant (grilled with butter)

napolitana nah-poh-lee-**tah**-nah
rolled pastry, usually filled with cream or chocolate

palmera pahl-**mehr**-ah
heart-shaped pastry (like an "elephant ear")

pantera rosa pahn-**tehr**-ah roh-sah
"pink panther" (a sugary pastry for kids)

rosquilla roh-**skee**-yah
doughnut (Madrid)

tortel (cabello de ángel) tor-**tehl** (kah-**beh**-yoh day **ahn**-hehl)
ring-shaped pastry (with sugared squash fibers called "angel hair")

In Madrid, a *rosquilla* (doughnut) comes either *tonta* ("dumb"—plain), *lista* ("ready to go"—frosted), or *francesa* ("French"—dusted with powdered sugar).

What's Probably Not for Breakfast

These items won't appear on a traditional Spanish breakfast table, but you may find them at international hotels or cafés catering to foreigners. Scrambled eggs (*huevos revueltos*, or simply *revuelto*) are more typically served at dinnertime.

eggs...	huevos... **weh**-bohs
...fried	...fritos / estrellados **free**-tohs / eh-streh-**yah**-dohs
...hard-boiled	...duros **doo**-rohs
...poached	...pochado poh-**chah**-doh
...scrambled	...revueltos reh-**bwehl**-tohs
yogurt	yogur yoh-**goor**
cereal	cereales theh-reh-**ah**-lehs

Sandwiches

Sandwiches are cheap and basic. A ham sandwich is just that—ham on bread, period. While a *sandwich* comes on square bread, the more popular and tastier *bocadillo* comes on a baguette.

baguette sandwich	bocadillo boh-kah-**dee**-yoh
square-bread sandwich	sandwich **sahnd**-weech
I'd like a sandwich.	Me gustaría un bocadillo. may goo-stah-**ree**-ah oon boh-kah-**dee**-yoh
white bread	pan pahn
wheat bread	pan integral pahn een-teh-**grahl**
toasted ham and cheese	tostado de jamón y queso toh-**stah**-doh day *h*ah-**mohn** ee **keh**-soh
cheese	queso **keh**-soh
tuna	atún ah-**toon**
fish	pescado peh-**skah**-doh
chicken	pollo **poh**-yoh
turkey	pavo **pah**-boh
ham (cured)	jamón *h*ah-**mohn**
ham (cooked)	jamón York *h*ah-**mohn** "York"
meat (beef)	carne **kar**-nay
salami	salami sah-**lah**-mee
egg salad	ensalada de huevo ehn-sah-**lah**-dah day **weh**-boh
lettuce	lechuga lay-**choo**-gah
tomato	tomate toh-**mah**-tay
onion	cebolla thay-**boh**-yah
mustard	mostaza moh-**stah**-thah
mayonnaise	mayonesa mī-yoh-**nay**-sah
on sandwich bread / on a roll	con pan de molde / con un bollo kohn pahn day **mohl**-day / kohn oon **boh**-yoh

toasted / grilled / heated	tostado / a la plancha / caliente toh-**stah**-doh / ah lah **plahn**-chah / kah-lee-**ehn**-tay
Does this come cold or warm?	¿Lo sirven frío o caliente? loh **seer**-behn **free**-oh oh kah-lee-**ehn**-tay

Types of Sandwiches

bocadillo boh-kah-**dee**-yoh
baguette sandwich

montado / montadito mohn-**tah**-doh / mohn-tah-**dee**-toh
small bun (or baguette slice) with a tapa "mounted" on top

pulga / pulguita / pepito **pool**-gah / pool-**gee**-tah / peh-**pee**-toh
various terms for a small baguette sandwich

flauta **flow**-tah
flute-thin baguette sandwich

canapé kah-nah-**pay**
tiny open-faced sandwich

tosta **toh**-stah
large, toasted, open-faced sandwich

sandwich **sahnd**-weech
American-style sandwich on square bread

pa amb tomàquet pah ahm toh-**mah**-keht
country bread rubbed with grated tomatoes and olive oil (Catalunya)

Say Cheese

cheese	queso **keh**-soh
cheese shop	quesería keh-seh-**ree**-ah
Do you have a cheese that is...?	¿Tiene un queso que sea...? tee-**ehn**-ay oon **keh**-soh kay **seh**-ah
...mild / sharp	...suave / fuerte **swah**-bay / **fwehr**-tay
...fresh / aged	...fresco / curado **freh**-skoh / koo-**rah**-doh

...soft / hard	...blando / duro **blahn**-doh / **doo**-roh
...from a cow / sheep / goat	...de vaca / oveja / cabra day **bah**-kah / oh-**beh**-*h*ah / **kah**-brah
sliced	a lonchas ah **lohn**-chahs
smoked	ahumado ah-oo-**mah**-doh
May I taste it?	¿Podría probarlo? poh-**dree**-ah proh-**bar**-loh
What is your favorite cheese?	¿Cuál es su queso favorito? kwahl ehs soo **keh**-soh fah-boh-**ree**-toh
I would like three types of cheese for a picnic.	Me gustaría comprar tres tipos de queso para hacer un picnic. may goo-stah-**ree**-ah kohm-**prar** trehs **tee**-pohs day **keh**-soh **pah**-rah ah-**thehr** oon **peek**-neek
Choose for me, please.	Elija por mí, por favor. eh-**lee**-*h*ah por mee por fah-**bor**
This much. (showing size)	Así. ah-**see**
More. / Less.	Más. / Menos. mahs / **meh**-nohs
Can you please slice it?	¿Puede cortarlo a lonchas, por favor? **pweh**-day kor-**tar**-loh ah **lohn**-chahs por fah-**bor**

Spanish Cheeses

burgos **boor**-gohs
fresh, creamy sheep's milk cheese (Castile)

cabrales kah-**brah**-lehs
tangy, strong, blue-veined cheese from raw goat, cow, and sheep milk

idiazábal ee-dee-ah-**thah**-bahl
raw sheep's milk cheese (Basque Country)

manchego mahn-**cheh**-goh
hard white or yellow sheep's milk cheese (La Mancha), best when made from raw milk (*leche cruda*)

palitos de queso   pah-**lee**-tohs day **keh**-soh
cheese sticks or straws

perilla / tetilla / teta   peh-**ree**-yah / teh-**tee**-yah / **teh**-tah
firm, bland cow's milk cheese (Galicia)

requesón   reh-keh-**sohn**
type of cottage cheese

roncal   rohn-**kahl**
smoked, strong, dry, sharp sheep's milk cheese (Navarre)

San Simón   sahn see-**mohn**
smoked but mild cheese (Galicia)

villalón   bee-yah-**lohn**
sheep's milk curdled and drained, pressed into molds, and salted

Soups

soup...	sopa... **soh**-pah
...of the day	...del día dehl **dee**-ah
...vegetable broth	...de verduras caldo day behr-**doo**-rahs **kahl**-doh
...chicken	...de pollo day **poh**-yoh
...meat	...de carne day **kar**-nay
...fish	...de pescado day peh-**skah**-doh
...with noodles	...con fideos kohn fee-**deh**-ohs
...with rice	...con arroz kohn ah-**rohth**

Salads

salad...	ensalada... ehn-sah-**lah**-dah
...green	...verde **behr**-day
...mixed	...mixta **meek**-stah
chef's salad...	ensalada de la casa... ehn-sah-**lah**-dah day lah **kah**-sah

...with ham and cheese	...con jamón y queso kohn hah-**mohn** ee keh-soh
...with egg	...con huevo kohn weh-boh
lettuce	lechuga leh-**choo**-gah
tomato	tomate toh-**mah**-tay
onion	cebolla theh-**boh**-yah
cucumber	pepino peh-**pee**-noh
carrot	zanahoria thah-nah-**oh**-ree-ah
oil / vinegar	aceite / vinagre ah-**thay**-tay / bee-**nah**-gray
dressing (on the side)	aliño (a parte) ah-**leen**-yoh (ah **par**-tay)
What is in this salad?	¿Qué tiene esta ensalada? kay tee-**ehn**-ay **eh**-stah ehn-sah-**lah**-dah

In Spanish restaurants, salad dressing is normally just the oil and vinegar at the table.

Soup and Salad Specialties

callos **kah**-yohs
tripe stew

cocido koh-**thee**-doh
meat stew with garbanzo beans and veggies

gazpacho gahth-**pah**-choh
cold soup with tomato, bread, garlic, and olive oil

salmorejo sahl-moh-**reh**-hoh
creamier variation of gazpacho (Córdoba)

sopa de almendras **soh**-pah day ahl-**mehn**-drahs
almond soup with saffron and red pepper (Granada)

sopa castellana **soh**-pah kah-steh-**yah**-nah
egg soup with garlic

sopa a la gitana **soh**-pah ah lah hee-**tah**-nah
pumpkin and chickpea soup (Andalucía)

ensaladilla Rusa ehn-sah-lah-**dee**-yah **roo**-sah
veggie salad in mayonnaise dressing

esqueixada eh-skay-**shah**-dah
salad of salted cod, onions, and peppers (Catalunya)

xató shah-**toh**
lettuce with tuna and anchovies in a spicy sauce (Catalunya)

Seafood

seafood	marisco mah-**ree**-skoh
assorted seafood	marisco variado mah-**ree**-skoh bah-ree-**ah**-doh
fish	pescado peh-**skah**-doh
shellfish	marisco mah-**ree**-skoh
anchovies	anchoas ahn-**choh**-ahs
anchovies cured in vinegar	boquerones en vinagre boh-keh-**roh**-nehs ehn bee-**nah**-gray
barnacles	percebes pehr-**theh**-behs
bream (fish)	besugo beh-**soo**-goh
clams	almejas ahl-**meh**-hahs
cod	bacalao bah-kahl-**ow**
crab	cangrejo kahn-**greh**-hoh
crayfish	cangrejo de río kahn-**greh**-hoh day **ree**-oh
cuttlefish	sepia **seh**-pee-ah
dogfish	cazón kah-**thohn**
eel	anguila ahn-**gee**-lah
hake (whitefish)	merluza (pescado blanco) mehr-**loo**-thah (pehs-**kah**-doh **blahn**-koh)
halibut	halibut ah-lee-**boot**
herring	arenque ah-**rehn**-kay
lobster	langosta lahn-**goh**-stah
monkfish	rape **rah**-pay
mussels	mejillones meh-hee-**yoh**-nehs

octopus	pulpo **pool**-poh
oysters	ostras **oh**-strahs
prawns	gambas **gahm**-bahs
...large prawns	...langostinos lahn-goh-**stee**-nohs
salmon	salmón sahl-**mohn**
sardines	sardinas sar-**dee**-nahs
scad (like mackerel)	jurel *hoo*-**rehl**
scallops	vieiras bee-**ay**-rahs
shrimp...	gambas... **gahm**-bahs
...in the shell	...en la cáscara ehn lah **kah**-skah-rah
...peeled	...peladas peh-**lah**-dahs
sole	lenguado lehn-**gwah**-doh
spider crab	centollo thehn-**toh**-yoh
squid	calamares kah-lah-**mah**-rehs
swordfish	pez espada / emperador
	pehth eh-**spah**-dah / ehm-peh-rah-**dor**
trout	trucha **troo**-chah
tuna	atún ah-**toon**
How much for a portion?	¿Cuánto cuesta una ración? **kwahn**-toh **kweh**-stah **oo**-nah rah-thee-**ohn**
What's fresh today?	¿Qué hay fresco hoy? kay ī **freh**-skoh oy
How do you eat this?	¿Cómo se come esto? **koh**-moh say **koh**-may **eh**-stoh
Do you eat this part?	¿Se come esta parte? say **koh**-may **eh**-stah **par**-tay
Just the head, please.	Sólo la cabeza, por favor. **soh**-loh lah kah-**beh**-thah por fah-**bor**

Fish is often prepared *en adobo*—marinated in a combination of stock, vinegar, garlic, paprika, oregano, and salt. Seafood is often served fried (*frito*). Shrimp (*gambas*) usually come in the shell (*en la cáscara*).

Seafood Specialties

bacalao a la vizcaína bah-kahl-**ow** ah lah beeth-kah-**ee**-nah
salt cod braised with peppers, tomatoes, and onions (Basque Country)

calamares con guisantes kah-lah-**mah**-rehs kohn gee-**sahn**-tehs
squid with garlic, peas, tomatoes, and mint

marmitako mar-mee-**tah**-koh
Basque tuna stew

paella pah-**eh**-yah
saffron rice, usually with seafood, sausage, and veggies

navaja de almeja nah-**bah**-hah day ahl-**meh**-hah
razor clam

romesco roh-**meh**-skoh
stewed fish and beans with tomatoes, green pepper, pimento, and garlic

zarzuela de mariscos thar-**thweh**-lah day mah-**ree**-skohs
seafood stew with an almond-cayenne pepper broth (Catalunya)

One of Spain's most famous dishes is *paella*, which features saffron-flavored rice with whatever the chef wants to mix in—seafood, sausage, chicken, peppers, and so on. Jump (like everyone else in the bar) at the opportunity to snare a small plate of *paella* when it appears hot out of the kitchen in a tapas bar.

Poultry

poultry	aves	**ah**-behs
chicken	pollo	**poh**-yoh
duck	pato	**pah**-toh
goose	ganso	**gahn**-soh
turkey	pavo	**pah**-boh
partridge	perdiz	pehr-**deeth**
breast	pechuga	peh-**choo**-gah
thigh / drumstick	muslo	**moo**-sloh

liver (pâté)	hígado (paté) **ee**-gah-doh (pah-**tay**)
eggs	huevos **weh**-bohs
free-range	de corral day koh-**rahl**
How long has this been dead?	¿Cuánto tiempo hace que lo mataron? **kwahn**-toh tee-**ehm**-poh ah-**thay** kay loh mah-**tah**-rohn

Meat

meat	carne **kar**-nay
cold cuts	fiambres fee-**ahm**-brehs
cured meats	embutidos ehm-boo-**tee**-dohs
cutlet / chop	chuleta choo-**leh**-tah
ribs	costillas koh-**stee**-yahs
shoulder	paletilla pah-leh-**tee**-yah
beef	carne de vaca **kar**-nay day **bah**-kah
beef steak	bistec **bee**-stehk
boar	jabalí hah-bah-**lee**
goat (kid)	cabrito / chato kah-**bree**-toh / **chah**-toh
ham...	jamón... hah-**mohn**
...smoked	...ahumado ah-oo-**mah**-doh
lamb	cordero kor-**dehr**-oh
mutton	oveja oh-**beh**-hah
ox	buey bway
pork	cerdo **thehr**-doh
rabbit	conejo koh-**neh**-hoh
roast beef	carne asada **kar**-nay ah-**sah**-dah
sausage (spicier / milder)	chorizo / salchichón choh-**ree**-toh / sahl-chee-**chohn**
...blood sausage	...morcilla mor-**thee**-yah
suckling pig	cochinillo koh-chee-**nee**-yoh

EATING

What's Cooking?

Avoiding Mis-Steaks

alive	vivo **bee**-boh
raw	crudo **kroo**-doh
very rare	muy poco hecha **moo**-ee **poh**-koh **eh**-chah
rare	poco hecho **poh**-koh **eh**-choh
medium	en su punto ehn soo **poon**-toh
well done	muy hecho **moo**-ee **eh**-choh
very well-done	bastante hecho bah-**stahn**-tay **eh**-choh
almost burnt	casi quemada **kah**-see keh-**mah**-dah
loin	lomo **loh**-moh
tenderloin / sirloin	solomillo soh-loh-**mee**-yoh
ribeye	entrecot ehn-treh-**koht**
T-bone	chuletón choo-leh-**tohn**
chop	chuleta choo-**leh**-tah
flank	falda **fahl**-dah
filet	filete fee-**leh**-tay

veal	ternera tehr-**nehr**-ah
venison	venado beh-**nah**-doh
Is this cooked?	¿Está hecho? eh-**stah eh**-choh

The two major types of Spanish sausage are **chorizo** (red and sometimes spicy, with paprika) and **salchichón** (milder, peppery, similar to salami). **Morcilla** is blood sausage, made with fresh pig's blood. Often mixed with rice, it is surprisingly light and mild.

Meat, but...

Spaniards pride themselves on using every part of the animal "except the walk." In markets, look for (or avoid) the *casquería* section, where you'll find some of these items:

brains	sesos **seh**-sohs
kidney	riñón reen-**yohn**
liver	hígado **ee**-gah-doh
neck	cuello **kweh**-yoh
organs	vísceras **bee**-theh-rahs
tongue	lengua **lehn**-gwah
bull testicles	criadillas / huevos de toro kree-ah-**dee**-yahs / **weh**-bohs day **toh**-roh
horse meat	caballo kah-**bah**-yoh
lamb intestines (fried)	gallinejas / zarajo gah-lee-**neh**-hahs / thah-**rah**-hoh
pig-brain omelet	tortilla Sacromonte tor-**tee**-yah sah-kroh-**mohn**-tay
pig's ear (fried)	oreja oh-**reh**-hah
sweetbreads	mollejas moh-**yeh**-hahs
tripe	tripa / callos **tree**-pah / **kah**-yohs

Orejas (fried pig's ears) are a popular snack, similar to pork rinds back home.

Jamón and Other Cured Meats

The prized staple of Spanish cuisine, *jamón* is prosciutto-like ham that's dry-cured and aged. It's generally sliced thin (right off the hock) and served raw and cold. Bars proudly hang hamhocks from the rafters.

jamón hah-**mohn**
dry-cured ham
jamón serrano hah-**mohn** seh-**rah**-noh
good quality, cured in the sierras (mountains)

jamón ibérico hah-**mohn** ee-**bay**-ree-koh
higher quality, from black-hooved Iberian pigs (*pata negra*)

jamón de bellota hah-**mohn** day beh-**yoh**-tah
top quality, from pigs fed acorns (*bellotas*)

jamón de recebeo / de cebo
hah-**mohn** day reh-theh-**beh**-oh / day **theh**-boh
lower quality, from grain-fed pigs

jamón blanco hah-**mohn blahn**-koh
jamón from "white" pigs

cecina (de vaca) theh-**thee**-nah (day **bah**-kah)
dry-cured beef

chorizo choh-**ree**-thoh
sausage with paprika, can be spicy

lomo **loh**-moh
pork tenderloin

morcilla mor-**thee**-yah
blood sausage

salchichón sahl-chee-**chohn**
mild, salami-like sausage

To sample the best *jamón* without paying high restaurant or bar prices, go to the local market and ask for 100 grams (about a quarter-pound) of top-quality ham *(cien gramos de jamón ibérico de bellota)*.

Main Course Specialties

Note that many items listed under "Tapas," on page 143, also show up as main courses.

butifarra boo-tee-**fah**-rah
pork sausage spiced with cinnamon, nutmeg, and cloves

cochinillo asado koh-chee-**nee**-yoh ah-**sah**-doh
roasted suckling pig marinated in herbs, olive oil, and white wine
(Castile and León)

cola de toro / rabo de toro
koh-lah day **toh**-roh / **rah**-boh day **toh**-roh
bull-tail stew

cordonices en hoja de parra
kor-doh-**nee**-thehs ehn **oh**-hah day **pah**-rah
sherry-braised quail wrapped in grape leaves and bacon

empanada gallega ehm-pah-**nah**-dah gah-**yeh**-gah
pizza-like pie, usually with pork tenderloin, onions, and bell peppers
(Galicia)

escudella i carn d'olla eh-skoo-**day**-ah ee karn **doy**-ah
minced pork meatballs

fabada asturiana fah-**bah**-dah ah-stoo-ree-**ah**-nah
pork, bean, and paprika stew (Asturias)

habas a la Catalana ah-bahs ah lah kah-tah-**lah**-nah
fava bean and chorizo sausage stew with mint and paprika

pastela pah-**steh**-lah
savory phyllo pie with poultry, seasoned with cinnamon (Andalucía)

pollo en pepitoria **poh**-yoh ehn peh-pee-**toh**-ree-ah
chicken fricassee with almonds and eggs

riñónes al jerez reen-**yoh**-nehs ahl heh-**rehth**
kidneys in sherry sauce

How Food Is Prepared

aged	madurado	mah-doo-**rah**-doh
assorted	variado	bah-ree-**ah**-doh
baked	cocido	koh-**thee**-doh
barbecued	a la parilla	ah lah pah-**ree**-yah
boiled	hervido	ehr-**bee**-doh
braised	estofado	eh-stoh-**fah**-doh
breaded	rebozado	reh-boh-**thah**-doh
broiled	a la parilla	ah lah pah-**ree**-yah
browned	dorado	doh-**rah**-doh

EATING

What's Cooking?

Spanish Regional Specialties

Asturias *(a la asturiana)*: Squeezed between the Picos de Europa mountains and the North Atlantic, Asturias combines seafood with hearty mountain grub—including *fabas* (giant, white, fava-like beans); the powerful, white, Roquefort-like *cabrales* cheese; and *sidra* (hard cider), used both for drinking and for cooking.

Galicia *(a la gallega)*: The green, rainy northwest of Spain is known for its octopus (*pulpo*, specifically *pulpo a la gallega*, chopped up and dusted with paprika) and its many pork dishes (such as *orejas*, fried pig's ears). Other specialties include *pimientos de Padrón* (deep-fried, small green peppers) and *ribeiro* wine, served in little ceramic bowls (to disguise its lack of clarity).

Andalucía: This region's food makes ample use of onion, tomatoes, and peppers, which combine deliciously in *sofrito*, a base for many dishes. The most famous Andalusian dish is the zesty cold tomato soup, *gazpacho*. Córdoba specializes in *pisto* (a ratatouille-like vegetable stew) and *salmorejo* (a creamier variation on gazpacho, often with ham and egg). From the Moorish influence, you'll find the Arabic-flavored *pastela*—a savory phyllo pie with poultry, seasoned with cinnamon.

Castilla y León *(castellano/leonese)*: This high, central plateau of Spain was the home of vast flocks of sheep in the Middle Ages. This

cold	frío	**free**-oh
cooked	cocinado	koh-thee-**nah**-doh
chopped	picado	pee-**kah**-doh
crispy	crujiente	kroo-hee-**ehn**-tay
cured	curado	koo-**rah**-doh
deep fried	rebozado	reh-boh-**thah**-doh
fresh	fresco	**freh**-skoh
fried	frito	**free**-toh

influence—in the form of lamb and the famous *manchego* sheep's cheese (from La Mancha)—persists today. Other popular Castilian and Leonese meats are sausages, *cochinillo asado* (roast suckling pig: 21 days of mother's milk, into the oven, and onto your plate—oh, Babe), and *cecina* (beef that's cured like *jamón serrano*).

Catalunya: Like its culture and language, Catalan food is a fusion of Spanish and French. Every meal starts with *pan con tomate* (or *pan amb tomaquet* in Catalan): a baguette rubbed with crushed tomatoes, garlic, and olive oil. Favorite dishes include *fideuà*, thin, flavor-infused noodles served with seafood, and *arròs negre*, black rice cooked in squid ink.

Basque Country: This is arguably the culinary capital of Spain, with inviting *pintxos* (tapas) bars that display a stunning array of help-your-self goodies (just grab what you like from the platters at the bar, and pay on the honor system). Top dishes include *txangurro* (spider crab), *antxoas* (tasty anchovies), *marmitako* (tuna stew), *ttoro* (seafood stew), and *txakoli* (fresh white wine, poured from high up). *Cazuelas* are hot meal-size servings (like *raciones* in Spanish). To find Basque-style bars elsewhere in Spain, look for bars with *vasca* or *euskal* (both mean "Basque") in their name.

garnished	con guarnición	kohn gwar-nee-thee-**ohn**
glazed	glaseado	glah-see-**ah**-doh
grated	rallado	rah-**yah**-doh
grilled (on a barbecue)	a la parrilla	ah lah pah-**ree**-yah
grilled (on a flat top)	a la plancha	ah lah **plahn**-chah
homemade	casera	kah-**sehr**-ah
hot	caliente	kah-lee-**ehn**-tay

in cream sauce	en salsa de crema ehn **sahl**-sah day **kreh**-mah
marinated	en adobo ehn ah-**doh**-boh
melted	fundido foon-**dee**-doh
minced	picado pee-**kah**-doh
mixed	mixto **meek**-stoh
pickled	en escabeche ehn eh-skah-**beh**-chay
poached	escalfado / pochado eh-skahl-**fah**-doh / poh-**chah**-doh
raw	crudo **kroo**-doh
roasted	asado ah-**sah**-doh
sautéed	salteado sahl-teh-**ah**-doh
skewer	brocheta broh-**cheh**-tah
smoked	ahumado ah-oo-**mah**-doh
steamed	al vapor ahl bah-**por**
stuffed	relleno reh-**yeh**-noh
with garlic mayonnaise	con alioli kohn ah-lee-**oh**-lee

When it comes to grilled dishes, Spaniards differentiate between *a la plancha* (on a flat-top grill, literally "by the iron") and *a la parrilla* (on a barbecue).

Flavors and Spices

spicy (flavorful)	con especias kohn eh-**speh**-thee-ahs
spicy (hot)	picante pee-**kahn**-tay
(too) salty	(demasiado) salado (deh-mah-see-**ah**-doh) sah-**lah**-doh
mild	templado tehm-**plah**-doh
sour	agrio **ah**-gree-oh
sweet	dulce **dool**-thay
bitter	amargo ah-**mar**-goh

cayenne	cayena kah-**yeh**-nah
cilantro	cilantro thee-**lahn**-troh
cinnamon	canela kah-**neh**-lah
citrus	cítrico **thee**-tree-koh
garlic	ajo **ah**-hoh
horseradish	rábano picante **rah**-bah-noh pee-**kahn**-tay
mint	menta **mehn**-tah
paprika	pimentón pee-mehn-**tohn**
pepper	pimienta pee-mee-**ehn**-tah
saffron	azafrán ah-thah-**frahn**
salt	sal sahl
sugar	azúcar ah-**thoo**-kar

You can look up more herbs and spices in the Menu Decoder (next chapter).

Veggies and Sides

vegetables	verduras behr-**doo**-rahs
mixed vegetables	menestra meh-**neh**-strah
artichoke	alcachofa ahl-kah-**choh**-fah
arugula (rocket)	rúcula **roo**-koo-lah
asparagus	espárragos eh-**spah**-rah-gohs
avocado	aguacate ah-gwah-**kah**-tay
bean	judía hoo-**dee**-ah
beet	remolacha reh-moh-**lah**-chah
broccoli	brécol / brócoli **bray**-kohl / **broh**-koh-lee
cabbage	col kohl
carrot	zanahoria thah-nah-**oh**-ree-ah
cauliflower	coliflor koh-lee-**flor**
corn	maíz mah-**eeth**

cucumber	pepino	peh-**pee**-noh
eggplant	berenjena	beh-rehn-**heh**-nah
endive	endivia	ehn-**dee**-bee-ah
fennel	hinojo	een-**oh**-hoh
French fries	patatas fritas	pah-**tah**-tahs **free**-tahs
garlic	ajo	**ah**-hoh
green bean	judías verde	hoo-**dee**-ahs **behr**-day
lentil	lenteja	layn-**tay**-hah
mushroom (regular / wild)	champiñon / seta	chahm-peen-**yohn** / **seh**-tah
olive	aceituna	ah-thay-**too**-nah
onion	cebolla	theh-**boh**-yah
pasta	pasta	"pasta"
pea	guisante	gee-**sahn**-tay
pepper...	pimiento...	pee-mee-**ehn**-toh
...green / red / hot	...verde / rojo / picante	**behr**-day / **roh**-hoh / pee-**kahn**-tay
pickle	pepinillo	peh-pee-**nee**-yoh
potato	patata	pah-**tah**-tah
rice	arroz	ah-**rohth**
spaghetti	espaguetis	eh-spah-**geh**-tees
spinach	espinacas	eh-spee-**nah**-kahs
tomato	tomate	toh-**mah**-tay
turnip	nabo	**nah**-boh
zucchini	calabacín	kah-lah-bah-**theen**

While you may know the Latin American word *frijoles* for "beans," Spaniards call them *judías*.

Fruits

fruit	fruta	**froo**-tah
fruit cup	macedonia	mah-theh-**doh**-nee-ah

fruit smoothie	batido de frutas bah-**tee**-doh day **froo**-tahs
apple	manzana mahn-**thah**-nah
apricot	albaricoque ahl-bah-ree-**koh**-kay
banana	plátano **plah**-tah-noh
berries	bayas **bī**-yahs
blueberry	arándano ah-**rahn**-dah-noh
cantaloupe	melon meh-**lohn**
cherry	cereza theh-**reh**-thah
cranberry	arándano rojo ah-**rahn**-dah-noh **roh**-hoh
date	dátil **dah**-teel
fig	higo **ee**-goh
grapefruit	pomelo poh-**meh**-loh
grapes	uvas **oo**-bahs
honeydew melon	melón verde meh-**lohn behr**-day
lemon	limón lee-**mohn**
mango	mango **mahn**-goh
orange	naranja nah-**rahn**-hah
peach	melocotón meh-loh-koh-**tohn**
pear	pera **peh**-rah
persimmon	caqui **kah**-kee
pineapple	piña **peen**-yah
plum	ciruela theer-**weh**-lah
pomegranate	granada grah-**nah**-dah
prune	ciruela pasa theer-**weh**-lah **pah**-sah
raisin	pasa **pah**-sah
raspberry	frambuesa frahm-**bweh**-sah
strawberry	fresa **freh**-sah
tangerine	mandarina mahn-dah-**ree**-nah
watermelon	sandía sahn-**dee**-ah

Nuts and Crunchy Munchies

Spaniards love *frutos secos*. Although literally "dried fruits," this broad category also includes all types of nuts. You'll see hole-in-the-wall *frutos secos* shops where locals stock up on snacks.

nuts	frutos secos **froo**-tohs **seh**-kohs
almond	almendra ahl-**mehn**-drah
cashew	anacardo ah-nah-**kar**-doh
chestnut	castaña kah-**stahn**-yah
coconut	coco **koh**-koh
hazelnut	avellana ah-beh-**yah**-nah
peanut	cacahuete kah-kah-**weh**-tay
pine nut	piñón peen-**yohn**
pistachio	pistachio pee-**stah**-choh
seed	pipa **pee**-pah
sunflower	girasól *hee*-rah-**sohl**
walnut	nuez nwehth

Spaniards like to snack on *pipas* (seeds), especially from sunflowers (*girasóls*) but also from pumpkins (*calabazas*). After a big event, the streets are littered with shells.

Just Desserts

I'd / We'd like...	Me / Nos gustaría... may / nohs goo-stah-**ree**-ah
dessert	postre **poh**-stray
cake	pastel pah-**stehl**
cookie	galleta gah-**yeh**-tah
candy	caramelos kah-rah-**meh**-lohs
caramel custard	flan flahn
cream cake	pastel de crema pah-**stehl** day **kreh**-mah
cream custard	natilla nah-**tee**-yah

Margin text: EATING / What's Cooking?

ice cream	helado eh-**lah**-doh
scoop of...	bola de... **boh**-lah day
cone of...	cucurucho de... koo-koo-**roo**-choh day
cup of...	copa de... **koh**-pah day
vanilla	vainilla bī-**nee**-yah
chocolate	chocolate choh-koh-**lah**-tay
strawberry	fresa **freh**-sah
lemon	limón lee-**mohn**
ice cream cake	tarta helada **tar**-tah eh-**lah**-dah
sherbet	sorbete sor-**beh**-tay
cupcake	magdalena mahg-dah-**leh**-nah
fruit cup	macedonia mah-theh-**doh**-nee-ah
tart	tarta **tar**-tah
whipped cream	nata montada **nah**-tah mohn-**tah**-dah
(chocolate) mousse	mousse (de chocolate) moos (day choh-koh-**lah**-tay)
pudding	pudín poo-**deen**
sweet egg pudding	natilla de huevo nah-**tee**-yah day **weh**-boh
low calorie	bajo en calorías **bah**-hoh ehn kah-loh-**ree**-ahs
homemade	hecho en casa / casera **eh**-choh ehn **kah**-sah / kah-**sehr**-ah
We'll split one.	Lo compartiremos. loh kohm-par-tee-**reh**-mohs
Two forks / spoons, please.	Dos tenedores / cucharas, por favor. dohs teh-neh-**doh**-rehs / koo-**chah**-rahs por fah-**bor**
I shouldn't, but...	No debería, pero... noh day-beh-**ree**-ah **pehr**-oh
Super-tasty!	¡Riquísimo! ree-**kee**-see-moh
Exquisite!	¡Exquisito! ehk-skee-**see**-toh

Death by chocolate.	Muerto por el chocolate. **mwehr**-toh por ehl choh-koh-**lah**-tay
Better than sex.	Mejor que el sexo. meh-**hor** kay ehl **sehk**-soh
A moment on the lips, forever on the hips.	Un momento en los labios, para el resto en las caderas. oon moh-**mehn**-toh ehn lohs **lah**-bee-ohs **pah**-rah ehl **reh**-stoh ehn lahs kah-**deh**-rahs

Spanish has various words for sweet shops: A *bollería* sells sweet rolls, a *pastelería* sells cakes, and a *confitería* is a candy store.

Dessert Specialties

amarguillo ah-marg-**ee**-yoh
confection of almonds, egg whites, and sugar

arroz con leche ah-**rohth** kohn **leh**-chay
rice pudding

brazo de gitano **brah**-thoh day hee-**tah**-noh
sponge cake filled with butter cream (Andalucía); "Gypsy's arm"

buñuelo boon-**weh**-loh
fried ball of dough

crema Catalana **kreh**-mah kah-tah-**lah**-nah
custard (like crème brulée)

cuajada kwah-**hah**-dah
cream-based dessert with honey

flan (de huevo) flahn (day **weh**-boh)
caramel custard

mel i mató mehl ee mah-**toh**
curd cheese drizzled with honey (Catalunya)

membrillo mehm-**bree**-yoh
sweetened quince

panellet pah-neh-**yeht**
sweet potato cookie with pine nuts and hazelnuts (Catalunya)

ponche segoviano   pohn-chay seh-goh-bee-**ah**-noh
layer cake with marzipan (Segovia)

postre de música   poh-stray day **moo**-see-kah
roasted nuts and dried fruit served with dessert wine

tarta de Santiago   **tar**-tah day sahn-tee-**ah**-goh
almond cake with powdered sugar (Galicia)

tocino de cielo   toh-**thee**-noh day thee-**eh**-loh
baked custard topped with caramelized sugar and often flavored
with lemon ("bacon from heaven")

toledana   toh-leh-**dah**-nah
nutty, crumbly, semi-sweet cookie with thread of squash filling

torrija   toh-**ree**-hah
sweet fritter

turrón   too-**rohn**
nougat made with almond, honey, and sugar (popular at Christmas)

yema   **yeh**-mah
sweets made from egg yolks and sugar

TAPAS

Bars called *tascas* or *tabernas* offer delicious snacks called *tapas*
throughout the day, a lifesaver for hungry tourists when Spanish restaurants are closed.

Although tapas are served all day, the real action begins late—21:00
at the earliest. But for beginners, an earlier start is easier and comes with
less commotion. For the least competition at the bar, go early, or on
Monday or Tuesday.

When you're ready to order, be assertive or you'll never be served.
Por favor is a key phrase—it grabs the bartender's attention. Don't
worry about paying until you're ready to leave—the bartender's keeping
track of your tab.

Tapas Basics

How much is it? (pointing)	¿Cuánto cuesta? kwahn-toh kweh-stah
How much per tapa?	¿Cuánto cuesta una tapa? kwahn-toh kweh-stah oo-nah tah-pah
I'd / We'd like...	Me / Nos gustaría... may / nohs goo-stah-ree-ah
...that.	...eso. eh-soh
...a plate of little sandwiches.	...una tabla de canapés variados. oo-nah tah-blah day kah-nah-pays bah-ree-ah-dohs
...an assortment of meats and cheeses.	...un surtido de charcutería y queso. oon soor-tee-doh day char-koo-teh-ree-ah ee keh-soh
How much so far?	¿Cuánto cuesta hasta ahora? kwahn-toh kweh-stah ah-stah ah-oh-rah
The bill, please.	La cuenta, por favor. lah kwehn-tah por fah-bor

For drinks, see page 152 for wine and page 155 for beer.

Tapas Terms

pincho **peen**-choh
bite-size portion

pinchito peen-**chee**-toh
a taste (smaller than a pincho)

tapa **tah**-pah
snack-size portion

media ración (½ ración) **meh**-dee-ah rah-thee-**ohn**
appetizer size, bigger than a tapa

ración rah-thee-**ohn**
large portion

surtido soor-**tee**-doh
assortment

frito   free-toh
fried

a la plancha   ah lah **plahn**-chah
grilled (on a flat-top griddle)

a la parilla   ah lah pah-**ree**-yah
barbecued

brocheta   broh-**cheh**-tah
shish kebab (on a stick)

con alioli   kohn ah-lee-**oh**-lee
with garlic mayonnaise

Many tapas come in sandwich form—tasty bites perched on top of a baguette. For more on sandwiches, see page 121.

Seafood Tapas

Be careful. While veggies are cheap, seafood can be expensive. Confirm the cost before you order.

almejas a la marinera   ahl-**meh**-*h*ahs ah lah mah-ree-**nehr**-ah
clams in white wine sauce with paprika

atún   ah-**toon**
tuna

bacalao   bah-kahl-**ow**
cod

boquerones en vinagre   boh-keh-**roh**-nehs ehn bee-**nah**-gray
anchovies cured in vinegar

calamares fritos / a la Romana
kah-lah-**mah**-rehs **free**-tohs / ah lah roh-**mah**-nah
rings of deep-fried squid

cazón en adabo   kah-**thohn** ehn ah-**dah**-boh
salty marinated dogfish

gambas a la plancha   **gahm**-bahs ah la **plahn**-chah
grilled prawns

gambas al ajillo gahm-bahs ahl ah-**hee**-yoh
prawns cooked in garlic and olive oil

mejillones meh-hee-**yoh**-nehs
mussels

merluza mehr-**loo**-thah
hake (whitefish)

paella pah-**eh**-yah
saffron rice dish with mix of seafood and meat

pescaditos fritos peh-skah-**dee**-tohs **free**-tohs
assortment of little fried fish

pescado en adobo peh-**skah**-doh ehn ah-**doh**-boh
marinated fish

pulpo **pool**-poh
octopus

rabas **rah**-bahs
squid tentacles

sardinas sar-**dee**-nahs
sardines

tortillitas de camarones tor-tee-**yee**-tahs day kah-mah-**roh**-nehs
shrimp fritters (Andalucía)

variado fritos bah-ree-**ah**-doh **free**-tohs
typical Andalusian mix of various fried fish

Even if you think you don't like anchovies, try *boquerones en vinagre*. These tasty little fish—deboned and headless—are deliciously marinated in olive oil, vinegar, and garlic. (*Boquerones fritos* are deep-fried and, for most, not as tasty.)

Meaty Tapas

Remember, the first and last word in meaty tapas is *jamón*—cured ham (see page 131).

albóndigas ahl-**bohn**-dee-gahs
seasoned meatballs with sauce

bomba   bohm-bah
fried ball of meat and potatoes

cabrillas   kah-**bree**-yahs
snails (cheap, but not as good as French escargot)

caracoles   kah-rah-**koh**-lehs
tree snails (May-Sept)

croqueta   kroh-**keh**-tah
croquette—fried dough ball with various fillings

empanadilla   ehm-pah-nah-**dee**-yah
pastry stuffed with meat or seafood

guiso   **gee**-soh
stew

morro   **moh**-roh
pig snout

pincho moruno   **peen**-choh moh-**roo**-noh
skewer of spicy lamb or pork

pollo alioli   **poh**-yoh ah-lee-**oh**-lee
chicken with garlic mayonnaise

sesos   **seh**-sohs
lamb brains

tabla serrana   **tah**-blah seh-**rah**-nah
plate of meat and cheese

Veggie and Egg Tapas

aceitunas   ah-thay-**too**-nahs
olives

almendras   ahl-**mehn**-drahs
almonds (usually fried)

banderilla   bahn-deh-**ree**-yah
skewer of pickled olives, peppers, carrots, and onions

champiñones   chahm-peen-**yoh**-nehs
mushrooms

ensaladilla Rusa   ehn-sah-lah-**dee**-yah **roo**-sah
potato salad with lots of mayo, peas, and carrots

espinaca (con garbanzos)   eh-spee-**nah**-kah (kohn gar-**bahn**-thohs)
spinach (with garbanzo beans)

gazpacho   gahth-**pah**-choh
cold soup, made with tomato, bread, garlic, and olive oil

judías verdes   hoo-**dee**-ahs **behr**-dehs
green beans

patatas bravas   pah-**tah**-tahs **brah**-bahs
fried potatoes with creamy, spicy tomato sauce

pimiento (relleno)   pee-mee-**ehn**-toh (reh-**yeh**-noh)
pepper (stuffed)

pimientos de Padrón   pee-mee-**ehn**-tohs day pah-**drohn**
lightly fried small green peppers, only a few of which are
jalapeño-hot

pinchos de queso   **peen**-chohs day **keh**-soh
pieces of cheese

queso manchego   **keh**-soh mahn-**cheh**-goh
classic Spanish sheep's milk cheese

revuelto de setas   reh-**bwehl**-toh day **seh**-tahs
scrambled eggs with wild mushrooms

tortilla   tor-**tee**-yah
omelet (usually made with potatoes)

tortilla española   tor-**tee**-yah eh-spahn-**yoh**-lah
potato and onion omelet

tortilla de jamón / queso   tor-**tee**-yah day hah-**mohn** / **keh**-soh
potato omelet with ham / cheese

DRINKING

Eating and drinking at a bar is usually cheapest if you sit or stand at the counter (*barra*). You may pay a little more to eat sitting at a table (*mesa or salón*) and still more for an outdoor table (*terraza*). It's bad form to order food at the bar, then take it to a table. If you want to confirm whether the price is the same at the bar or a table, ask *¿Es el mismo precio en la barra que en la mesa?*

Water

mineral water...	agua mineral...	**ah**-gwah mee-neh-**rahl**
...with / without carbonation	...con / sin gas	kohn / seen gahs
tap water	agua del grifo	**ah**-gwah dehl **gree**-foh
(not) drinkable	(no) potable	(noh) poh-**tah**-blay
Is the water safe to drink?	¿Es el agua potable?	ehs ehl **ah**-gwah poh-**tah**-blay

If ordering mineral water in a restaurant, request the more economical *botella grande de agua* (big bottle). For a glass of tap water, specify *un vaso de agua del grifo*. The waiter may counter with "*¿Embotellada?*"— "Bottled?"—hoping to sell you something. Be strong and insist on tap water (*del grifo*), and you'll get it.

Milk

whole milk	leche entera	**leh**-chay ehn-**tehr**-ah
skim milk	leche desnatada	**leh**-chay dehs-nah-**tah**-dah
fresh milk	leche fresca	**leh**-chay **freh**-skah
cold / warm	fría / caliente	**free**-ah / kah-lee-**ehn**-tay
straw	pajita	pah-**hee**-tah
hot chocolate	chocolate caliente	choh-koh-**lah**-tay kah-lee-**ehn**-tay

Key Phrases: Drinking

drink	bebida	bay-**bee**-dah
(mineral) water	agua (mineral)	ah-gwah (mee-neh-**rahl**)
big bottle	botella grande	boh-**teh**-yah **grahn**-day
tap water	agua del grifo	ah-gwah dehl **gree**-foh
milk	leche	**leh**-chay
juice	zumo	**thoo**-moh
coffee	café	kah-**fay**
tea	té	tay
wine	vino	**bee**-noh
beer	cerveza	thehr-**beh**-thah
Cheers!	¡Salud!	sah-**lood**

Juice and Other Drinks

fruit juice	zumo de fruta	**thoo**-moh day **froo**-tah
100% juice	cien por ciento zumo	thee-**ehn** por thee-**ehn**-toh **thoo**-moh
orange juice (pure)	zumo (puro) de naranja	**thoo**-moh (**poo**-roh) day nah-**rahn**-hah
apple juice	zumo de manzana	**thoo**-moh day mahn-**thah**-nah
grape juice	zumo de uva / mosto	**thoo**-moh day **oo**-vah / **moh**-stoh
pineapple juice	zumo de piña	**thoo**-moh day **peen**-yah
fruit smoothie	batido de frutas	bah-**tee**-doh day **froo**-tahs
lemonade	limonada	lee-moh-**nah**-dah
(diet) soda	refresco ("lite")	reh-**freh**-skoh ("lite")
energy drink	bebida energética	beh-**bee**-dah eh-nehr-**hay**-tee-kah

with / without...	con / sin... kohn / seen
...sugar	...azúcar ah-**thoo**-kar
...ice	...hielo **yeh**-loh

Fun Spanish beverages include the chilled almond-flavored drink called **horchata** (or-**chah**-tah); the refreshing drink of honey and water called **aloja** (ah-**loh**-*h*ah); and **llet mallorquina** (yeht mah-yor-**kee**-nah, "Mallorcan milk," most common in Catalunya), milk with cinnamon and lemon.

Coffee and Tea

coffee...	café... kah-**fay**
...black	...americano ah-meh-ree-**kah**-noh
...with a little milk	...cortado kor-**tah**-doh
...with a lot of milk	...con leche kohn **leh**-chay
...with sugar	...con azúcar kohn ah-**thoo**-kar
...iced	...con hielo kohn **yeh**-loh
espresso	espresso / café solo eh-**spreh**-soh / kah-**fay** soh-loh
espresso with a touch of brandy	carajillo kah-rah-**hee**-yoh
instant coffee	Nescafé nehs-kah-**fay**
decaffeinated	descafeinado deh-skah-fay-**nah**-doh
hot water	agua caliente **ah**-gwah kah-lee-**ehn**-tay
tea	té / infusión tay / een-foo-see-**ohn**
lemon	limón lee-**mohn**
tea bag	bolsa de té **bohl**-sah day tay
herbal tea	té de hierbas tay day **yehr**-bahs
chamomile	manzanilla mahn-thah-**nee**-yah
black tea	té negro tay **neh**-groh
English breakfast tea	té clásico tay **klah**-see-koh
green tea	té verde tay **behr**-day
lemon tea	té de limón tay day lee-**mohn**

orange tea	té de naranja tay day nah-**rahn**-hah
fruit tea	té de frutas tay day **froo**-tahs
mint tea	té de menta tay day **mehn**-tah
chai tea	té tipo chai tay **tee**-poh chī

Wine Words

For a basic glass of red wine, you can order *un tinto*. But for quality wine, ask for *un crianza* (old), *un reserva* (older), or *un gran reserva* (oldest)—though you'll rarely see *gran reserva* served by the glass. The single most important tip for good, economical wine drinking is to ask for *un crianza*—for little or no extra money than a basic *tinto*, you'll get a quality, aged wine.

wine	vino **bee**-noh
red	tinto **teen**-toh
white	blanco **blahn**-koh
rosé	rosado roh-**sah**-doh
house wine	vino de la casa **bee**-noh day lah **kah**-sah
glass of basic red wine	un tinto oon **teen**-toh
glass of better red wine	un crianza oon kree-**ahn**-thah
glass of pricey, aged wine	un reserva / un gran reserva oon reh-**sehr**-bah / oon grahn reh-**sehr**-bah
sparkling white wine	cava **kah**-bah
fruit punch with wine	sangría sahn-**gree**-yah
wine and lemonade	tinto de verano **teen**-toh day beh-**rah**-noh
wine and cola	calimocho kah-lee-**moh**-choh
local	local loh-**kahl**
of the region	de la región day lah reh-hee-**ohn**

sparkling	espumoso eh-spoo-**moh**-soh
light	ligero lee-**heh**-roh
sweet	dulce **dool**-thay
semi-dry	semi-seco seh-mee-**seh**-koh
(very) dry	(muy) seco (**moo**-ee) **seh**-koh
full-bodied	de cuerpo day **kwehr**-poh
mature	maduro mah-**doo**-roh
fruity	afrutado ah-froo-**tah**-doh
chilled	fresco **freh**-skoh
at room temperature	a temperatura natural ah tehm-peh-rah-**too**-rah nah-too-**rahl**
cork	corcho **kor**-choh
corkscrew	sacacorchos sah-kah-**kor**-chohs
vineyard	viña **been**-yah
harvest	vendimia behn-**dee**-mee-ah

Except in winter, red wine is served chilled (*fresco*); if you want it at room temperature, ask for *temperatura natural.*

For a refreshing blend of red wine, seltzer, fruit, and fruit juice, you can try *sangría,* but most Spaniards prefer *tinto de verano,* a wine-lemon soda mix. In the Basque Country, it's *calimocho* (or *kalimotxo*)—wine and cola. *Mosto* is non-alcoholic grape juice on the verge of being wine.

Cava is a champagne-like sparkling white wine produced in the northern region of Penedés. The best-known brands are Cordoniú and Freixenet.

Ordering Wine

I'd / We'd like...	Me / Nos gustaría... may / nohs goo-stah-**ree**-ah
...the wine list.	...la carta de vinos. lah **kar**-tah day **bee**-nohs
...a glass...	...una copa... **oo**-na **koh**-pah

...a small glass...	...un chato... oon **chah**-toh
...a carafe...	...una jarra... **oo**-nah **hah**-rah
...a bottle...	...una botella... **oo**-nah boh-**teh**-yah
...of red wine.	...de vino tinto. day **bee**-noh **teen**-toh
...of white wine.	...de vino blanco. day **bee**-noh **blahn**-koh
What do you recommend?	¿Qué recomienda? kay reh-koh-mee-**ehn**-dah
Choose for me, please.	Elija por mí, por favor. eh-**lee**-hah por mee por fah-**bor**
Around _____ euros.	Unos _____ euros. **oo**-nohs _____ **yoo**-rohs
Another, please.	Otro, por favor. **oh**-troh por fah-**bor**

Conoisseurs will find delicious wines at reasonable prices. Rioja wines are excellent, especially the reds. Navarra, Aragón, and Castilla-La Mancha produce good budget reds. Whites and reds from the Penedés region near Barcelona are also a good value. Valdepeñas wines are usually cheap and forgettable.

Wine Labels

Deciphering the information on a Spanish wine label can be confusing. Listed below are terms that can help you judge the quality of a wine. The terms *reserva* and *gran reserva* do not refer to quality per se, but to the wine's potential as it ages.

Gran reserva: Aged at least five years
Reserva: Aged at least three years for reds and two years for whites
DOC (DO+calificada): Highest-quality guarantee for winemaking
DO: High-quality standards for wine production
DOP (DO+provisional): Next best in quality, after DO
Vino de la tierra: Regional wine of good quality
Vino de mesa: Table wine
Vino joven: Young wine
Vino de maceración carbónica: New wine

Beer

I'd / We'd like...	Me / Nos gustaría... may / nohs goo-stah-**ree**-ah
beer	cerveza thehr-**beh**-thah
from the tap	de barril day bah-**reel**
bottle	botella boh-**teh**-yah
light / dark	rubia / negra **roo**-bee-ah / **neh**-grah
local / imported	local / importada loh-**kahl** / eem-por-**tah**-dah
small / large	pequeña / grande peh-**kehn**-yah / **grahn**-day
wheat	trigo **tree**-goh
microbrew	cerveza artesana thehr-**beh**-thah ar-teh-**sah**-nah
small glass of draft beer	caña **kahn**-yah
large glass of draft beer	doble doh-**blay**
draft beer in tall glass	tubo **too**-boh
large draft beer in glass with handle	jarra de cerveza **hah**-rah day thehr-**beh**-thah
fifth-sized bottle	quinto / botellín **keen**-toh / boh-teh-**yeen**
half-liter bottle	mediana meh-dee-**ah**-nah
low-calorie ("lite")	light "lite"
non-alcoholic	sin alcohol seen ahl-**kohl**

A *clara con limón* is beer made refreshing by a touch of lemon soda (or with soda water—*clara con casera*). For a non-alcholic beer, you can just ask for *una sin* ("one without"). In most bars in Spain, you pay when you leave instead of when you order. In college towns, you may find a *chupitería* (shot shop), where students—most of them visiting from other countries—throw back *chupitos* (shots).

Drink Specialties

BEFORE A MEAL

Cuba libre koo-bah **lee**-bray
rum and Coke

leche de pantera **leh**-chay day pahn-**tehr**-ah
"panther milk," cocktail of milk and gin

jerez heh-**reth**
sherry, a fortified wine from Jerez in Andalucía

jerez amontillado / fino / manzanilla
heh-**reth** ah-mohn-tee-**yah**-doh / **fee**-noh / mahn-thah-**nee**-yah
rich, dry sherries (such as Tío Pepe and La Ina)

sidra **see**-drah
fermented cider (poured theatrically from high above to aerate it)

vermút vehr-**moot**
vermouth, red or white

AFTER A MEAL

aguardiente / orujo ah-gwar-dee-**yehn**-tay / oh-**roo**-hoh
clear grape-based liqueur (Spanish grappa)

chinchón cheen-**chohn**
anise-flavored liqueur

coñac / brandy **kohn**-yahk / **brahn**-dee
Spanish brandy (such as Centario, Magro, and Soberano)

jerez oloroso heh-**reth** oh-loh-**roh**-soh
richest and fullest of all dry sherries

madroño mah-**drohn**-yoh
liqueur distilled from Madrid's mascot berry tree

moscatel moh-skah-**tehl**
sweet white dessert wine

pacharán pah-chah-**rahn**
aniseed and sloe liqueur

Spanish *jerez* is not the sweet dessert wine sold in the States as "sherry." Spanish sherry, often served chilled with appetizers, is most commonly a very dry white. Spain also produces thick, sweet dessert sherries (such as Pedro Ximénez).

Bar Talk

Shall we go for a drink?	¿Vamos a tomar una copa? **bah**-mohs ah toh-**mar oo**-nah **koh**-pah
I'll buy you a drink.	Te invito a una copa. tay een-**bee**-toh ah **oo**-nah **koh**-pah
It's on me.	Pago yo. **pah**-goh yoh
The next one's on me.	Invito a la próxima. een-**bee**-toh ah lah **prohk**-see-mah
What would you like?	¿Qué quiere? kay kee-**ehr**-ay
I'll have _____.	Me apetece _____. may ah-peh-**teh**-thay _____
I don't drink alcohol.	No bebo alcohol. noh **beh**-boh ahl-**kohl**
What's the local specialty?	¿Cuál es la especialidad regional? kwahl ehs lah eh-speh-thee-ah-lee-**dahd** reh-hee-oh-**nahl**
Straight.	Sólo. **soh**-loh
With / Without ice.	Con / Sin hielo. kohn / seen **yeh**-loh
One more.	Otro. **oh**-troh
Cheers!	¡Salud! sah-**lood**
Long live Spain!	¡Viva España! **bee**-bah eh-**spahn**-yah
I'm feeling...	Me siento... may see-**ehn**-toh
...tipsy.	...achispado[a]. ah-chee-**spah**-doh
...a little drunk.	...un poco borracho[a]. oon **poh**-koh boh-**rah**-choh
...wasted.	...borracho[a]. boh-**rah**-choh
I'm hung over.	Tengo resaca. **tehn**-goh reh-**sah**-kah

At a bar, Spaniards generally take turns buying a round for their group.

PICNICKING

While you can opt for the one-stop *supermercado,* it's more fun to assemble your picnic and practice your Spanish visiting the small shops or *mercados al aire libre* (open-air markets).

Tasty Picnic Words

picnic	picnic **peek**-neek
sandwich (on baguette)	bocadillo boh-kah-**dee**-yoh
bread	pan pahn
whole-wheat bread	pan integral pahn een-teh-**grahl**
roll	panecillo pah-neh-**thee**-yoh
cured ham	jamón hah-**mohn**
sausage (like salami)	salchichón sahl-chee-**chohn**
cheese	queso **keh**-soh
mustard...	mostaza... moh-**stah**-thah
mayonnaise...	mayonesa... mī-yoh-**neh**-sah
...in a tube	...en tubo ehn **too**-boh
olives...	aceitunas... ah-thay-**too**-nahs
pickles...	pepinillos... peh-pee-**nee**-yohs
...in a jar	...en conserva ehn kohn-**sehr**-bah
yogurt	yogur yoh-**goor**
fruit	fruta **froo**-tah
box of juice	lata de zumo **lah**-tah day **thoo**-moh
cold drinks	bebidas frías beh-**bee**-dahs **free**-ahs
spoon / fork...	cuchara / tenedor... koo-**chah**-rah / teh-neh-**dor**
...made of plastic	...de plástico day **plah**-stee-koh
cup / plate...	vaso / plato... **bah**-soh / **plah**-toh
...made of paper	...de papel day pah-**pehl**

To get real juice, look for 100% on the label. Or get wine for your picnic. Europeans see no problem with sipping a glass of wine outside—in parks, on benches, or along the riverbank.

Picnic-Shopping Phrases

Meat and cheese are sold by the gram. One hundred grams is about a quarter pound, enough for two sandwiches.

Self-service?	¿Autoservicio?	ow-toh-sehr-**bee**-thee-oh
Fifty grams.	Cincuenta gramos. theen-**kwehn**-tah **grah**-mohs	
One hundred grams.	Cien gramos.	thee-**ehn grah**-mohs
More. / Less.	Más. / Menos.	mahs / **meh**-nohs
A piece.	Un trozo.	oon **troh**-thoh
A slice.	Una rodaja.	oo-nah roh-**dah**-hah
Four slices.	Cuatro lonchas.	**kwah**-troh **lohn**-chahs
Cut into slices (fine).	Cortado en lonchas (finas). kor-**tah**-doh ehn **lohn**-chahs (**fee**-nahs)	
Half.	Medio.	**meh**-dee-oh
A small bag.	Una bolsita.	oo-nah bohl-**see**-tah
A bag, please.	Una bolsa, por favor. oo-nah **bohl**-sah por fah-**bor**	
Ripe for today?	¿Maduro para hoy? mah-**doo**-roh **pah**-rah oy	
May I taste it?	¿Podría probarlo? poh-**dree**-ah proh-**bar**-loh	
Will you make me / us..?	¿Me / Nos puede hacer....? may / nohs **pweh**-day ah-**thehr**	
...a sandwich	...un bocadillo	oon boh-kah-**dee**-yoh
...two sandwiches	...dos bocadillos dohs boh-kah-**dee**-yohs	
To take out.	Para llevar.	**pah**-rah yeh-**bar**
Can you please slice it?	¿Puede cortarlo en lonchas? **pweh**-day kor-**tar**-loh ehn **lohn**-chahs	

Does it need to be cooked?	¿Esto necesita cocinarse? **eh**-stoh neh-theh-**see**-tah koh-thee-**nar**-say
Can I use the microwave?	¿Puedo usar el microondas? **pweh**-doh oo-**sar** ehl mee-kroh-**ohn**-dahs
May I borrow a...?	¿Puedo pedir prestado un...? **pweh**-doh peh-**deer** preh-**stah**-doh oon
Do you have a...?	¿Tiene un...? tee-**ehn**-ay oon
Where can I buy / find a...?	¿Dónde puedo comprar / encontrar un...? **dohn**-day **pweh**-doh kohm-**prar** / ehn-kohn-**trar** oon
...**corkscrew**	...sacacorchos sah-kah-**kor**-chohs
...**can opener**	...abrelatas ah-breh-**lah**-tahs
...**bottle opener**	...abrebotellas ah-breh-boh-**teh**-yahs
Is there a park nearby?	¿Hay un parque cerca de aquí? Ī oon **par**-kay **thehr**-kah day ah-**kee**
Where is a good place to picnic?	¿Dónde hay un buen lugar para hacer un picnic? **dohn**-day Ī oon bwehn loo-**gar pah**-rah ah-**thehr** oon **peek**-neek
Is picnicking allowed here?	¿Se puede hacer picnic aquí? say **pweh**-day ah-**thehr peek**-neek ah-**kee**

To weigh and price produce at the grocery store, put it on the scale, and push the photo or number (keyed to the bin it came from); a sticker will pop out—just place it on the produce.

To borrow a shopping cart *(carrito de la compra)*, put a coin into a lock to release one. When you return the cart, your coin pops out again.

Very flimsy bags are free, but if you have a lot of groceries, you can buy a much sturdier bag *(bolsa)* for a token amount.

Produce Markets

It's considered rude for customers to touch produce; instead, tell the clerk what you want. Pointing and gesturing go a long way. Pay careful attention, as the unit of measure can differ. It could be *por* (per) *kilo* or *kg* (for *kilogram*), *por ½ kg, por ¼ kg, por 100 g, por 500 g,* and so on. If a price is listed without a unit, then it's usually per kilo, but confirm just in case, *¿Es por kilo?* One quarter of a kilo is *un quarto*—that is, 250 grams (about a half-pound). You'll also see items priced by the piece, bunch, and container.

kilo (kilogram; 1,000 grams)	kilo **kee**-loh
½ kilo (500 grams)	medio kilo **meh**-dee-oh **kee**-loh
¼ kilo (250 grams)	cuarto **kwar**-toh **kee**-loh
100 grams	cien gramos thee-**ehn grah**-mohs
that	eso **eh**-soh
this much	así ah-**see**
more / less	más / menos mahs / **meh**-nohs
too much	demasiado deh-mah-see-**ah**-doh
enough	suficiente soo-fee-thee-**ehn**-tay
in one piece	unidad oo-nee-**dahd**
one / two	uno / dos **oo**-noh / dohs
bunch (handful)	puñado poon-**yah**-doh
bunch (a lot)	mucho **moo**-choh
container	envase ehn-**bah**-say

MENU DECODER

This handy menu decoder, in Spanish and English, won't unlock every word on the menu, but it'll help get you *ostras* (oysters) instead of *orejas* (pig's ears).

Menu Categories

When you pick up a menu, you'll likely see these categories of offerings:

Desayuno	Breakfast
Almuerzo / Comida	Lunch
Cena	Dinner
Aperitivos / Entrantes / Entremeses	Appetizers
Platos Calientes	Hot Dishes
Platos Fríos	Cold Dishes
Tapas / Pinchos	Small Plates
Bocadillos	Sandwiches
Ensaladas	Salads
Sopas	Soups
Menú(s)	Fixed-Price Meal(s)
Especialidades	Specialties
Platos	Dishes
(Platos) Principales	Main Dishes
Carne	Meat
Cerdo	Pork
Aves	Poultry
Pescados	Fish
Mariscos	Seafood
A Parte / Complementos	Side Dishes

Arroz	Rice Dishes
Tortillas	Egg Omelets
Verduras	Vegetables
Pan	Bread
(Carta de) Bebidas	Drink (Menu)
(Carta de) Vinos	Wine (List)
Postres	Dessert
Plato de Niños	Children's Plate
Nuestros	"Our"
Selección de	Selection of

And for the fine print:

precio de entrada	cover charge
servicio (no) incluido	service (not) included
IVA (no) incluido	tax (not) included

Small Words

a la / al	in the style of
con	with
de / del	of
en	in
o	or
sin	without
solo	only
y	and

SPANISH / ENGLISH

a parte side dish, on the side
acedía dab (flatfish)
aceite oil
aceituna olive
acelgas Swiss chard
acompañado accompanied
adobo, en in marinade of vinegar, garlic, and spices
afrutado fruity, aromatic (wine)
agua water
aguacate avocado
agua del grifo tap water
aguardiente Spanish grappa
ahumado smoked
ajete garlic stalk
ajillo, al in oil and garlic
ajo garlic
ajo blanco almond-based garlic soup
albaricoque apricot
albóndiga meatball
alcachofa artichoke
alcaparra caper
aliño dressing
alioli garlic mayonnaise
almeja clam
almejas a la marinera clams in paprika sauce
almendra almond
almíbar sugar syrup (as in canned fruit)
almuerzo lunch
aloja spiced water and honey drink

amarguillo almond/egg confection
amontillado sherry type (pale and dry)
anacardo cashew
anchoa anchovy
anguila eel
angula young eel (elver)
añojo aged
antxoa anchovy (Basque)
aperitivo appetizer
arenque herring
arroz rice
arroz caldero variation on paella (soupy rice)
arroz con leche rice pudding
asado roasted
asturiana, a la in the style of Asturias (region)
atún tuna
avellana hazelnut
aves poultry
azafrán saffron
azúcar sugar
bacalao cod
bacalao a la vizcaína salt cod braised with vegetables
bacón bacon
bamba de nata cream puff
bandeja tray
banderilla skewer of pickled veggies
barra at the bar
barra de pan baguette loaf

bastante hecha very well-done (meat)

batida whipped

bebida beverage

bellota, de top-quality Iberian ham from pigs fed acorns

berberecho cockle

berenjena eggplant

berro watercress

besugo bream (fish)

bistec beef steak

bizcocho sponge cake

blanco white

blando soft (cheese)

bocadillo sandwich (on baguette)

bocadillo chiquito tiny sandwich

bola scoop

bollos sweet rolls

bomba fried ball of meat and potatoes

bonito tuna-like fish

boquerón fresh anchovy

botella bottle

brazo de gitano sponge cake filled with cream

brazuelo shin

brécol broccoli

brocheta shish kebab, skewer

brócoli broccoli

buey ox, steer

buñuelo fried dough ball

burbujas carbonation

burgos fresh cow's milk cheese

butifarra sweetly spiced pork sausage

caballo horse

cabello de ángel sweet pumpkin preserve ("angel hair")

cabrales tangy blue cheese

cabrilla snail

cabrito kid goat

cacahuete peanut

cachelo small potato

café... coffee...

    americano black

    con azúcar with sugar

    con hielo iced

    con leche with milk

    cortado with a little milk

    solo espresso

calabacín zucchini

calamar squid

calamares a la Romana rings of deep-fried squid

calamares con guisantes squid with garlic, peas, mint, and tomatoes

caldo broth

caldo gallego Galician soup

caliente hot (not cold)

calimocho half red wine, half cola

callos tripe, tripe stew

caña small draft beer

canape tiny open-faced sandwich

cangrejo crab

cangrejo de río crayfish

canónigo lamb's lettuce (mâche)

capón capon (high-quality rooster)

caracol snail

caracola spiral-shaped pastry ("conch")

carajillo espresso with a touch of brandy

caramelo candy

carbón de encina charcoal

carne meat

carne de vaca beef

carrillera / carrillada cheek

casa house

casa, de la speciality "of the house"

cáscara shell

casera homemade

castaña chestnut

castellano in the style of Castille (region)

cava sparkling white wine

cayena cayenne

caza game

cazón dogfish

cazón en adabo marinated white fish

cazuela casserole, stew

cebo, de grain-fed cured ham

cebolla onion

cebón fattened

cecina (de vaca) cured beef

centollo spider crab

cerdo pork

cereales cereal

cereza cherry

cerveza beer

chacina canned, marinated, or otherwise preserved meat

champiñón mushroom

champiñones rellenos stuffed mushrooms

chato kid goat

chinchón anise-flavored liqueur

chino Chinese

chistorra spicy Basque sausage

chocos baby squid

chopitos baby squid, usually deep-fried

chorizo sausage (spicy)

chorizo a la sidra spicy sausage cooked in cider

chufa tiger nut (used in horchata)

chuleta cutlet, chop

chuletón T-bone steak

chupito small glass (shot)

churrasco grilled meat

churro fritter

cigala crayfish

cinta de lomo pork loin

ciruela plum

ciruela pasa prune

clara con casera beer with soda water

clara con limón beer with lemon soda

cochinillo suckling pig

cocido baked (adj); also a chickpea stew

cocido maragato traditional stew from northern Spain eaten in three stages: meats, veggies, broth

cocinado cooked

coco coconut

coctel cocktail

codillo knuckle
cogollo heart or bulb
col cabbage
cola de toro bull-tail stew
coliflor cauliflower
combinado combination
comida food
conejo rabbit
confitado candied
cono cone
copa cup (ice cream)
coquina small clam
cordero lamb
cordonices en hoja de parra quail in grape leaves
cordoniz quail
corto small, short
cosecha harvest
costilla rib
crema Catalana custard (like crème brulée)
crianza good, reasonably priced red wine
crocantino light honey-and-almond loaf
croqueta croquette (fried dough ball with various fillings)
cruasán de chocolate chocolate croissant
crudo raw
cuajada cream with honey
cuchara spoon, scoop
cucharón scoop (ice cream)
cucurucho cone (ice cream)
cuerpo, de full-bodied (wine)
curado cured
dátil date

del día of the day
delicia delicacy
delicioso delicious
deshuesado boneless
diablo, al spicy ("of the devil")
dorado browned ("golden")
dulce sweet
duro hard (cheese)
edulcorante artificial sweetener
embutidos cured meats
empanada meat pie
empanada gallega pizza-like pie
empanadilla pastry stuffed with meat or seafood
ensalada salad
ensalada de arroz rice salad
ensaladilla Rusa vegetable salad in mayonnaise
entrañas innards
entrecot ribeye steak (sometimes sirloin)
entremeses appetizers
eperlano smelt
escalfado poached
escalivada roasted eggplant, peppers, and onions
escudella i carn d'olla minced pork meatball
espaguetis spaghetti
espalda, a la skin-side down ("on the back")
espárragos asparagus (white)
espárragos trigueros asparagus (green)
especial special
espinacas spinach
espresso espresso

espuma foam

espumoso sparkling

esqueixada salted cod, onion, and peppers salad

estofada braised

fabada asturiana pork and bean stew

fabe giant, fava-like white bean (Asturias)

fideo noodle

fideuà paella made with noodles (instead of rice)

filete fillet

filete empanado breaded veal or beef fillet

fino sherry type (dry)

flan caramel custard

flauta sandwich on thin baguette bread

fondo on a bed of

frambuesa raspberry

franceca (tortilla) fluffy mini-omelet

fresa strawberry

fresco fresh

frijol bean

frío cold

frito fried

fritura modesto fried seafood plate

fruta fruit

frutos secos dried fruit and nut mix

fuerte sharp (cheese), heavy (hard to digest)

gallega, a la in the style of Galicia (region); seasoned with sea salt and paprika

galleta cookie

gallinejas fried lamb intestines

gallineta game hen

gamba prawn

gambas a la plancha grilled prawns

garrafa carafe

gas carbonation

gaseosa sweetened soda water

gazpacho chilled tomato soup

gelatina jelly, gelatin

girasól sunflower

gitana, a la "gypsy" style

gordo (n) fat

grande large

gran reserva aged "grand reserve" wine

gratinado au gratin

grelo turnip top, rapini

guarnición garnish

guisante pea

guiso stew

haba lima bean, fava bean

habas a la Catalana fava bean and chorizo stew

hamburguesa hamburger

hecho en casa homemade

helado ice cream

hervido boiled

hielo ice

hierba herb

hígado liver

higo fig

horchata sweet milky drink made from tiger nuts or almonds

horneado baked

horno, al oven-baked

hueva roe (fish eggs)

huevo egg

huevo del toro bull testicle

huevo estrellado fried egg

ibérico top-quality cured ham ("Iberian")

idiazábal raw sheep's milk cheese (Basque)

importada imported

jabalí wild boar

jabugo, de special type of cured Iberian ham

jamón ham

jamón ibérico ham from acorn-fed pigs

jamón serrano cured ham

jarra carafe for wine or large draft beer glass

jerez sherry

judía bean

judía verde green bean

judiones de La Granja soup made with flat white beans

jurel scad (like mackerel)

lacón pork shoulder

langosta lobster

langostino large prawn

lechal suckling

leche milk

leche de pantera cocktail of milk and gin ("panther milk")

lechuga lettuce

lengua tongue

lenguado sole

lenteja lentil

ligero light

limón lemon

lomo loin

loncha slice

lubina sea bass

macedonia fruit cup

macerado macerated (lightly pickled)

madrileño Madrid style

madroño berry liqueur

maduro mature (wine)

magdalena cupcake, muffin

maíz corn

manchego cured sheep's milk cheese, from La Mancha (region)

mandarina tangerine

manitas de cerdo pig's feet

mantequilla butter

mantequilla de cacahuete peanut butter

manzana apple

manzanilla sherry type, chamomile tea

mar y montaña / mar y terra chicken or rabbit with lobster or scampi ("surf and turf")

margarina margarine

marinera, a la with seafood; also a white wine sauce with paprika ("sailor style")

marisco seafood, shellfish

marmitako Basque tuna stew

mayonesa mayonnaise
mazapán marzipan
medallón medallion
mediana half-liter bottle of beer
medio half
mejillón mussel
mel i mató curd cheese with honey
melocotón peach
melón cantaloupe
membrillo quince, quince jelly or jam
menestra mixed vegetables, vegetable stew
merengada milkshake
merienda late-afternoon snack
merluza hake (fish)
mermelada jam
mesa table
microondas microwave
miel honey
mixto mixed
mojama salt- and dry-cured tuna
molde, pan de white bread
mollejas sweetbreads
mollete bread roll (Andalucía)
montadito tiny open-faced sandwich
morcilla blood sausage
morro pig snout
moscatel sweet dessert wine
mostaza mustard
mosto grape juice
muy hecha well-done (meat)
muy poco hecha very rare (meat)
nabo turnip

napolitana cream-filled pastry
naranja orange
nata cream
nata montada whipped cream
natilla cream custard
natilla de huevo sweet egg pudding
navaja de almeja razor clam
negra dark (beer)
nuez walnut
obela big, flat wafer cracker
oca goose
olla, a la cooked in a pot
oloroso sherry type (rich and dark)
oreja pig's ear
orgánico organic
ortiguilla anemone
orujo Spanish grappa
ostra oyster
oveja sheep
pa amb tomàquet country bread with grated tomatoes and olive oil (Catalunya)
pacharán aniseed and sloe liqueur
paella saffron rice and seafood dish
país, del country style
pajita straw (drinking)
paletilla shoulder blade
palillo toothpick
palito de queso cheese straw or stick
palmera heart-shaped pastry
pan bread

panadilla fried savory pie, like an empanada
panecillo roll
panellet sweet potato cookie with nuts
para llevar "to go"
parradilla mixed grill (plate of barbecued meat)
parrilla, a la barbecued
pasa raisin
pasta pastry
pastel cake, pastry
pastela savory phyllo pie with poultry and cinnamon
patata potato
patatas bravas fried potatoes with creamy, spicy tomato sauce
patatas fritas French fries
patatas meneadas mashed potatoes with paprika and bacon
pato duck
pavo turkey
pelada peeled
pepinillo pickle
pepino cucumber
pepito little sandwich
pepitoria, en fricassee
pequeño small
pera pear
percebe barnacle
perdiz partridge
perilla mild cow's milk cheese (Galicia)
perrito caliente hot dog
pescadilla whiting (cod-like fish)
pescaditos fritos assortment of little fried fish

pescado fish
pescado en adobo marinated whitefish
pez espada swordfish
picadillo hash
picante spicy hot
pico breadstick
pieza piece
pijota small hake (whitefish)
pimentón paprika
pimienta pepper (seasoning)
pimiento bell pepper
pimientos de Padrón small green peppers, sometimes hot
pimientos de piquillo sweet, small red peppers (Basque)
pinchito tiny pincho
pincho snack
pincho moruno skewer of spicy lamb or pork
piña pineapple
piñón pine nut
pistacho pistachio
pisto stewed zucchini, tomatoes, and peppers
plancha, a la grilled (on a flat-top)
plátano banana
platija plaice (whitefish)
plato plate
plato de niños children's plate
poco hecha rare (meat)
pollo chicken
pollo en pepitoria chicken fricassee with almonds and hard-boiled eggs
pomelo grapefruit

ponche segoviano layer cake with marzipan (from Segovia)

postre dessert

postre de música roasted nuts and dried fruit with a glass of moscatel wine

precio de mercado market price

presa tender cut of pork

pudín pudding

puerro leek

pulga / pulguita small closed baguette sandwich

pulpo octopus

punta tip

puntilla / puntillita crisp, golden edge, from frying in oil

punto, en su medium (meat)

puré thick soup

puro pure

quemada burned (adj)

queso cheese

queso ahumado smoked cheese

queso rallado grated cheese

quinto fifth-sized bottle

raba squid tentacle

rabo de toro bull-tail stew

ración portion

rallado grated (cheese)

rape monkfish

rebozado breaded

recebeo, de ham from grain-fed pigs

regañá flat, hard, cracker-like bread (Andalucía)

rehogado sautéed lightly

relleno stuffed (adj), filling (n)

remolacha beet

requesón type of ricotta cheese

reserva aged "reserve" wine

revueltos egg "scramble"

riñón kidney

riñones al jerez kidneys in sherry sauce

riojana, a la hearty dish of sausage and potatoes ("Rioja style")

rodaja slice

rojo red

rollito de huevo sweet egg roll

Romana, a la fried ("Roman style")

romesco spicy sauce or fish and vegetable stew

roncal strong, sharp, dry sheep's cheese

ropa vieja shredded meat ("old clothes")

rosado rosé (wine)

rosquilla doughnut (Madrid)

rubia light (beer color)

sacacorchos corkscrew

sal salt

salchichón sausage (mild)

salmón salmon

salmorejo (Cordobes) creamy variation on gazpacho, often with ham and egg (from Córdoba)

salón dining room

salpicón salmagundi (mixed salad)

salteado sautéed

San Simón smoked mild cheese from cow's milk

sancochado hard-boiled
sandía watermelon
sangría red wine, juice, and
  brandy
sardina sardine
seco dry (wine)
semi-seco semi-dry (wine)
sepia cuttlefish
serrano usually refers to cured
  ham ("from the Sierras")
sesos brains
seta wild mushroom
sidra hard cider
silvestre wild
sofrito sauce of onion, tomato,
  and peppers
solomillo sirloin
sopa... soup...
  a la gitana pumpkin and
  chickpea
  de almendras almond with
  saffron
  de castellana egg and garlic
  de espárragos asparagus
  de mariscos seafood (often
  shellfish)
sorbete sherbet
suave mild (cheese)
suis hot chocolate with whipped
  cream ("Swiss")
surtido assortment (mixed plate)
tabla combination plate
tabla serrana plate of meat and
  cheese
tajada slice, chunk
tajada de bacalao deep-fried
  cod slices

tapa appetizer
taquito rolled, filled, fried savory
  pastry
tarrina cup
tarta tart
tarta de Santiago almond cake
  with powdered sugar (Galicia)
taza cup
té... tea...
  de frutas fruit
  de hierbas herbal
  de limón lemon
  de menta mint
  de naranja orange
templado lukewarm
ternera veal
tetilla firm, mild cow's milk
  cheese (Galicia)
tinto red wine ("dark red")
tinto de verano red wine and
  lemon soda
típico typical
tocino bacon, pork belly
tocino(illo) de cielo baked
  custard dessert ("bacon from
  heaven")
Toledana nutty cookie with
  squash filling
tolosa type of red bean
tomate tomato
torrija sweet fritter (bread)
tortel ring-shaped pastry
tortilla... omelet...
  de camarones shrimp
  de jamón ham
  de queso cheese
  española potato

Sacromonte spicy pig's brain and other organs (Granada)

tosta toasted open-face sandwich

tostada toast

tostón crouton, bruschetta (Andalucía)

trigo wheat

tripa tripe

trozo piece

trucha trout

tubo draft beer

turrón nougat made with almond, honey, and sugar (popular at Christmas)

uva grape

vacuno beef

vainilla vanilla

vapor, al steamed

variado assorted

vaso glass

vegetal vegetable

vegetariano vegetarian

venado venison

ventresca belly

verde green

verdura vegetables, greens

vermút vermouth

vieira scallop

villalón curd sheep's cheese in a mold

vinagre vinegar

vinagreta vinaigrette

vino... wine...

  blanco white

  de crianza aged red

  de la casa house

de la region of the region

de mesa table

de reserva / de gran reserva pricier aged red

joven young

rojo / tinto red

vizcaína, a la Basque style

xató lettuce, tuna, and anchovy salad with spicy sauce

yema yolk; also a sweet made from egg yolks and sugar

yogur yogurt

York (jamón York) cooked (rather than cured) ham

zafra container for olive oil

zamburiña tiny scallop

zanahoria carrot

zancarrón shank

zapatilla "slipper"-sized patty melt

zarajo (de Cuenca) cooked lamb intestines (from the town of Cuenca)

zarzuela de mariscos shellfish stew

zumo... juice...

  de fruta fruit

  de manzana apple

  de naranja orange

  de piña pineapple

  de uva (or mosto) grape

ENGLISH / SPANISH

almond almendra
anchovy anchoa, antxoa (Basque)
anchovy, fresh boqueron
anemone ortiguilla
appetizer tapa, aperitivo, entremese
apple manzana
apricot albaricoque
artichoke alcachofa
asparagus (green) espárragos trigueros
asparagus (white) espárragos
assorted variado
assortment (mixed plate) surtido
au gratin gratinado
avocado aguacate
bacon tocino, bacón
baguette loaf pan de barra
baked cocido, horneado
banana plátano
barbecued a la parilla
barnacle percebe
bass, sea lubina
bean judía, frijol
beef carne de vaca
beef, cured cecina de vaca
beef steak bistec
beer cerveza
beer, dark negra
beer, large draft tubo
beer, light-colored rubia
beer, small draft caña

beer with lemon soda / with soda water clara con limón / con casera
beet remolacha
bell pepper pimiento
belly ventresca
beverage bebida
boar jabalí
boiled hervido
boneless deshuesado
bottle botella
braised estofada
bread pan
bread, white pan de molde
breaded rebozado
breadstick pico
breakfast desayuno
broccoli brócoli, brécol
broth caldo
browned dorado ("golden")
bull-tail stew cola de toro, rabo de toro
burned (adj) quemada
butter mantequilla
cabbage col
cake pastel, tarta
candied confitado
candy caramelo
cantaloupe melón
caper alcaparra
carafe garrafa, jarra
carbonation gas, burbujas
carrot zanahoria
cashew anacardo
casserole cazuela

cauliflower coliflor
cayenne cayena
cereal cereales
charcoal carbón de encina
cheek carrillera, carrillada
cheese queso
cheese, smoked queso ahumado
cheese straw or stick palito de
  queso
cherry cereza
chestnut castaña
chicken pollo
children's plate plato de niños
Chinese chino
chocolate chocolate
chop (meat) chuleta
cider, hard sidra
clam almeja
clam, razor navaja de almeja
clam, small coquina
cockle berberecho
cocktail coctel
coconut coco
cod bacalao
coffee... café...
  black americano
  espresso espresso, café solo
  iced con hielo
  with a little milk cortado
  with milk con leche
  with sugar con azúcar
cold frío
combination combinado
combination plate tabla
cone (ice cream) cono,
  cucurucho
cooked cocinado

cookie galleta
corkscrew sacacorchos
corn maíz
country style del país
crab cangrejo
crab (spider) centollo
crayfish cigala
cream nata
cream puff bamba de nata
croissant cruasán
cucumber pepino
cup taza, tarrina
cup (ice cream) copa
cupcake magdalena
cured curado
custard, caramel flan
custard, cream natilla
cutlet chuleta
dab (flatfish) acedía
dark (beer) negra
date dátil
day, of the del día
dessert postre
dining room salón
dinner cena
dogfish cazón
doughnut (Madrid) rosquilla
dressing aliño
dried fruits (includes
  nuts) frutos secos
drink menu carta de bebidas
dry / very dry (wine) seco /
  muy seco
duck pato
eel anguila
egg huevo
egg, fried huevo estrellado

egg "scramble" revueltos
eggplant berenjena
espresso espresso, café solo
espresso with brandy carajillo
fat (n) grasa
fava bean haba
fig higo
fillet filete
filling (n) relleno
fish pescado
foam espuma
food comida
French fries patatas fritas
fresh fresco
fricassee en pepitoria
fried frito
fritter churro
fruit fruta
fruit cup macedonia
fruit tea té de frutas
fruity (wine) afrutado
full-bodied (wine) de cuerpo
game caza
game hen gallineta
garlic ajo
garlic mayonnaise alioli
garnish guarnición
glass vaso
goat (kid) cabrito
goose oca
grape uva
grapefruit pomelo
grappa aguardiente, orujo
grated (cheese) rallado
green bean judía verde
grilled (on a barbecue) a la parrilla

grilled (on a flat-top) a la plancha
hake (whitefish) merluza
hake, small pijota
half medio
halibut halibut
ham, cooked jamón York
ham, cured (typical quality / top quality) jamón (serrano / ibérico)
hamburger hamburguesa
hard duro
hard-boiled sancochado
hash picadillo
hazelnut avellana
herb hierba
herbal tea té de hierbas
herring arenque
homemade hecho en casa, casera
honey miel
hot (temperature) caliente
hot (spicy) picante
hot chocolate with whipped cream suis ("Swiss")
hot dog perrito caliente
house casa
house wine vino de la casa
ice hielo
ice cream helado
imported importada
innards tripas, entrañas
jam mermelada
jelly gelatina
juice... zumo...
  apple de manzana
  fruit de fruta

grape de uva (or mosto)
orange de naranja
pineapple de piña
kidney riñón
knuckle codillo
lamb cordero
lamb intestines, fried gallinejas
large grande
leek puerro
lemon limón
lentil lenteja
lettuce / lamb's lettuce
  (mâche) lechuga / cordero
light (wine) ligero
light-colored (beer) rubia
lima bean haba
liver hígado
lobster langosta
loin lomo
lukewarm templado
lunch almuerzo, comida
macerated macerado
mango mango
margarine margarina
market price precio de mercado
marzipan mazapán
mature (wine) maduro
mayonnaise mayonesa
meat... carne...
  medium en su punto
  rare / very rare poco hecha /
  muy poco hecha
  well done / very well-
  done muy hecha / bastante
  hecha
meat, cured embutidos
meat, grilled churrasco

meat, raw carne cruda
meatball albóndiga
medallion medallón
mild (cheese) suave
milk leche
milkshake merengada
mineral water agua mineral
mint tea té de menta
mixed mixto
monkfish rape
muffin magdalena
mushroom champiñon
mushroom, wild seta
mussel mejillón
mustard mostaza
noodle fideo
nougat (almond) turrón
octopus pulpo
oil aceite
olive aceituna
omelet... tortilla...
  potato española
on the side a parte
onion cebolla
orange naranja
organic orgánico
oven-baked al horno
ox buey
oyster ostra
paprika pimentón
partridge perdiz
pastry pastel
peach melocotón
peanut cacahuete
peanut butter mantequilla de
  cacahuete
pea guisante

pear pera
peeled pelada
pepper (seasoning) pimienta
pepper, bell pimiento
pickle pepinillo
piece pieza
pig's ear oreja
pine nut piñón
pineapple piña
pistachio pistacho
plaice (whitefish) platija
plate plato
plum ciruela
poached escalfado
pork cerdo
pork loin cinta de lomo
pork shoulder lacón
portion ración
potato patata
poultry aves
prawn gamba, langostino (large)
prune ciruela pasa
pudding pudín
pure puro
quail cordoniz
quince membrillo
rabbit conejo
raisin pasa
rare / very rare (meat) poco
  hecha / muy pocho hecha
raspberry frambuesa
raw crudo
ribeye steak entrecot
ribs costillas
receipt recibo
red rojo
rice arroz

rice pudding arroz con leche
roasted asado
roe (fish eggs) hueva
roll panecillo
rosé rosado
saffron azafrán
salad ensalada
salmon salmón
salt sal
sandwich (on square white
  bread) sandwich
sandwich (on
  baguette) bocadillo
sardine sardina
sausage chorizo (spicy),
  salchichón (mild)
sausage, blood morcilla
sautéed / sautéed
  lightly salteado / rehogado
scad (like mackerel) jurel
scallop vieira
scallop (tiny) zamburiña
scoop (ice cream) bola
scrambled revueltos
sea bass lubina
seafood marisco
seafood soup sopa de mariscos
seed pipa
semi-dry (wine) semi-seco
shank zancarrón
sheep oveja
shell cáscara
shellfish marisco
shellfish stew zarzuela de
  mariscos
sherbet sorbete
sherry jerez

shish kebab brocheta	**sweet rolls** bollos, bollería
shoulder blade paletilla	**sweetbreads** mollejas
side dish a parte	**sweetener, artificial** edulcorante
sirloin solomillo	**swordfish** pez espada
skewer brocheta	**table** mesa
slice tajada	**tangerine** mandarina
small pequeño, corto	**tart** tarta
smelt eperlano	**T-bone steak** chuletón
smoked ahumado	**tea** té
snack pincho	**tilapia** tilapia
snail caracol, cabrilla	**tip (point)** punta
soft (cheese) blando	**tip (for service)** propina
sole lenguado	**"to go"** para llevar
soup sopa	**toast** tostada
spaghetti espaguetis	**tomato** tomate
sparkling espumoso	**tongue** lengua
special especial	**toothpick** palillo
spicy hot picante	**tray** bandeja
spinach espinacas	**tripe** tripa
sponge cake bizcocho	**trout** trucha
spoon cuchara	**tuna** atún
squid calamares	**turkey** pavo
squid, deep-fried calamares a la Romana	**turnip** nabo
squid tentacle raba	**typical** típico
steak bistec	**vanilla** vainilla
steamed al vapor	**veal** ternera
steer buey	**vegetable** vegetal, verdura
stew guiso, cazuela	**vegetables, mixed** menestra
straw (drinking) pajita	**vegetarian** vegetariano
strawberry fresa	**venison** venado
stuffed relleno	**vermouth** vermút
suckling lechal	**very dry (wine)** muy seco
suckling pig cochinillo	**very rare (meat)** muy poco hecha
sugar azúcar	**very well-done (meat)** bastante hecha
sunflower girasól	**vinaigrette** vinagreta
sweet dulce	

vinegar vinagre
walnut nuez
water... agua...
  mineral mineral
  tap del grifo
  with carbonation con gas
  without carbonation sin gas
watercress berro
watermelon sandía
well-done / very well done
  (meat) muy hecha / bastante
  hecha
wheat trigo
whipped batida
whipped cream nata montada
white blanco

whiting (cod-like fish) pescadilla
wild silvestre
wine... vino...
  house de la casa
  of the region de la región
  red rojo, tinto
  red, aged de crianza
  red, aged (pricier) de reserva,
  de gran reserva
  table de mesa
  young joven
  white blanco
wine list carta de vinos
yogurt yogur
yolk yema
zucchini calabacín

SIGHTSEEING

W hether you're touring a museum, going on a city walking tour, visiting a church, or conquering a castle, these phrases will help you make the most of your sightseeing time.

WHERE?

Where is the...?	¿Dónde está el / la...? **dohn**-day eh-**stah** ehl / lah
Where are the...?	¿Dónde están los / las...? **dohn**-day eh-**stahn** lohs / lahs
tourist information office	oficina de turismo oh-fee-**thee**-nah day too-**rees**-moh
toilets	servicios sehr-**bee**-thee-ohs
main square	plaza mayor **plah**-thah mah-**yor**
old town center	casco antiguo **kahs**-koh ahn-**tee**-gwoh
entrance	entrada ehn-**trah**-dah
exit	salida sah-**lee**-dah
museum	museo moo-**seh**-oh
cathedral	catedral kah-teh-**drahl**
church	iglesia ee-**gleh**-see-ah
castle	castillo kah-**stee**-yoh
palace	palacio pah-**lah**-thee-oh
ruins	ruinas **rwee**-nahs
amusement park	parque de atracciones **par**-kay day ah-trahk-thee-**oh**-nehs
aquarium	acuario ah-**kwah**-ree-oh
zoo	zoo zoh
best view	mejor vista meh-**hor** **bee**-stah
viewpoint	mirador mee-rah-**dor**
Is there a fair / festival nearby?	¿Hay una feria / fiesta cerca? ī **oo**-nah **feh**-ree-ah / fee-**eh**-stah **thehr**-kah

Key Phrases: Sightseeing

ticket	billete / entrada bee-**yeh**-tay / ehn-**trah**-dah
How much is it?	¿Cuánto cuesta? **kwahn**-toh **kweh**-stah
Is there a guided tour (in English)?	¿Hay un tour guiado (en inglés)? ī oon tor gee-**ah**-doh (ehn een-**glays**)
When?	¿Cuándo? **kwahn**-doh
What time does this open / close?	¿A qué hora abren / cierran? ah kay **oh**-rah **ah**-brehn / thee-**ehr**-ahn

Many Spanish cities (most notably Madrid and Salamanca) have a grand *plaza mayor*—a vast and inviting main square that serves as the living room for the entire community.

AT SIGHTS

Tickets and Discounts

ticket office	taquilla / venta tah-**kee**-yah / **behn**-tah
ticket	billete / entrada bee-**yeh**-tay / ehn-**trah**-dah
combo-ticket	ticket combinado tee-**keht** kohm-bee-**nah**-doh
price	tarifa tah-**ree**-fah
discount	descuento dehs-**kwehn**-toh
Is there a discount for...?	¿Hay un descuento para...? ī oon dehs-**kwehn**-toh **pah**-rah
...children	...niños **neen**-yohs
...youths	...jóvenes **hoh**-beh-nehs
...students	...estudiantes eh-stoo-dee-**ahn**-tehs

...families	...familias fah-**meel**-yahs
...seniors	...jubilados *hoo*-bee-**lah**-dohs
...groups	...grupos **groo**-pohs
I am...	Tengo... **tehn**-goh
He / She is...	Él / Ella tiene... ehl / **ay**-yah tee-**ehn**-ay
... _____ years old.	... _____ años. ... _____ **ahn**-yohs
I am extremely old.	Soy muy, muy viejo[a]. soy **moo**-ee **moo**-eebee-**eh**-*h*oh
Is the ticket good all day?	¿El billete está válido para todo el día? ehl bee-**yeh**-tay eh-**stah bah**-lee-doh **pah**-rah **toh**-doh ehl **dee**-ah
Can I get back in?	¿Puedo volver a entrar? **pweh**-doh bohl-**behr** ah ehn-**trar**

Tickets for transportation are typically called *billetes,* while those sold for events or the theater are *entradas.* Museums use either term.

Information and Tours

information	información een-for-mah-thee-**ohn**
tour	tour tor
in English	en inglés ehn een-**glays**
Is there a...?	¿Hay un / una...? ī oon / **oo**-nah
...city walking tour	...visita guiada a pie por la ciudad bee-**see**-tah gee-**ah**-dah ah pee-**ay** por lah thee-oo-**dahd**
...guided tour	...tour guiado tor gee-**ah**-doh
...audioguide	...audioguía ow-dee-oh-**gee**-ah
...local guide (I can hire)	...guía local (que puedo contratar) **gee**-ah loh-**kahl** (kay **pweh**-doh kon-trah-**tar**)
...city guidebook	...guía sobre la ciudad **gee**-ah **soh**-bray lah thee-oo-**dahd**

...museum guidebook	...guía sobre el museo gee-ah soh-bray ehl moo-seh-oh
Is it free?	¿Es gratis? ehs grah-tees
How much is it?	¿Cuánto cuesta? kwahn-toh kweh-stah
How long does it last?	¿Cuánto tiempo dura? kwahn-toh tee-ehm-poh doo-rah
When is the next next tour in English?	¿Cuándo es la siguiente visita en inglés? kwahn-doh ehs lah seeg-ee-ehn-tay bee-see-tah ehn een-glays

Some sights are tourable only by groups with a guide (*guía*—pronounced with a hard *g* as in *gracias*). Individuals usually end up with the next Spanish tour. To get an English tour, call in advance to see if one's scheduled; individuals can often tag along with a large tour group.

Visiting Sights

opening times	horario de apertura oh-rah-ree-oh day ah-pehr-too-rah
last entry	última entrada ool-tee-mah ehn-trah-dah
What time does this open / close?	¿A qué hora abren / cierran? ah kay oh-rah ah-brehn / thee-ehr-ahn
When is the last entry?	¿A qué hora es la última entrada? ah kay oh-rah ehs lah ool-tee-mah ehn-trah-dah
Do I have to check this (bag)?	¿Tengo que dejar este (bolso) en consigna? tehn-goh kay deh-har eh-stay (bohl-soh) ehn kohn-seeg-nah
bag check	consigna kohn-seeg-nah
information	información een-for-mah-thee-ohn
floor plan	plano plah-noh
floor	planta plahn-tah

collection	colección koh-lehk-thee-**ohn**
exhibition...	exposición... ehk-poh-see-thee-**ohn**
...temporary / special	...temporal / especial tehm-poh-**rahl** / eh-speh-thee-**ahl**
...permanent	...permanente pehr-mahn-**ehn**-tay
café	cafetería kah-feh-teh-**ree**-ah
elevator	ascensor ah-thehn-**sor**
toilets	servicios sehr-**bee**-thee-ohs
Where is _____?	¿Dónde está _____? **dohn**-day eh-**stah** _____
I'd like to see _____.	Me gustaría ver _____. may goo-stah-**ree**-ah behr _____
Photo / Video OK?	¿Foto / Vídeo OK? **foh**-toh / **bee**-deh-oh "OK"
(No) flash.	(No) flash. (noh) flahsh
(No) tripod.	(No) trípode. (noh) **tree**-poh-day
Will you take my / our photo?	¿Me / Nos hace una foto? may / nohs **ah**-thay **oo**-nah **foh**-toh
Please let me / let us in. (if room or sight is closing)	Por favor, déjeme / déjenos entrar. por fah-**bor day**-heh-may / **day**-heh-nohs ehn-**trar**
I promise I'll be fast.	Le prometo que no tardaré vendré rápido. lay proh-**meh**-toh kay noh tar-dar-**ay** behn-**dray rah**-pee-doh
It was my mother's dying wish that I see this.	Fue el último deseo de mi madre que yo viera esto. fweh ehl **ool**-tee-moh deh-**seh**-oh day mee **mah**-dray kay yoh bee-**ehr**-ah **eh**-stoh

Once at the sight, get your bearings by viewing the *plano* (floor plan). *Usted está aquí* means "You are here." Many museums have an official, one-way route that all visitors take—just follow signs for *Sentido de la visita.*

Signs at Sights

First figure out which line is for buying tickets (*taquilla* or *venta*) and which is for the entrance (*entrada*). Some larger museums have separate entrances for individuals (*para individuales*), for groups (*para grupos*), and for people who already have tickets reserved (*retirada de reservas*).

Entrada	Entrance
Reservas	Reservations
Taquilla	Ticket office
Entradas	Tickets
Adultos	Adults
Niños	Children
Jóvenes	Youths
Estudiantes	Students
Jubilados	Seniors
Ticket combinado	Combo-ticket
Descuento	Discount
Tour guiado	Guided tour
Exposición	Exhibition
Plano (de orientación)	Map (orientation)
Usted está aquí	You are here (on map)
Guardarropas	Cloakroom
Consigna	Bag check
Obligatorio	Required
Táquillas	Lockers
Audioguía	Audioguide
Ascensores	Elevators
A la exposición	To the exhibition
Colección	Collection
Sentido de la visita	Direction of visit ("this way")
No fotos	No photography
No flash / trípode	No flash / tripod
No tocar	Do not touch
No comer / beber	No eating / drinking
No se permite	Not allowed
Prohibido	Forbidden
Silencio	Silence
Obra en restauración	Work in restoration
Obra prestada	Work on loan

Taller (de educación)	Classroom
Sólo personal	Staff only
No hay salida	Not an exit
Salida	Exit
Salida de emergencia	Emergency exit

MUSEUMS

Types of Museums

museum	museo	moo-**seh**-oh
gallery	galería	gahl-leh-**ree**-ah
art gallery	galería de arte gah-leh-**ree**-ah day **ar**-tay	
painting gallery	galería de pinturas gah-leh-**ree**-ah day peen-**too**-rahs	
modern art	arte moderno	**ar**-tay mo-**dehr**-noh
contemporary art	arte contemporáneo **ar**-tay kohn-tehm-poh-**rah**-nee-oh	
folk	arte folclórico	**ar**-tay fohl-**kloh**-ree-koh
history	historia	ee-**stoh**-ree-ah
town / city	pueblo / ciudad **pweh**-bloh / thee-**oo-dahd**	
children's	para niños	**pah**-rah **neen**-yohs
Jewish	judío	hoo-**dee**-oh
memorial	conmemorativo kohn-mehm-oh-rah-**tee**-boh	

Art Appreciation

I like it.	Me gusta.	may **goo**-stah
It's so...	Es tan...	ehs tahn
...beautiful.	...bonito.	boh-**nee**-toh

...ugly.	...feo. **feh**-oh
...strange.	...extraño. ehk-**strahn**-yoh
...boring.	...aburrido. ah-boo-**ree**-doh
...interesting.	...interesante. een-teh-reh-**sahn**-tay
...thought-provoking.	...que te hace pensar. kay tay **ah**-thay pehn-**sar**
...B.S.	...mierda. mee-**ehr**-dah
I don't get it.	No lo entiendo. noh loh ehn-tee-**ehn**-doh
Is it upside down?	¿Está bocarriba? eh-**stah** boh-kah-**ree**-bah
Who did this?	¿Quién lo hizo? kee-**ehn** loh **ee**-thoh
How old is this?	¿Cuánto tiempo tiene esto? **kwahn**-toh tee-**ehm**-poh tee-**ehn**-ay **eh**-stoh
Wow!	¡Vaya! **bī**-ah
My feet hurt!	¡Me duelen los pies! may **dweh**-lehn lohs pee-**ays**

Art and Architecture Terms

art	arte **ar**-tay
artist	artista ar-**tee**-stah
painting	cuadro **kwah**-droh
sculptor	escultor eh-skool-**tor**
sculpture	escultura eh-skool-**too**-rah
architect	arquitecto ar-kee-**tehk**-toh
architecture	arquitectura ar-kee-tehk-**too**-rah
original	original oh-ree-hee-**nahl**
restored	restaurado reh-stow-**rah**-doh
B.C. / A.D.	A.C. / D.C. ah thay / day thay
century	siglo **see**-gloh

style	estilo	eh-**stee**-loh
prehistoric	prehistórico	preh-ee-**stoh**-ree-koh
Iberian (pre-Roman)	ibérico	ee-**bay**-ree-koh
ancient	antiguo	ahn-**tee**-gwoh
classical	clásico	**klah**-see-koh
Roman	romano	roh-**mah**-noh
Byzantine	bizantino	bee-thahn-**tee**-noh
Moorish	moros	**moh**-rohs
Islamic	islámico	ees-**lah**-mee-koh
medieval	medieval	meh-dee-eh-**bahl**
Romanesque	románico	roh-**mah**-nee-koh
Gothic	gótico	**goh**-tee-koh
Renaissance	renacimiento	reh-nah-thee-mee-**ehn**-toh
Baroque	barroco	bah-**roh**-koh
Neoclassical	neoclásico	neh-oh-**klah**-see-koh
Romantic	romántico	roh-**mahn**-tee-koh
Impressionist	impresionista	eem-preh-see-oh-**nee**-stah
Art Nouveau	modernista	moh-dehr-**nee**-stah
Modern	moderno	moh-**dehr**-noh
abstract	abstracto	ahb-**strahk**-toh
contemporary	contemporáneo kohn-tehm-poh-**rah**-neh-oh	

Historical Terms

Moors	Moros	**moh**-rohs
Christian Reconquest	Reconquista	reh-kohn-**kee**-stah
Catholic Monarchs	Reyes Católicos **reh**-ehs kah-**toh**-lee-kohs	
Inquisition	Inquisición	een-kee-see-thee-**ohn**
Christopher Columbus	Cristóbal Colón kree-**stoh**-bahl koh-**lohn**	

Age of Discovery	Era de los Descubrimientos **eh**-rah day los dehs-koo-bree-mee-**ehn**-tohs
Golden Age	Siglo de Oro **see**-gloh day **oh**-roh
World War I	Primera Guerra Mundial pree-**mehr**-ah **gehr**-ah moon-dee-**ahl**
World War II	Segunda Guerra Mundial seh-**goon**-dah **gehr**-ah moon-dee-**ahl**
Spanish Civil War	Guerra Civil Española **gehr**-ah thee-**beel** ehs-pahn-**yoh**-lah
European Union (EU)	Unión Europea (UE) oo-nee-**ohn** eh-oo-roh-**peh**-ah (oo ay)

CHURCHES

cathedral	catedral kah-teh-**drahl**
church	iglesia ee-**gleh**-see-ah
chapel	capilla kah-**pee**-yah
prayer hall	oratorio oh-rah-**toh**-ree-oh
altar	altar ahl-**tar**
bells	campanas kahm-**pah**-nahs
carillon	carillón / campana kah-ree-**yohn** / kahm-**pah**-nah
chapter house (meeting room)	salas capitular **sah**-lahs kah-pee-too-**lar**
choir	coro **koh**-roh
cloister	claustro **klow**-stroh (klow rhymes with cow)
cross	cruz krooth
crypt	cripta **kreep**-tah
dome	cúpula **koo**-poo-lah
organ	órgano **or**-gah-noh
pulpit	púlpito **pool**-pee-toh
relic	reliquia reh-**lee**-kee-ah

sacristy	sacristía	sah-kree-**stee**-ah
stained glass	vidriera	vee-dree-**ehr**-ah
steeple / bell tower	campanario	kahm-pah-**nah**-ree-oh
treasury	tesoro	teh-**soh**-roh
pope	papa	**pah**-pah
Mass	misa	**mee**-sah
When is the Mass?	¿A qué hora es la misa?	
	ah kay **oh**-rah ehs lah **mee**-sah	
Are there church concerts?	¿Hay conciertos en la iglesia?	
	ī kohn-thee-**ehr**-tohs ehn lah	
	ee-**gleh**-see-ah	
Can I climb the tower?	¿Puedo subir la torre?	
	pweh-doh soo-**beer** lah **toh**-ray	

At many churches, you may not be allowed to enter with shorts or bare shoulders.

MORE SIGHTS

Castles and Palaces

castle	castillo	kah-**stee**-yoh
palace	palacio	pah-**lah**-thee-oh
royal residence	residencia real	
	reh-see-**dehn**-thee-ah reh-**ahl**	
fortress	alcázar / fortaleza	
	ahl-kah-**thar** / for-tah-**leh**-thah	
kitchen	cocina	koh-**thee**-nah
dungeon	calabozo	kah-lah-**boh**-thoh
moat	foso	**foh**-soh
fortified walls	murallas fortificadas	
	moo-**rī**-ahs for-tee-fee-**kah**-dahs	
tower	torre	**toh**-ray
fountain	fuente	**fwehn**-tay

garden	jardín	har-**deen**
king	rey	ray
queen	reina	**reh**-ee-nah
knight	caballero	kah-bah-**yehr**-oh
fair maiden	doncella bella	dohn-**theh**-yah **beh**-yah
dragon	dragón	drah-**gohn**

A Moorish castle is called an *alcazaba,* and a Moorish fortress or palace is an *alcázar.*

Ancient Sites

ancient sites	yacimientos antiguos	
	yah-thee-mee-**ehn**-tohs ahn-**tee**-gwohs	
Iberian	ibérico	ee-**bay**-ree-koh
Roman	romano	roh-**mah**-noh
walls	murallas	moo-**rī**-ahs
forum (main square)	foro	**foh**-roh
temple	templo	**tehm**-ploh
column	columna	koh-**loom**-nah
mosaic	mosaico	moh-**sah**-ee-koh
theater	teatro	teh-**ah**-troh
arena	arena	ah-**reh**-nah
aqueduct	acueducto	ah-kweh-**dook**-toh

RECREATION AND ENTERTAINMENT

T his chapter offers phrases for your recreational pleasure, whether you're going to the park or beach, swimming, biking, hiking, or enjoying other sports. It also covers your options for nightlife and entertainment.

RECREATION

Outdoor Fun

Where is the best place for...?	¿Dónde está el mejor lugar para...? **dohn**-day eh-**stah** ehl meh-**hor** loo-**gar** pah-**rah**
...biking	...montar en bicicleta mohn-**tar** ehn bee-thee-**kleh**-tah
...walking	...caminar kah-mee-**nar**
...hiking	...hacer senderismo ah-**thehr** sehn-deh-**rees**-moh
...running	...correr koh-**rehr**
...picnicking	...hacer un picnic ah-**thehr** oon **peek**-neek
...sunbathing	...tomar el sol toh-**mar** ehl sohl
Where is a...?	¿Dónde está...? **dohn**-day eh-**stah**
...park	...un parque oon **par**-kay
...playground	...un parque infantíl oon **par**-kay een-fahn-**teel**
...snack shop	...una tienda de alimentación **oo**-nah tee-**ehn**-dah day ah-lee-**mehn**-tah-thee-**ohn**
...toilet	...un servicio oon sehr-**bee**-thee-oh
Where can I rent...?	¿Dónde puedo alquilar...? **dohn**-day **pweh**-doh ahl-kee-**lar**
...a bike	...una bicicleta **oo**-nah bee-thee-**kleh**-tah
...that	...eso **eh**-soh

What's a fun activity...?	¿Qué sería una actividad divertida...? kay seh-**ree**-ah **oo**-nah ahk-tee-bee-**dahd** dee-behr-**tee**-dah
...for a boy / a girl...	...para un niño / una niña... **pah**-rah oon **neen**-yoh / **oo**-nah **neen**-yah
... _____ years old	...de _____ años day _____ **ahn**-yohs

At bigger parks, you can sometimes rent a rowboat *(barco de remo)* or see a puppet show *(espectáculo de títeres)*—fun to watch in any language.

Swimming and Water Sports

swimming	natación nah-tah-thee-**ohn**
to swim	nadar nah-**dar**
Where is...?	¿Dónde está...? **dohn**-day eh-**stah**
...a swimming pool	...una piscina **oo**-nah pee-**thee**-nah
...a water park	...un parque aquático oon **par**-kay ah-**kwah**-tee-koh
...a (good) beach	...una playa (buena) **oo**-nah **plah**-yah (**bweh**-nah)
...a nude beach	...una playa nudista **oo**-nah **plah**-yah noo-**dee**-stah
Is it safe for swimming?	¿Es una zona segura para bañarse? ehs **oo**-nah **thoh**-nah seh-**goo**-rah **pah**-rah bahn-**yar**-say
Where can I buy / rent...?	¿Dónde puedo comprar / alquilar...? **dohn**-day **pweh**-doh kohm-**prar** / ahl-kee-**lar**
swimsuit	bañador bahn-yah-**dor**
towel	toalla toh-**ī**-yah
sunscreen	protección de sol proh-tehk-thee-**ohn** day sohl
sunglasses	gafas de sol **gah**-fahs day sohl

Renting

Whether you're renting a bike or a boat, here's what to ask.

Where can I rent...?	¿Dónde puedo alquilar...?
	dohn-day **pweh**-doh ahl-kee-**lar**
Can I rent...?	¿Puedo alquilar...?
	pweh-doh ahl-kee-**lar**
...a bike	...una bicicleta
	oo-nah bee-thee-**kleh**-tah
...a boat	...un barco oon **bar**-koh
How much per...?	¿Cuánto es por...? **kwahn**-toh ehs por
...hour	...hora **oh**-rah
...half-day	...medio día **meh**-dee-oh **dee**-ah
...day	...día **dee**-ah
Is a deposit required?	¿Se requiere un depósito?
	say reh-kee-**ehr**-ay oon deh-**poh**-see-toh

flip-flops	chancletas chahn-**kleh**-tahs
water shoes	zapatos para el agua
	thah-**pah**-tohs **pah**-rah ehl **ah**-gwah
umbrella	paraguas pah-**rah**-gwahs
lounge chair	tumbona toom-**boh**-nah
inner tube	tubo **too**-boh
goggles	gafas de natación
	gah-fahs day nah-tah-thee-**ohn**
snorkel and mask	tubo de respiración y máscara
	too-boh day reh-spee-rah-thee-**ohn** ee
	mahs-kah-rah
surfing	surfing **soor**-feeng
surfboard	tabla de surf **tah**-blah day soorf
windsurfing	windsurfing **weend**-soor-feeng

waterskiing	esquí acuático eh-**skee** ah-**kwah**-tee-koh
jet ski	jet ski "jet ski"
paddleboard	tabla de natación **tah**-blah day nah-tah-thee-**ohn**
boat	barco **bar**-koh
rowboat	barco de remo **bar**-koh day **reh**-moh
paddleboat	barca de pedales **bar**-kah day peh-**dah**-lehs
canoe / kayak	canoa / kayak kah-**noh**-ah / "kayak"
sailboat	barco de vela **bar**-koh day **beh**-lah

In Spain, nearly any beach is topless. For privacy when changing clothes, look for a little *cabina*. Many beaches have inviting shacks called *chiringuitos* that sell snacks and drinks.

Bicycling

bicycle / bike	bicicleta / bici bee-thee-**kleh**-tah / **bee**-thee
I'd like to rent a bicycle.	Me gustaría alquilar una bicicleta. may goo-stah-**ree**-ah ahl-kee-**lar oo**-nah bee-thee-**kleh**-tah
two bicycles	dos bicicletas dohs bee-thee-**kleh**-tahs
kid's bike	bicicleta de niños bee-thee-**kleh**-tah day **neen**-yohs
mountain bike	bicicleta de montaña bee-thee-**kleh**-tah day mohn-**tahn**-yah
helmet	casco **kahs**-koh
map	mapa **mah**-pah
lock	candado kahn-**dah**-doh
chain	cadena kah-**dehn**-ah
pedal	pedal peh-**dahl**

wheel	rueda roo-**eh**-dah
tire	neumático neh-oo-**mah**-tee-koh
air / no air	aire / sin aire **ī**-ray / seen **ī**-ray
pump	bomba de aire **bohm**-bah day **ī**-ray
brakes	frenos **freh**-nohs
How does this work?	¿Cómo funciona? **koh**-moh foon-thee-**oh**-nah
How many gears?	¿Cuántas marchas? **kwahn**-tahs **mar**-chahs
Is there a bike path?	¿Hay una ruta para bicicletas? ī **oo**-nah **roo**-tah **pah**-rah bee-thee-**kleh**-tahs
I don't like hills or traffic.	No me gustan las cuestas o el tráfico. noh may **goo**-stahn lahs **kweh**-stahs oh ehl **trah**-fee-koh
I brake for bakeries.	Me paro en las pastelerías. may **pah**-roh ehn lahs pah-steh-leh-**ree**-ahs

Hiking

hiking	senderismo sehn-deh-**rees**-moh
a hike	una caminata **oo**-nah kah-mee-**nah**-tah
trail	senda **sehn**-dah
Where can I buy a...?	¿Dónde se puede comprar...? **dohn**-day say **pweh**-day kom-**prar**
...hiking map	...un mapa de senderismo oon **mah**-pah day sehn-deh-**rees**-moh
...compass	...un compass oon **kohm**-pass
Where's the trailhead?	¿Dónde está el nacimiento de la ruta? **dohn**-day eh-**stah** ehl nah-thee-mee- **ehn**-toh day lah **roo**-tah
How do I get there?	¿Cómo llego allí? **koh**-moh **yeh**-goh ī-**yee**

Way to Go!

Whether you're biking or hiking, you'll want to know the best way to go.

Can you recommend a route / hike that is...?	¿Me podría recomendar una ruta / caminata que sea...? may poh-**dree**-ah reh-koh-mehn-**dar** oo-nah **roo**-tah / kah-mee-**nah**-tah kay **seh**-ah
...easy	...fácil **fah**-theel
...moderate	...moderado moh-deh-**rah**-doh
...strenuous	...difícil dee-**fee**-theel
...safe	...segura seh-**goo**-rah
...scenic	...panorámica pah-noh-**rah**-mee-kah
...about _____ kilometers	...de unos _____ kilómetros day **oo**-nohs _____ kee-**loh**-meh-trohs
How many minutes / hours?	Cuántos minutos / horas? **kwahn**-tohs mee-**noo**-tohs / **oh**-rahs
uphill / level / downhill	cuesta arriba / plano / cuesta abajo **kweh**-stah ah-**ree**-bah / **plah**-noh / **kweh**-stah ah-**bah**-hoh

Show me?	¿Me enseñaría? may ehn-sehn-yah-**ree**-ah
How is the trail marked?	¿Cómo está señalizada la senda? **koh**-moh eh-**stah** sehn-yah-lee-**thah**-dah lah **sehn**-dah

Most hiking trails are well-marked with signs listing the destination and the duration in hours (*horas*) and minutes (*minutos*).

Sports Talk

sports	deportes	deh-**por**-tehs
sports bar	bar deportivo	bar deh-por-**tee**-boh
game	partido	par-**tee**-doh
team	equipo	eh-**kee**-poh
championship	campeonato	kahm-peh-oh-**nah**-toh
field	campo	**kahm**-poh
court	pista	**pee**-stah
fitness club	gimnasio	heem-**nah**-see-oh
I like to play...	Me gusta jugar...	may **goo**-stah hoo-**gar**
I like to watch...	Me gusta ver...	may **goo**-stah behr
American football	fútbol americano **foot**-bohl ah-meh-ree-**kah**-noh	
baseball	béisbol	**bays**-bohl
basketball	baloncesto	bah-lohn-**theh**-stoh
golf	golf	gohlf
miniature golf	minigolf	mee-nee-**gohlf**
soccer	fútbol	**foot**-bohl
tennis	tenis	**teh**-nees
volleyball	vóleibol	**voh**-lay-bohl
Where can I play?	¿Dónde puedo jugar? **dohn**-day **pweh**-doh hoo-**gar**	
Where can I rent / buy sports equipment?	¿Dónde puedo alquilar / comprar equipo deportivo? **dohn**-day **pweh**-doh ahl-kee-**lar** / kohm-**prar** eh-**kee**-poh deh-por-**tee**-boh	
Where can I see a game?	¿Dónde puedo ver un partido? **dohn**-day **pweh**-doh behr oon par-**tee**-doh	

As in most of the world, *fútbol* (soccer) is hugely popular. Spain's elite division, *La Liga*, is dominated by FC Barcelona (nicknamed *Barça*) and *Real* ("Royal") *Madrid*. Matches between these heated rivals are called *El Clásico*.

ENTERTAINMENT

What's Happening

event guide	guía del ocio **gee**-ah dehl **oh**-thee-oh
What's happening tonight?	¿Qué hay esta noche? kay ī **eh**-stah **noh**-chay
What do you recommend?	¿Qué recomienda? kay reh-koh-mee-**ehn**-dah
Where is it?	¿Dónde está? **dohn**-day eh-**stah**
How do I / we get there?	¿Cómo llego / llegamos allí? **koh**-moh **yeh**-goh / yeh-**gah**-mohs ī-**yee**
Is it free?	¿Es gratis? ehs **grah**-tees
Are there seats available?	¿Hay asientos disponibles? ī ah-see-**ehn**-tohs dee-spoh-**nee**-blehs
Where can I buy a ticket?	¿Dónde puedo comprar una entrada? **dohn**-day **pweh**-doh kohm-**prar oo**-nah ehn-**trah**-dah
Do you have tickets for today / tonight?	¿Tiene entradas para hoy / esta noche? tee-**ehn**-ay ehn-**trah**-dahs **pah**-rah oy / **eh**-stah **noh**-chay
When does it start?	¿Cuándo empieza? **kwahn**-doh ehm-pee-**eh**-thah
When does it end?	¿Cuándo acaba? **kwahn**-doh ah-**kah**-bah
Where is the best place to stroll?	¿Dónde está el mejor paseo? **dohn**-day eh-**stah** ehl meh-**hor** pah-**seh**-oh

Many Spanish cities have an events guide *(guía del ocio)* that you can buy cheaply at a newsstand. For free, enjoyable entertainment, join the locals for a *paseo*—an evening stroll through town.

Music and Dance

Where's a good place for...?	¿Dónde está un buen sitio para...? dohn-day eh-stah oon bwehn seet-yoh pah-rah
...dancing	...bailar bī-lar
...(live) music	...música (en vivo) moo-see-kah (ehn bee-boh)
rock	rock "rock"
jazz	jazz "jazz"
blues	blues "blues"
classical	clásica klah-see-kah
choir	coro koh-roh
folk	folclórica fohk-loh-ree-kah
folk dancing	baile folclórico bī-lay (fohk-loh-ree-koh)
flamenco	flamenco flah-mehn-koh
disco	disco "disco"
karaoke	karaoke kah-rah-oh-kay
singer	cantante kahn-tahn-tay
band	grupo de música groo-poh day moo-see-kah
bar with live music	bar con música en vivo bar kohn moo-see-kah ehn bee-boh
nightclub	club nocturno kloob nohk-toor-noh
(no) cover charge	(sin) entrada (seen) ehn-trah-dah
concert	concierto kohn-thee-ehr-toh
opera	ópera oh-peh-rah
symphony	sinfónica seen-foh-nee-kah
show	espectáculo eh-spehk-tah-koo-loh
theater	teatro teh-ah-troh
best / cheap seats	mejores / baratos asientos meh-hoh-rehs / bah-rah-tohs ah-see-ehn-tohs
sold out	agotadas ah-goh-tah-dahs

Movies

movie	película peh-**lee**-koo-lah
Where is a movie theater?	¿Dónde está un cine? **dohn**-day eh-**stah** oon **thee**-nay
Is this movie in English?	¿La película está en inglés? lah peh-**lee**-koo-lah eh-**stah** ehn een-**glays**
original version	versión original behr-thee-**ohn** oh-ree-*hee*-**nahl**
with subtitles	con subtítulos kohn soob-**tee**-too-lohs
dubbed	doblada doh-**blah**-dah
3D	tres "D" trehs "dee"
show times	horarios oh-**rah**-ree-ohs
matinee	primera sesión pree-**mehr**-ah seh-see-**ohn**
ticket	entrada ehn-**trah**-dah
discount	descuento dehs-**kwhen**-toh
popcorn	palomitas pah-loh-**mee**-tahs
I liked it.	Me ha gustado. may ah goo-**stah**-doh
The book is better.	El libro es mejor. ehl **lee**-broh ehs meh-**hor**

In Spain, most foreign films are dubbed into Spanish. But you can sometimes find American movies screened in the "original version" (English with Spanish subtitles)—look for *V.O.* and *en inglés sub*.

SHOPPING

These phrases will give you the basics on browsing and bargaining; help you shop for various items, including souvenirs, clothes, and jewelry; and assist you in shipping items home.

SHOP TILL YOU DROP

Shop Talk

opening hours	horario de apertura oh-**rah**-ree-oh day ah-pehr-**too**-rah
sale	rebajas reh-**bah**-hahs
special offer	oferta oh-**fehr**-tah
cheap	barato bah-**rah**-toh
affordable	asequible ah-seh-**kee**-blay
(too) expensive	(demasiado) caro (deh-mah-see-**ah**-doh) **kah**-roh
a good value	un buen precio oon bwehn **preh**-thee-oh
Pardon me.	Perdóneme. pehr-**dohn**-eh-may
Where can I buy _____?	¿Dónde puedo comprar _____? **dohn**-day **pweh**-doh kohm-**prar** _____
How much is it?	¿Cuánto cuesta? **kwahn**-toh **kweh**-stah
I'm / We're just browsing.	Estoy / Estamos sólo mirando. eh-stoy / eh-**stah**-mohs **soh**-loh mee-**rahn**-doh
I'd like...	Me gustaría... may goo-stah-**ree**-ah
Do you have...?	¿Tiene usted...? tee-**ehn**-ay oo-**stehd**
...more	...más mahs
...something cheaper	...algo más barato **ahl**-goh mahs bah-**rah**-toh
...something nicer	...algo más bonito **ahl**-goh mahs boh-**nee**-toh
Can I see more?	¿Puedo ver más? **pweh**-doh behr mahs
This one.	Este. **eh**-stay

Key Phrases: Shopping

How much is it?	¿Cuánto cuesta? **kwahn**-toh **kweh**-stah
I'm just browsing.	Estoy sólo mirando. **eh**-stoy **soh**-loh mee-**rahn**-doh
Can I see more?	¿Puedo ver más? **pweh**-doh behr mahs
I'll think about it.	Voy a pensármelo. boy ah pehn-**sar**-meh-loh
I'll take it.	Me lo llevo. may loh **yeh**-boh
Do you accept credit cards?	¿Se aceptan tarjetas de crédito? say ah-**thehp**-tahn tar-**heh**-tahs day **kray**-dee-toh
Can I try it on?	¿Puedo probarlo? **pweh**-doh proh-**bar**-loh
It's too expensive / big / small.	Es demasiado caro / grande / pequeño. ehs deh-mah-see-**ah**-doh **kah**-roh / **grahn**-day / peh-**kehn**-yoh

I'll think about it.	Voy a pensármelo. boy ah pehn-**sar**-meh-loh
I'll take it.	Me lo llevo. may loh **yeh**-boh
What time do you close?	¿A qué hora cierran? ah kay **oh**-rah thee-**ehr**-ahn
What time do you open tomorrow?	¿A qué hora abren mañana? ah kay **oh**-rah **ah**-brehn mahn-**yah**-nah

Bargain hunters keep an eye out for sales: *rebajas, ofertas,* and *oportunidades*.

If there's a line, you might have to take a number—look for the box marked *su turno* (your turn). When the vendor is ready for the next customer, she might say *Siguiente* (seeg-ee-**ehn**-tay) or *El próximo?* (ehl **prohk**-see-moh).

Pay Up

Where do I pay?	¿Dónde pago? **dohn**-day **pah**-goh
the cashier	la caja lah **kah**-hah
Do you accept credit cards?	¿Se aceptan tarjetas de crédito? say ah-**thehp**-tahn tar-**heh**-tahs day **kray**-dee-toh
VAT (Value-Added Tax)	IVA (Impuesto al Valor Agregado) **ee**-bah (eem-**pweh**-stoh ahl bah-**lor** ah-greh-**gah**-doh)
Can I get...?	¿Me puede dar...? may **pweh**-doh dar
I need the paperwork for...	Necesito el formulario para... neh-theh-**see**-toh ehl for-moo-**lah**-ree-oh **pah**-rah
...a VAT refund.	...la devolución del IVA. lah deh-bohl-loo-thee-**ohn** dehl **ee**-bah
Can you ship this?	¿Puede enviar esto? **pweh**-day ehn-bee-**ar eh**-stoh

When you're ready to pay, look for a *caja* (cashier). The cashier might ask you something like *¿Tienes quince céntimos?* (Do you have 15 cents?) or *¿Quieres una bolsa?* (Do you want a bag?).

If you make a major purchase from a single store, you may be eligible for a VAT refund; for details, see www.ricksteves.com/vat.

WHERE TO SHOP

Types of Shops

Where is a...?	¿Dónde hay un / una...? **dohn**-day ī oon / **oo**-nah
antique shop	tienda de antigüedades tee-**ehn**-dah day ahn-tee-gway-**dah**-dehs
art gallery	galería de arte gah-leh-**ree**-ah day **ar**-tay

bakery	panadería pah-nah-deh-**ree**-ah
barber shop	barbería bar-beh-**ree**-ah
beauty salon	peluquería peh-loo-keh-**ree**-ah
bookstore...	librería... lee-breh-**ree**-ah
used bookstore...	tienda de libros de segundo mano... tee-**ehn**-dah day **lee**-brohs day seh-**goon**-doh **mah**-noh
...with books in English	...de libros en inglés day **lee**-brohs ehn een-**glays**
camera shop	tienda de fotos tee-**ehn**-dah day **foh**-tohs
call shop (for making cheap long-distance calls)	locutorio loh-koo-**tor**-ee-oh
cheese shop	quesería keh-seh-**ree**-ah
clothing boutique	tienda de ropa tee-**ehn**-dah day **roh**-pah
coffee shop	cafetería kah-feh-teh-**ree**-ah
computer store	tienda de informática tee-**ehn**-dah day een-for-**mah**-tee-kah
crafts shop	tienda de artesanía tee-**ehn**-dah day ar-teh-sah-**nee**-ah
delicatessen	delicatessen deh-lee-kah-**teh**-sehn
department store	grandes almacenes **grahn**-dehs ahl-mah-**theh**-nehs
electronics store	tienda de informática y electrónica tee-**ehn**-dah day een-for-**mah**-tee-kah ee eh-lehk-**troh**-nee-kah
fabric store	tienda de telas tee-**ehn**-dah day **teh**-lahs
flea market	rastro **rahs**-troh
flower market	floristería floh-ree-steh-**ree**-ah
grocery store	supermercado soo-pehr-mehr-**kah**-doh
hardware store	ferretería feh-reh-teh-**ree**-ah

Internet café	café de Internet kah-**fay** day **een**-tehr-neht
jewelry shop (fine)	joyería hoy-eh-**ree**-ah
jewelry shop (cheap)	bisutería bee-soo-teh-**ree**-ah
launderette	lavandería lah-vahn-deh-**ree**-ah
liquor store	tienda de vinos y licores tee-**ehn**-dah day **bee**-nohs ee lee-**kor**-ehs
mobile-phone shop	tienda de teléfonos móviles tee-**ehn**-dah day teh-**lay**-foh-nohs **moh**-bee-lehs
newsstand	kiosco kee-**oh**-skoh
office supply shop	papelería pah-peh-leh-**ree**-ah
open-air market	mercado al aire libre mehr-**kah**-doh ahl ī-ray **lee**-bray
optician	óptico **ohp**-tee-koh
pastry shop	pastelería pah-steh-leh-**ree**-ah
pharmacy	farmacia far-**mah**-thee-ah
photocopy shop	tienda de fotocopias tee-**ehn**-dah day foh-toh-**koh**-pee-ahs
shoe store	zapatería thah-pah-teh-**ree**-ah
shopping mall	centro comercial **thehn**-troh koh-mehr-thee-**ahl**
souvenir shop	tienda de souvenirs tee-**ehn**-dah day soo-beh-**neers**
supermarket	supermercado soo-pehr-mehr-**kah**-doh
sweets shop	tienda de dulces / caramelos tee-**ehn**-dah day **dool**-thehs / kah-rah-**meh**-lohs
toy store	juguetería hoo-geh-teh-**ree**-ah
travel agency	agencia de viajes ah-**hehn**-thee-ah day bee-**ah**-hehs
wine shop	tienda de vinos tee-**ehn**-dah day **bee**-nohs

In Spain, shops are often closed for a long lunch (generally between 1:00 and 4:00 p.m.) and all day on Sundays. For tips and phrases on shopping for a picnic—at grocery stores or open-air markets—see page 159 in the Eating chapter.

Department Stores

department store	grandes almacenes **grahn**-dehs ahl-mah-**theh**-nehs
floor	planta **plahn**-tah
Pardon me.	Perdóneme. pehr-**dohn**-eh-may
Where is / are...?	¿Dónde está / están...? **dohn**-day eh-**stah** / eh-**stahn**
men's / women's	moda para hombres / mujeres **moh**-dah **pah**-rah **ohm**-brehs / moo-**hehr**-ehs
children's	de niño day **neen**-yoh
accessories	complementos kohm-pleh-**mehn**-tohs
books	libros **lee**-brohs
electronics	electrónicos eh-lehk-**troh**-nee-kohs
fashion	moda **moh**-dah
footwear	calzado kahl-**thah**-doh
groceries	supermercado soo-pehr-mehr-**kah**-doh
housewares / kitchenware	electrodomésticos / utensilios de cocina eh-lehk-troh-doh-**may**-stee-kohs / oo-tehn-**see**-lee-ohs day koh-**thee**-nah
intimates	lencería lehn-theh-**ree**-ah
jewelry	joyas **hoy**-ahs
maternity (wear)	(ropa) premamá (**roh**-pah) preh-mah-**mah**
mobile phones	teléfonos móviles teh-**lay**-foh-nohs **moh**-bee-lehs
stationery (office supplies, cards)	papelería pah-peh-leh-**ree**-ah

Department stores, like the popular *El Corte Inglés* chain, sell nearly everything and are a good place to get cheap souvenirs and postcards. Most have a directory (often with English) by the escalator or elevator.

Street Markets

Did you make this?	¿Hizo usted esto? **ee**-thoh oo-**stehd eh**-stoh
Is this made in Spain?	¿Está hecho en España? eh-**stah eh**-choh ehn eh-**spahn**-yah
How much is it?	¿Cuánto cuesta? **kwahn**-toh **kweh**-stah
Cheaper?	¿Hay uno más barato? ī **oo**-noh mahs bah-**rah**-toh
And if I give you _____? (name price)	¿Y si le doy _____? ee see lay doy _____
Cheaper if I buy two or three?	¿Es más barato si compro dos o tres? ehs mahs bah-**rah**-toh see **kohm**-proh dohs oh trehs
Good price.	Buen precio. bwehn **preh**-thee-oh
My last offer.	Mi última oferta. mee **ool**-tee-mah oh-**fehr**-tah
I'll take it.	Me lo llevo. may loh **yeh**-boh
We'll take it.	Nos lo llevamos. nohs loh yeh-**bah**-mohs
I'm / We're nearly broke.	Estoy / Estamos a dos velas. eh-stoy / eh-**stah**-mohs ah dohs **beh**-lahs
My friend (m / f)...	Mi amigo / Mia amiga... mee ah-**mee**-goh / **mee**-ah ah-**mee**-gah
My husband / My wife...	Mi marido / Mia mujer... mee mah-**ree**-doh / **mee**-ah moo-**hehr**
...has the money.	...tiene el dinero. tee-**ehn**-ay ehl dee-**nehr**-oh

It's OK to bargain at street markets, though not every vendor will drop prices. Expect to pay cash and be wary of pickpockets. For help with numbers and prices, see page 24.

WHAT TO BUY

Here are some of the items you might buy, ranging from souvenirs to clothing to jewelry. For personal care items, see page 270. For electronics, see page 232.

Souvenirs

Do you have a...?	¿Tiene usted un / una...? tee-**ehn**-ay oo-**stehd** oon / **oo**-nah
I'm looking for a...	Estoy buscando un / una... **eh**-stoy boos-**kahn**-doh oon / **oo**-nah
book	libro **lee**-broh
guidebook	guía turístico **gee**-ah too-**ree**-stee-koh
children's book	libro para niños **lee**-broh **pah**-rah **neen**-yohs
bookmark	marcador de libros mar-kah-**dor** day **lee**-brohs
calendar	calendario kah-lehn-**dah**-ree-oh
candle	vela **beh**-lah
doll	muñeca moon-**yeh**-kah
journal	diario dee-**ah**-ree-oh
magnet	imán ee-**mahn**
notecards	tarjeta para dejar una nota tar-**heh**-tah **pah**-rah deh-**har oo**-nah **noh**-tah
ornament	ornamento or-nah-**mehn**-toh
pen / pencil	bolígrafo / un lápiz boh-**lee**-grah-foh / oon **lah**-peeth
postcard	tarjeta postal tar-**heh**-tah poh-**stahl**
poster	póster **poh**-stehr
print	grabado grah-**bah**-doh
toy	juguete *hoo*-**geh**-tay
umbrella	paraguas pah-**rah**-gwahs

Specifically Spanish Souvenirs

castanets	castañuelas	kas-tahn-noo-**eh**-lahs
espadrilles (shoes)	alpargatas	ahl-par-**gah**-tahs
fan	abanico	ah-bah-**nee**-koh
hair comb (ornamental)	peineta	pay-**neh**-tah
fancy head scarf	mantilla	mahn-**tee**-yah
shawl	mantón	mahn-**tohn**

Andalusian women wear colorful, flamenco-style gowns during Sevilla's April Fair. In addition, they wear an ornate head scarf called a *mantilla*, secured by a *peineta* (ornamental comb). They use *abanicos* (fans) as accessories to match different dresses.

Clothing

clothing	ropa	**roh**-pah
This one.	Este.	**eh**-stay
Can I try it on?	¿Puedo probarlo?	
	pweh-doh proh-**bar**-loh	
Do you have a...?	¿Tiene un...?	tee-**ehn**-ay oon
...mirror	...espejo	eh-**speh**-hoh
...fitting room	...probador	proh-bah-**dor**
It's too...	Es demasiado...	
	ehs deh-mah-see-**ah**-doh	
...expensive.	...caro.	**kah**-roh
...big / small.	...grande / pequeño.	
	grahn-day / peh-**kehn**-yoh	
...short / long.	...corto / largo.	**kor**-toh / **lar**-goh
...tight / loose.	...apretado / ligero.	
	ah-preh-**tah**-doh / lee-**heh**-roh	
...dark / light.	...oscuro / claro.	
	oh-**skoo**-roh / **klah**-roh	

Do you have a different color / pattern?	¿Tiene usted otro color / diseño?
	tee-**ehn**-ay oo-**stehd** oh-troh koh-**lor** / dee-**sehn**-yoh
What's this made of?	¿De qué está hecho esto?
	day kay eh-**stah** eh-choh **eh**-stoh
Is it machine washable?	¿Se puede lavar en la lavadora?
	say **pweh**-day lah-**var** ehn lah lah-vah-**doh**-rah
Will it shrink?	¿Esto se encogerá?
	eh-stoh say ehn-koh-hehr-**ah**
Will it fade in the wash?	¿Desteñirá en la lavadora?
	deh-stehn-yee-**rah** ehn lah lah-vah-**doh**-rah
Dry clean only?	¿Limpiar en seco sólo?
	leem-pee-**ar** ehn **seh**-koh **soh**-loh

For lists of colors and fabrics, see page 225.

Types of Clothes and Accessories

For a...	Para un / una... pah-rah oon / **oo**-nah
...man.	...hombre. **ohm**-bray
...woman.	...mujer. moo-**hehr**
...male teen.	...adolescente hombre.
	ah-doh-leh-**sehn**-tay ohm-bray
...female teen.	...adolescente mujer.
	ah-doh-leh-**sehn**-tay moo-**hehr**
...child. (m / f)	...niño / niña. **neen**-yoh / **neen**-yah
...baby.	...bebé. beh-**bay**
I'm looking for a...	Estoy buscando un / una...
	eh-stoy boos-**kahn**-doh oon / **oo**-nah
I want to buy a...	Me gustaría comprar un / una...
	may goo-stah-**ree**-ah kohm-**prar** oon / **oo**-nah
bathrobe	albornoz ahl-bor-**nohth**

bib	peto **peh**-toh
belt	cinturón theen-too-**rohn**
bra	sujetador soo-*heh*-tah-**dor**
dress	vestido behs-**tee**-doh
flip-flops	chancletas chahn-**kleh**-tahs
gloves	guantes **gwahn**-tehs
handbag	bolso **bohl**-soh
hat	sombrero sohm-**brehr**-oh
jacket	chaqueta chah-**keh**-tah
jeans	vaqueros bah-**kehr**-ohs
leggings	leggings **leh**-geengs
nightgown	camisón kah-mee-**sohn**
nylons	medias **meh**-dee-ahs
pajamas	pijama pee-*hah*-mah
pants	pantalones pahn-tah-**loh**-nehs
raincoat	gabardina gah-bar-**dee**-nah
sandals	sandalias sahn-**dah**-lee-ahs
scarf	bufanda boo-**fahn**-dah
shirt...	camisa... kah-**mee**-sah
...long-sleeved	...de manga larga day **mahn**-gah **lar**-gah
...short-sleeved	...de manga corta day **mahn**-gah **kor**-tah
...sleeveless	...sin mangas seen **mahn**-gahs
shoelaces	cordones kor-**doh**-nehs
shoes	zapatos thah-**pah**-tohs
shorts	pantalones cortos pahn-tah-**loh**-nehs **kor**-tohs
skirt	falda **fahl**-dah
sleeper (for baby)	canguro kahn-**goo**-roh

slip	calzoncillo para mujeres kahl-thohn-**thee**-yoh **pah**-rah moo-**hehr**-ehs
slippers	zapatillas thah-pah-**tee**-yahs
socks	calcetines kahl-theh-**tee**-nehs
sweater	jersey **hehr**-see
swimsuit	bañador bahn-yah-**dor**
tank top	camiseta de tirantes kah-mee-**seh**-tah day tee-**rahn**-tehs
tennis shoes	zapatillas de tenis thah-pah-**tee**-yahs day **teh**-nees
tie	corbata kor-**bah**-tah
tights	medias **meh**-dee-ahs
T-shirt	camiseta kah-mee-**seh**-tah
underwear	ropa interior **roh**-pah een-teh-ree-**or**
vest	chaleco chah-**leh**-koh
wallet	cartera kar-**teh**-rah

Clothing Sizes

extra-small	extra pequeño **ehk**-strah peh-**kehn**-yoh
small	pequeño peh-**kehn**-yoh
medium	mediano meh-dee-**ah**-noh
large	grande **grahn**-day
extra-large	extra grande **ehk**-strah **grahn**-day
I need a bigger / smaller size.	Necesito un tamaño más grande / más pequeño. neh-theh-**see**-toh oon tah-**mahn**-yoh mahs **grahn**-day / mahs peh-**kehn**-yoh
What's my size?	¿Cuál es mi tamaño? kwahl ehs mee tah-**mahn**-yoh

US-to-European Comparisons

When shopping for clothing, use these US-to-European comparisons as a guideline (but note that no conversion is perfect).

Women's dresses and blouses: Add 30 (US size 10 = EU size 40)
Men's suits and jackets: Add 10 (US size 40 regular = EU size 50)
Men's shirts: Multiply by 2 and add about 8 (US size 15 collar = EU size 38)
Women's shoes: Add about 30 (US size 8 = EU size 38 1/2)
Men's shoes: Add 32-34 (US size 9 = EU size 41; US size 11 = EU size 45)
Children's clothing: Small children, subtract 1 (US size 10 = EU size 9); juniors, subtract 4 (US size 14 = EU size 10)
Girls' shoes: Add 16-17 (US size 10 = EU size 26); over size 13 use women's sizes
Boys' shoes: Add 17.5-18 (US size 11 = EU size 29); over size 13 use men's sizes

Sew What?

Traveling is hard on clothes.

I need...	Necesito... neh-theh-**see**-toh
...a button.	...un botón. oon boh-**tohn**
...a needle.	...una aguja. **oo**-nah ah-**goo**-hah
...thread.	...hilo. **ee**-loh
...scissors.	...unas tijeras. **oo**-nahs tee-**heh**-rahs
...stain remover.	...un quitamanchas. oon kee-tah-**mahn**-chahs
...a new zipper.	...una nueva cremallera. **oo**-nah **nweh**-bah kreh-mah-**yeh**-rah
Can you fix it?	¿Lo puede arreglar? loh **pweh**-day ah-reh-**glar**

Colors

black	negro **neh**-groh
blue	azul ah-**thool**
brown	marrón mah-**rrohn**
gray	gris grees
green	verde **behr**-day
orange	naranja nah-**rahn**-hah
pink	rosa **roh**-sah
purple	morado moh-**rah**-doh
red	rojo **roh**-hoh
white	blanco **blahn**-koh
yellow	amarillo ah-mah-**ree**-yoh
dark(er)	(más) oscuro (mahs) oh-**skoo**-roh
light(er)	(más) claro (mahs) **klah**-roh
bright(er)	(más) brillante (mahs) bree-**yahn**-tay

Fabrics

What's this made of?	¿De qué está hecho esto? day kay eh-**stah eh**-choh **eh**-stoh
A mix of...	Una mezcla de... **oo**-nah **mehth**-klah day
cashmere	cachemir kah-cheh-**meer**
cotton	algodón ahl-goh-**dohn**
denim	tela vaquero **teh**-lah bah-**keh**-roh
flannel	franela frah-**neh**-lah
fleece	vellón beh-**lohn**
lace	encaje ehn-**kah**-hay
leather	piel pee-**ehl**
linen	lino **lee**-noh
nylon	nilón nee-**lohn**
polyester	poliéster poh-lee-**eh**-stehr

silk	seda **seh**-dah
velvet	terciopelo tehr-thee-oh-**peh**-loh
wool	lana **lah**-nah

Jewelry

jewelry	joyas **hoy**-ahs
fine jewelry shop	joyería hoy-eh-**ree**-ah
cheap fashion jewelry shop	bisutería bee-soo-teh-**ree**-ah
bracelet	pulsera pool-**seh**-rah
brooch	broche **broh**-chay
cuff links	gemelos heh-**meh**-lohs
earrings	pendientes pehn-dee-**ehn**-tehs
necklace	collar koh-**yar**
ring	anillo ah-**nee**-yoh
watch	reloj **reh**-loh
watch battery	batería de reloj bah-teh-**ree**-ah day **reh**-loh
silver / gold	plata / oro **plah**-tah / **oh**-roh
Is this...?	¿Es esto...? ehs **eh**-stoh
...sterling silver	...plata de ley **plah**-tah day lay
...real gold	...oro puro **oh**-roh **poo**-roh
...handmade	...hecha a mano **eh**-chah ah **mah**-noh
...made in Spain	...hecho en España **eh**-choh ehn eh-**spahn**-yah
...stolen	...robado roh-**bah**-doh

SHIPPING AND MAIL

If you need to ship packages home, head for the *correos* (post office).
Otherwise, you can often get stamps at a *kiosco* (newsstand) or an
estanco (tobacco shop).

At the Post Office

post office	correos koh-**reh**-ohs
Where is the post office?	¿Dónde está correos? **dohn**-day eh-**stah** koh-**reh**-ohs
stamps	sellos **seh**-yohs
postcard	tarjeta postal tar-**heh**-tah poh-**stahl**
letter	carta **kar**-tah
package	paquete pah-**keh**-tay
window	ventana behn-**tah**-nah
line	cola **koh**-lah
Which window...?	¿Cuál es la ventana...? **kwahl** ehs lah behn-**tah**-nah
Is this the line...?	¿Es ésta la cola...? ehs **eh**-stah lah **koh**-lah
I need...	Tengo que... **tehn**-goh kay
...to buy stamps	...comprar sellos kohm-**prar** **seh**-yohs
...to mail a package	...enviar un paquete ehn-bee-**ar** oon pah-**keh**-tay
to the United States	a los Estados Unidos ah lohs eh-**stah**-dohs oo-**nee**-dohs
by air mail	por avión por ah-bee-**ohn**
by express mail	urgente oor-**hehn**-tay
by surface mail	vía terrestre **bee**-ah teh-**reh**-stray
slow and cheap	lento y barato **lehn**-toh ee bah-**rah**-toh
How much is it?	¿Cuánto cuesta? **kwahn**-toh **kweh**-stah

How much to send a letter / postcard to _____?	¿Cuánto cuesta enviar una carta / tarjeta postal a _____? **kwahn**-toh **kweh**-stah ehn-bee-**ar oo**-nah **kar**-tah / tar-**heh**-tah poh-**stahl** ah _____
Pretty stamps, please.	Sellos bonitos, por favor. **seh**-yohs boh-**nee**-tohs por fah-**bor**
Can I buy a box?	¿Se vende cajas de embalaje? say **behn**-day **kah**-hahs day ehm-bah-**lah**-hay
This big.	Así de grande. ah-**see** day **grahn**-day
Do you have tape?	¿Tiene cinta adhesiva? tee-**ehn**-ay **theen**-tah ah-deh-**see**-bah
How many days will it take?	¿Cuántos días tardará? **kwahn**-tohs **dee**-ahs tar-dar-**ah**
I always choose the slowest line.	Siempre elijo la cola más lenta. see-**ehm**-pray eh-**lee**-hoh lah **koh**-lah mahs **lehn**-tah

Bigger post offices may have windows labeled *Entrega* for mailing and *Recogida* for picking up packages. Watch the *su turno* (your turn) board, which lists the *número* (number currently being served) and *puesto* (window) to report to.

Licking the Postal Code

to / from	a / desde ah / **dehs**-day
address	dirección dee-rehk-thee-**ohn**
zip code	código postal **koh**-dee-goh poh-**stahl**
envelope	sobre **soh**-bray
package	paquete pah-**keh**-tay
box	caja **kah**-hah
packing material	material de relleno para paquetes mah-teh-ree-**ahl** day reh-**yeh**-noh **pah**-rah pah-**keh**-tehs

tape	cinta adhesiva **theen**-tah ah-deh-**see**-bah
string	cuerda **kwehr**-dah
mailbox	buzón boo-**thohn**
book rate	tarifa tah-**ree**-fah
weight limit	peso máximo **peh**-soh **mahk**-see-moh
registered	certificada thehr-tee-fee-**kah**-dah
insured	asegurada ah-seh-goo-**rah**-dah
fragile	frágil **frah**-heel
contents	contenido kohn-teh-**nee**-doh
customs	aduana ah-**dwah**-nah
tracking number	número de rastreo **noo**-mehr-oh day rahs-**treh**-oh

Post offices sell sturdy boxes, which you can assemble, fill with souvenirs, and mail home...so you can keep packing light.

TECHNOLOGY

This chapter covers phrases for your tech needs—from buying earbuds to taking photos, from making phone calls (using mobile or landline phones) to getting online (using your portable device or a public Internet terminal).

TECH TERMS

Portable Devices and Accessories

I need a...	Necesito un / una...
	neh-theh-**see**-toh oon / **oo**-nah
Do you have a...?	¿Tiene usted un / una...?
	tee-**ehn**-ay oo-**stehd** oon / **oo**-nah
Where can I buy a...?	¿Dónde puedo comprar un / una...?
	dohn-day **pweh**-doh kohm-**prar** oon / **oo**-nah
battery (for my _____)	batería / pila (para mi _____)
	bah-teh-**ree**-ah / **pee**-lah (**pah**-rah mee _____)
battery charger	cargador de pilas
	kar-gah-**dor** day **pee**-lahs
charger	cargador kar-gah-**dor**
computer	ordenador or-deh-nah-**dor**
convertor	convertidor kohn-vehr-tee-**dor**
CD / DVD	CD / DVD thay day / day **oo**-vay day
ebook reader	kindle **keen**-duhl
electrical adapter	adaptador eléctrico
	ah-dahp-tah-**dor** eh-**lehk**-tree-koh
flash drive	pendrive **pehn**-drive
headphones / earbuds	auriculares
	ow-ree-koo-**lah**-rehs
iPod / MP3 player	iPod / reproductor de MP3
	"iPod" / reh-proh-dook-**tor** day **eh**-may pay trehs
laptop	portátil por-**tah**-teel

memory card	tarjeta de memoria tar-**heh**-tah day meh-**moh**-ree-ah
mobile phone	móvil **moh**-beel
SIM card	tarjeta SIM tar-**heh**-tah seem
speakers **(for my _____)**	altavoces (para mi _____) ahl-tah-**boh**-thehs (**pah**-rah mee _____)
tablet	tableta tah-**bleh**-tah
(mini) USB cable	(pequeño) cable USB (peh-**kehn**-yoh) **kah**-blay oo **ehs**-ay bay
video game	videojuego bee-deh-oh-**hweh**-goh
Wi-Fi	Wi-Fi **wee**-fee

Familiar brands (like iPad, Facebook, YouTube, Instagram, or whatever the latest craze) are just as popular in Europe as they are back home. These go by their English names, sometimes with a Spanish accent.

Cameras

camera	cámara **kah**-mah-rah
digital camera	cámara digital **kah**-mah-rah dee-hee-**tahl**
video camera	cámara de vídeo **kah**-mah-rah day **bee**-deh-oh
lens cap	tapa de lente **tah**-pah day **lehn**-tay
film	carrete para la cámara kah-**reh**-tay **pah**-rah lah **kah**-mah-rah
Can I download my **photos onto a CD?**	¿Puedo copiar mis fotos a un CD? **pweh**-doh koh-pee-**ar** mees **foh**-tohs ah oon thay day
Will you take my / **our photo?**	¿Me / Nos hace una foto? may / nohs **ah**-thay **oo**-nah **foh**-toh
Can I take a photo **of you?**	¿Puedo hacerle una foto? **pweh**-doh ah-**thehr**-lay **oo**-nah **foh**-toh
Smile!	¡Sonría! sohn-**ree**-ah

You'll find words for batteries, chargers, and more in the previous list.

TELEPHONES

Travelers have several phoning options: A mobile phone provides the best combination of practicality and flexibility. Public pay phones are available, but are becoming rare, and require buying an insertable phone card. You can also make calls online (using Skype or a similar program) or from your hotel-room phone. As this is a fast-changing scene, check my latest tips at www.ricksteves.com/phoning.

Telephone Terms

telephone	teléfono teh-**lay**-foh-noh
phone call...	llamada telefónica... yah-**mah**-dah teh-leh-**foh**-nee-kah
...local	...local loh-**kahl**
...domestic	...nacional nah-thee-oh-**nahl**

Key Phrases: Telephones

telephone	teléfono teh-**lay**-foh-noh
phone call	llamada telefónica yah-**mah**-dah teh-leh-**foh**-nee-kah
mobile phone	móvil **moh**-beel
Where is the nearest phone?	¿Dónde está el teléfono más cercano? **dohn**-day eh-**stah** ehl teh-**lay**-foh-noh mahs thehr-**kah**-noh
May I use your phone?	¿Puedo usar su teléfono? **pweh**-doh oo-**sar** soo teh-**lay**-foh-noh
Where can I buy a...?	¿Dónde puedo comprar una...? **dohn**-day **pweh**-doh kohm-**prar** oo-nah
...SIM card	...tarjeta SIM tar-**heh**-tah seem
...telephone card	...tarjeta telefónica tar-**heh**-tah teh-leh-**foh**-nee-kah

...international	...internacional een-tehr-nah-thee-oh-**nahl**
...toll-free	...gratuita grah-**twee**-tah
...with credit card	...con tarjeta de crédito kohn tar-**heh**-tah day **kray**-dee-toh
...collect	...a cobro revertido ah **koh**-broh reh-behr-**tee**-doh
mobile phone	móvil / teléfono móvil **moh**-beel / teh-**lay**-foh-noh **moh**-beel
mobile number	número de móvil **noo**-mehr-oh day **moh**-beel
landline	teléfono fijo teh-**lay**-foh-noh **fee**-hoh
fax	fax fahks
operator	operador oh-peh-rah-**dor**
directory assistance	información telefónica een-for-mah-thee-**ohn** teh-lay-**foh**-nee-kah
phone book	guía telefónica **gee**-ah teh-lay-**foh**-nee-kah

Spain has a direct-dial phone system (no area codes). For phone tips—including a calling chart for dialing European numbers—see Appendix, page 417.

Making Calls

Where is the nearest phone?	¿Dónde está el teléfono más cercano? **dohn**-day eh-**stah** ehl teh-**lay**-foh-noh mahs thehr-**kah**-noh
May I use your phone?	¿Puedo usar su teléfono? **pweh**-doh oo-**sar** soo teh-**lay**-foh-noh
Can you talk for me?	¿Puede hablar usted por mí? **pweh**-day ah-**blar** oo-**stehd** por mee
It's busy.	Está ocupado. eh-**stah** oh-koo-**pah**-doh
It doesn't work.	No funciona. noh foon-thee-**oh**-nah

out of service	fuera de servicio **fwehr**-ah day sehr-**bee**-thee-oh
Try again?	¿Intente de nuevo? een-**tehn**-tay day **nweh**-boh

On the Phone

Hello, this is ____.	Hola, soy ____. **oh**-lah soy ____
My name is ____.	Me llamo ____. may **yah**-moh ____
Do you speak English?	¿Habla usted inglés? **ah**-blah oo-**stehd** een-**glays**
Sorry, I speak only a little Spanish.	Lo siento, sólo hablo un poco de español. loh see-**ehn**-toh **soh**-loh **ah**-bloh oon **poh**-koh day eh-spahn-**yohl**
Speak slowly, please.	Hable despacio, por favor. **ah**-blay dehs-**pah**-thee-oh por fah-**bor**
Wait a moment.	Un momento. oon moh-**mehn**-toh

Spaniards answer a call by saying simply *Diga* or *Dígame* ("Talk to me"), or just plain *Sí* ("Yes").

In this book, you'll find the phrases you need to reserve a hotel room (page 78) or a table at a restaurant (page 103). To spell your name over the phone, refer to the code alphabet on page 15.

Mobile Phones

Your US mobile phone should work in Europe if it's GSM-enabled, tri-band or quad-band, and on a calling plan that includes international service. Alternatively, you can buy a phone in Europe.

mobile phone	móvil / teléfono móvil **moh**-beel / teh-**lay**-foh-noh **moh**-beel
smartphone	smartphone "smartphone"
roaming	roaming "roaming"

text message	SMS / mensaje de texto **ehs**-ay **ehm**-ay **ehs**-ay / mehn-sah-**hay** day **tehks**-toh
Where is a mobile-phone shop?	¿Dónde hay una tienda de móviles? **dohn**-day ī **oo**-nah tee-**ehn**-dah day **moh**-bee-lehs
I'd like to buy...	Me gustaría comprar... may goo-stah-**ree**-ah kohm-**prar**
...a (cheap) mobile phone.	...un móvil (barato). oon **moh**-beel (bah-**rah**-toh)
...a SIM card.	...una tarjeta SIM. **oo**-nah tar-**heh**-tah seem
prepaid credit	prepago **pray**-**pah**-goh
calling time	saldo **sahl**-doh
contract	contrato kohn-**trah**-toh
band	banda **bahn**-dah
tri-band / quad-band	tribanda / cuatribanda tree-**bahn**-dah / kwah-tree-**bahn**-dah
locked	bloqueado bloh-keh-**ah**-doh
unlocked	liberado **lee**-beh-**rah**-doh
Is this phone unlocked?	¿Está liberado este móvil? eh-**stah** lee-beh-**rah**-doh eh-stay **moh**-beel
Can you unlock this phone?	¿Puede liberar este móvil? **pweh**-day lee-beh-**rar** eh-stay **moh**-beel
How do I...?	¿Cómo...? **koh**-moh
...make calls	...llamo **yah**-moh
...receive calls	...recibo llamadas reh-**thee**-boh yah-**mah**-dahs
...send a text message	...mando un SMS **mahn**-doh oon **ehs**-ay **ehm**-ay **ehs**-ay
...check voicemail	...escucho el buzón de voz eh-**skoo**-choh ehl boo-**thohn** day bohth

...set the language to English	...lo cambio al inglés loh **kahm**-bee-oh ahl een-**glays**
...mute the ringer	...quito el sonido **kee**-toh ehl soh-**nee**-doh
...change the ringer	...cambio el tono del timbre **kahm**-bee-oh ehl **toh**-noh dehl **teem**-bray
...turn it on	...lo enciendo loh ehn-see-**ehn**-doh
...turn it off	...lo apago loh ah-**pah**-goh

Buying a Mobile-Phone SIM Card

The simplest (but potentially most expensive) solution is to roam with your US phone in Europe. If your phone is unlocked *(liberado)*, you can save money by buying a cheap European SIM card (which usually comes with some calling credit) at a mobile-phone shop or a news-stand. After inserting a SIM card in your phone, you'll have a European number and pay lower European rates.

Where can I buy...?	¿Dónde puedo comprar...? **dohn**-day **pweh**-doh kohm-**prar**
I'd like to buy...	Me gustaría comprar... may goo-stah-**ree**-ah kohm-**prar**
...a SIM card	...una tarjeta SIM **oo**-nah tar-**heh**-tah seem
...more calling time	...más saldo mahs **sahl**-doh
Will this SIM card work in my phone?	¿Esta tarjeta SIM funciona en mi móvil? **eh**-stah tar-**heh**-tah seem foon-thee-**oh**-nah ehn mee **moh**-beel
Which SIM card is best for my phone?	¿Cuál tarjeta SIM es lo mejor para mi móvil? kwahl tar-**heh**-tah seem ehs loh meh-**hor** **pah**-rah mee **moh**-beel

How much per minute for...?	¿Cuánto vale el minuto para...? **kwan**-toh **bah**-lay ehl mee-**noo**-toh **pah**-rah
...making...	...hacer... ah-**thehr**
...receiving...	...recibir... reh-thee-**beer**
...domestic calls	...llamadas nacionales yah-**mah**-dahs nah-thee-oh-**nah**-lehs
...international calls	...llamadas internacionales yah-**mah**-dahs een-tehr-nah-thee-oh-**nah**-lehs
...calls to the US	...llamadas a los Estados Unidos yah-**mah**-dahs ah lohs eh-**stah**-dohs oo-**nee**-dohs
How much to send a text message?	¿Cuánto cuesta mandar un SMS? **kwahn**-toh **kweh**-stah mahn-**dar** oon **ehs**-ay **ehm**-ay **ehs**-ay
How much credit is included?	¿Cuánto crédito viene incluido? **kwan**-toh **kray**-dee-toh bee-**ehn**-ay een-kloo-**ee**-doh
Can I roam with this card in another country?	¿Puedo hacer llamadas roaming desde otro país? **pweh**-doh ah-**thehr** yah-**mah**-dahs "roaming" **dehs**-day **oh**-troh pī-**ees**
Do you have a list of rates?	¿Tiene una lista de tarifas? tee-**ehn**-ay **oo**-nah **lee**-stah day tah-**ree**-fahs
How do I...?	¿Cómo...? **koh**-moh
...insert this into the phone	...meto esto en el teléfono **meh**-toh **eh**-stoh ehn ehl teh-**lay**-foh-noh
...check the credit balance	...averiguo el crédito ah-beh-**ree**-gwoh ehl **kray**-dee-toh
...buy more time	...compro más saldo **kohm**-proh mahs **sahl**-doh

...change the language to English	...lo cambio al inglés loh **kahm**-bee-oh ahl een-**glays**
...turn off the SIM PIN	...desactivo el PIN de la tarjeta SIM deh-sahk-**tee**-boh ehl peen day lah tar-**heh**-tah seem

Each time you turn on your phone, you'll be prompted to punch in the **SIM PIN** (the numerical code that came with your SIM card). Before leaving the shop, have the clerk help you set up your new SIM card. Ask to have the prompts and messages changed to English; find out if it's possible to turn off the SIM PIN feature; and be sure you know how to check your balance and add more time (typically you can buy top-ups at mobile-phone shops, newsstands, and grocery stores—wherever you see the symbol of your mobile-phone company).

Pay Phones and Hotel-Room Phones

If you want to use a phone booth or your hotel-room phone, buy a phone card at a newsstand or tobacco shop. There are two types: The insertable card (*tarjeta telefónica,* tar-**heh**-tah teh-leh-**foh**-nee-kah) is designed to stick directly into a slot in a public pay phone. The cheap international PIN card (*tarjeta telefónica con código,* tar-**heh**-tah teh-leh-**foh**-nee-kah kohn **koh**-dee-goh) comes with a toll-free access number and a PIN that work from any phone.

Where is a public pay phone?	¿Dónde está una cabina telefónica? **dohn**-day eh-**stah oo**-nah kah-**bee**-nah teh-leh-**foh**-nee-kah
Can I call from my room?	¿Puedo llamar desde mi habitación? **pweh**-doh yah-**mar dehs**-day mee ah-bee-tah-thee-**ohn**
How do I dial out?	¿Cómo marco una línea exterior? **koh**-moh **mar**-koh **oo**-nah **lee**-neh-ah ehks-teh-ree-**or**

How much per minute for a...?	¿Cuánto vale el minuto para una...? **kwahn**-toh **bah**-lay ehl mee-**noo**-toh **pah**-rah **oo**-nah
...local call	...llamada local yah-**mah**-dah loh-**kahl**
...domestic call	...llamada nacional yah-**mah**-dah nah-thee-oh-**nahl**
...international call	...llamada internacional yah-**mah**-dah een-tehr-nah-thee-oh-**nahl**
Can I dial this number for free?	¿Puedo marcar este número gratis? **pweh**-doh mar-**kar** eh-stay **noo**-mehr-oh **grah**-tees

GETTING ONLINE

To get online in Europe, you can bring your own portable device or use public Internet terminals (at an Internet café, library, or your hotel).

Internet Terms

Internet access	acceso a Internet ahk-**seh**-soh ah **een**-tehr-neht
Wi-Fi	Wi-Fi **wee**-fee
email	email "email"
computer	ordenador or-deh-nah-**dor**
Internet café	ciber café thee-**behr** kah-**fay**
surf the Web	navegar la red nah-beh-**gar** lah rehd
username	usuario oo-**swah**-ree-oh
password	contraseña kohn-trah-**sehn**-yah
network key	clave de red **klah**-bay day rehd
secure network	red segura rehd seh-**goo**-rah
website	página web **pah**-hee-nah wehb
homepage	inicio ee-**nee**-thee-oh
download	bajar bah-**har**

Key Phrases: Getting Online

Where is a Wi-Fi hotspot?	¿Dónde hay una zona Wi-Fi? **dohn**-day ī **oo**-nah **thoh**-nah **wee**-fee
Where can I get online?	¿Dónde me puedo conectar a Internet? **dohn**-day may **pweh**-doh koh-nehk-**tar** ah **een**-tehr-neht
Where is an Internet café?	¿Dónde hay un ciber café? **dohn**-day ī oon thee-**behr** kah-**fay**
Can I check my email?	¿Puedo mirar mi email? **pweh**-doh mee-**rar** mee "email"

print	imprimir eem-pree-**meer**
My email address is ____.	Mi email es ____. mee "email" ehs ____
What's your email address?	¿Cuál es tu email? kwahl ehs too "email"

The *www* found at the beginning of most URLs is called *tres w* (literally "three w's") and pronounced "trehs **doh**-blay **oo**-bay."

Tech Support

Help me, please.	Me puede ayudar, por favor. may **pweh**-day ī-oo-**dar** por fah-**bor**
How do I...?	¿Cómo....? **koh**-moh
...start this	...empiezo esto ehm-pee-**eh**-thoh **eh**-stoh
...get online	...me conecto a Internet may koh-**nehk**-toh ah **een**-tehr-neht
...get this to work	...consigo que este funcione kohn-**see**-goh kay **eh**-stay foon-thee-**oh**-nay

...stop this	...paro esto	**pah**-roh **eh**-stoh
...send this	...envio esto	**ehn**-bee-oh **eh**-stoh
...print this	...imprimo esto eem-**pree**-moh **eh**-stoh	
...make this symbol	...hago este símbolo **ah**-goh **eh**-stay **seem**-boh-loh	
...copy and paste	...copio y pego	**koh**-pee-oh ee **peh**-goh
...type @	...escribo arroba eh-**skree**-boh ah-**roh**-bah	
This doesn't work.	Esto no funciona. **eh**-stoh noh foon-thee-**oh**-nah	

Using Your Own Portable Device

If you have a smartphone, tablet computer, laptop, or other wireless device, you can get online at many hotels, cafés, and public hotspots. Most Internet access is Wi-Fi (pronounced **wee**-fee), but occasionally you'll connect by plugging an Ethernet cable directly into your laptop. While Internet access is often free, sometimes you'll have to pay.

laptop	portátil	por-**tah**-teel
tablet	tableta	tah-**bleh**-tah
smartphone	smartphone	"smartphone"
Where is a Wi-Fi hotspot?	¿Dónde hay una zona Wi-Fi? **dohn**-day ī **oo**-nah **thoh**-nah **wee**-fee	
Do you have Wi-Fi?	¿Tiene Wi-Fi?	tee-**ehn**-ay **wee**-fee
What is...?	¿Qué es...?	kay ehs
...the network name	...el nombre de la red ehl **nom**-bray day lah rehd	
...the username	...el usuario	ehl oo-**swah**-ree-oh
...the password	...la contraseña lah kohn-trah-**sehn**-yah	
Do I need a cable?	¿Necesito un cable? neh-theh-**see**-toh oon **kah**-blay	

Do you have a...?	¿Tiene un...? tee-**ehn**-ay oon
Can I borrow a...?	¿Me puede dejar un...? may **pweh**-day deh-**har** oon
...charging cable	...cable para cargar **kah**-blay **pah**-rah kar-**gar**
...Ethernet cable	...cable Ethernet **kah**-blay **eh**-thehr-neht
...USB cable	...cable USB **kah**-blay oo **ehs**-ay bay
Free?	¿Gratis? **grah**-tees
How much?	¿Cuánto cuesta? **kwahn**-toh **kweh**-stah
Do I have to buy something to use the Internet?	¿Tengo que comprar algo para usar Internet? **tehn**-goh kay kohm-**prar ahl**-goh **pah**-rah oo-**sar een**-tehr-neht

Using a Public Internet Terminal

Many hotels have terminals in the lobby for guests to get online; otherwise, an Internet café is usually nearby.

Where can I get online?	¿Dónde me puedo conectar a Internet? **dohn**-day may **pweh**-doh koh-nehk-**tar** ah **een**-tehr-neht
Where is an Internet café?	¿Dónde está un ciber café? **dohn**-day eh-**stah** oon thee-**behr** kah-**fay**
May I use this computer to...?	¿Puedo usar este ordenador para...? **pweh**-doh oo-**sar eh**-stay or-deh-nah-**dor** **pah**-rah
...get online	...conectarme a Internet koh-nehk-**tar**-may ah **een**-tehr-neht
...check my email	...mirar mi email mee-**rar** mee "email"
...download my photos	...copiar mis fotos koh-pee-**ar** mees **foh**-tohs
...print (something)	...imprimir (algo) eem-pree-**meer** (**ahl**-goh)

boarding passes	tarjetas de embarque tar-**heh**-tahs day ehm-**bar**-kay
tickets	billetes bee-**yeh**-tehs
reservation confirmation	confirmación de reserva kohn-feer-mah-thee-**ohn** day reh-**sehr**-bah
Free?	¿Gratis? **grah**-tees
How much (for... minutes)?	¿Cuánto cuesta (por... minutos)? **kwahn**-toh **kweh**-stah (por... mee-**noo**-tohs)
...10	...diez dee-**ehth**
...15	...quince **keen**-thay
...30	...treinta **trayn**-tah
...60	...sesenta seh-**sehn**-tah
I have a...	Tengo un / una... **tehn**-goh oon / **oo**-nah
Do you have a...?	¿Tiene un / una...? tee-**ehn**-ay oon / **oo**-nah
...webcam	...webcam "webcam"
...headset	...auriculares ow-ree-koo-**lah**-rehs
...USB cable	...cable USB **kah**-blay oo **ehs**-ay bay
...memory card	...tarjeta de memoria tar-**heh**-tah day meh-**moh**-ree-ah
...flash drive	...pendrive **pehn**-drive
Can you switch the keyboard to American?	¿Me puede cambiar el teclado a la versión americana? may **pweh**-day kahm-bee-**ar** ehl teh-**klah**-doh ah lah behr-see-**ohn** ah-meh-ree-**kah**-nah

If you're using a public Internet terminal, the keyboard, menus, and on-screen commands will likely be designed for Spanish speakers. Some computers allow you to make the Spanish keyboard work as if it were an American one (ask the clerk if it's possible).

Spanish Keyboards

Spanish keyboards differ from American ones (for example, you'll find the Spanish letter **Ñ** in the place of the **;** key). Here's a rundown of how major commands are labeled on a Spanish keyboard:

YOU'LL SEE...	IT MEANS...	YOU'LL SEE...	IT MEANS...
Intro	Enter	**Supr**	Delete
↑	Shift	**←**	Backspace
Control	Ctrl	**Insert**	Insert
Alt	Alt	**Inicio**	Home
Bloq Mayús	Caps Lock	**Fin**	End
Bloq Num	Num Lock	**Re Pág**	Page Up
→|	Tab	**Av Pág**	Page Down
Esc	Esc		

The Alt key to the right of the space bar is actually a different key, called "Alt Gr" (for "Alternate Graphics"). Press this key to insert the extra symbol that appears on some keys (such as the # in the lower-right corner of the 3 key).

A few often-used keys look the same, but have different names in Spanish:

@ sign	arroba	ah-**roh**-bah
dot	punto	**poon**-toh
hyphen (-)	guión	gee-**ohn**
underscore (_)	guión bajo	gee-**ohn** bah-*hoh*
slash (/)	barra	**bah**-rah

Spanish-speakers call the @ sign *arroba*. When saying an email address, you say *arroba* in the middle.

To type @, press **Alt Gr** and **2** at the same time. If that doesn't work, try copying-and-pasting the @ sign from elsewhere on the page.

On Screen

YOU'LL SEE...	IT MEANS...	YOU'LL SEE...	IT MEANS...
Red	Network	**Vista**	View
Usuario	User (name)	**Insertar**	Insert
Contraseña / Clave	Password	**Formato**	Format
Tecla	Key	**Herramientas**	Tools
Carpeta	Folder	**Ayuda**	Help
Ajustes	Settings	**Opciones**	Options
Archivo	File	**Correo**	Mail
Nuevo	New	**Mensaje**	Message
Abrir	Open	**Responder (a todos)**	Reply (to All)
Cerrar	Close	**CC**	CC
Guardar	Save	**Reenviar**	Forward
Imprimir	Print	**Enviar**	Send
Borrar	Delete	**Recibir**	Receive
Buscar	Search	**Buzón**	Inbox
Editar	Edit	**Adjunto**	Attach
Cortar	Cut	**Subir**	Upload
Copiar	Copy	**Bajar**	Download
Pegar	Paste		

TECHNOLOGY

Getting Online

HELP!

These phrases will help you in case of a medical emergency, theft, loss, fire, or—if you're a woman—harassment. To phone for help in Spain, dial **091** for police or **112** in any emergency (medical or otherwise). If you're lost, see the phrases on page 73.

EMERGENCIES

Medical Help

Help!	¡Socorro! soh-**koh**-roh
Help me, please.	Ayúdeme, por favor. ī-**yoo**-deh-may por fah-**bor**
emergency	emergencia eh-mehr-**hehn**-thee-ah
accident	accidente ahk-thee-**dehn**-tay
clinic / hospital	clínica / hospital **klee**-nee-kah / oh-spee-**tahl**
Call...	Llame a... **yah**-may ah
...a doctor.	...un médico. oon **may**-dee-koh
...the police.	...la policía. lah poh-lee-**thee**-ah
...an ambulance.	...una ambulancia. **oo**-nah ahm-boo-**lahn**-thee-ah
I need / We need a doctor.	Necesito / Necesitamos un médico. neh-theh-**see**-toh / neh-theh-see-**tah**-mohs oon **may**-dee-koh
I / We have to go to the hospital.	Tengo / Tenemos que ir al hospital. **tehn**-goh / teh-**neh**-mohs kay eer ahl oh-spee-**tahl**
It's urgent.	Es urgente. ehs oor-**hehn**-tay
injured	herido eh-**ree**-doh
bleeding	sangrando sahn-**grahn**-doh
choking	ahogando ah-oh-**gahn**-doh
unconscious	inconsciente een-koh-see-**ehn**-tay
not breathing	no respira noh reh-**spee**-rah

Key Phrases: Help!

Help!	¡Socorro! soh-**koh**-roh
emergency	emergencia eh-mehr-**hehn**-thee-ah
clinic / hospital	clínica / hospital **klee**-nee-kah / oh-spee-**tahl**
Call a doctor.	Llame a un medico. **yah**-may ah oon **may**-dee-koh
police	policía poh-lee-**thee**-ah
ambulance	ambulancia ahm-boo-**lahn**-thee-ah
thief	ladrón lah-**drohn**
Stop, thief!	¡Detengan al ladrón! deh-**tehn**-gahn ahl lah-**drohn**

Thank you for your help.	Gracias por su ayuda. **grah**-thee-ahs por soo ah-**yoo**-dah
You are very kind.	Usted es muy amable. oo-**stehd** ehs **moo**-ee ah-**mah**-blay

For related words, see the Personal Care and Health chapter.

Theft and Loss

thief	ladrón lah-**drohn**
pickpocket	carterista kar-teh-**ree**-stah
police	policía poh-lee-**thee**-ah
embassy	embajada ehm-bah-**hah**-dah
Stop, thief!	¡Detengan al ladrón! deh-**tehn**-gahn ahl lah-**drohn**
Call the police!	¡Llame a la policía! **yah**-may ah lah poh-lee-**thee**-ah

I've / We've been robbed.	Me / Nos han robado. meh / nohs ahn roh-**bah**-doh
A thief took...	Un ladrón se llevó... oon lah-**drohn** say yeh-**boh**
Thieves took...	Los ladrones se llevaron... lohs lah-**droh**-nehs say yeh-**bah**-rohn
I've lost my...	He perdido mi / mia... eh pehr-**dee**-doh mee / **mee**-ah
We've lost our...	Hemos perdido nuestro / nuestra... **eh**-mohs pehr-**dee**-doh **nweh**-stroh / **nweh**-strah
money	dinero dee-**nehr**-oh
credit card	tarjeta de crédito tar-**heh**-tah deh **kray**-dee-toh
passport	pasaporte pah-sah-**por**-tay
ticket	billete bee-**yeh**-tay
railpass	abono de tren ah-**boh**-noh day trehn
baggage	equipaje eh-kee-**pah**-hay
purse	bolso **bohl**-soh
wallet	cartera kar-**tehr**-ah
watch	reloj **reh**-loh
jewelry	joyas **hoy**-ahs
camera	cámara **kah**-mah-rah
mobile phone	teléfono móvil teh-**lay**-foh-noh **moh**-beel
iPod / iPad	iPod / iPad "iPod" / "iPad"
tablet	tableta tah-**bleh**-tah
computer	ordenador or-deh-nah-**dor**
laptop	portátil por-**tah**-teel
faith in humankind	confianza en la especie humana kohn-fee-**ahn**-thah ehn lah eh-**speh**-thee-ay oo-**mah**-nah

I want to contact my embassy.	Quiero ponerme en contacto con mi embajada. kee-**ehr**-oh poh-**nehr**-may ehn kohn-**tahk**-toh kohn mee ehm-bah-**hah**-dah
I need to file a police report (for my insurance).	Tengo que hacer una denuncia (para mi seguro). **tehn**-goh kay ah-**thehr oo**-nah deh-**noon**-thee-ah (**pah**-rah mee seh-**goo**-roh)
Where is the police station?	¿Dónde está la comisaría? **dohn**-day eh-**stah** lah koh-mee-sah-**ree**-ah

To replace a passport, you'll need to go in person to your embassy (see page 419). Cancel and replace your credit and debit cards by calling your credit-card company (as of this printing, these are the 24-hour US numbers that you can call collect: Visa—tel. 303/967-1096, MasterCard—tel. 636/722-7111, American Express—tel. 336/393-1111). If you'll want to submit an insurance claim for lost or stolen gear, be sure to file a police report, either on the spot or within a day or two. For more info, see www.ricksteves.com/help. Precautionary measures can minimize the effects of loss—back up your photos and other files frequently.

Fire!

fire	fuego **fweh**-goh
smoke	humo **oo**-moh
exit	salida sah-**lee**-dah
emergency exit	salida de emergencia sah-**lee**-dah day eh-mehr-**hehn**-thee-ah
fire extinguisher	el extintor ehl ehk-steen-**tor**
Call the fire department.	Llame a los bomberos. **yah**-may ah lohs bohm-**beh**-rohs

HELP FOR WOMEN

Whenever macho males threaten to turn leering into a contact sport, local women will stroll holding hands or arm-in-arm. Wearing conservative clothes and avoiding smiley eye contact also convey a "No way, José" message.

No!	¡No! noh
Stop it!	¡Para! **pah**-rah
Enough!	¡Basta! **bah**-stah
Don't touch me.	No me toques. noh meh **toh**-kehs
Go away.	Déjame. **day**-hah-may
Leave me alone.	Déjame en paz. **day**-hah-may ehn pahth
Get lost!	¡Lárgate! **lar**-gah-tay
Drop dead!	¡Piérda de vista! pee-**ayr**-dah day **bee**-stah
Police!	¡Policía! poh-lee-**thee**-ah

Safety in Numbers

If a guy is bugging you, approach a friendly-looking couple, family, or business for a place to stay safe.

A man is bothering me.	Un hombre me está molestando. oon **ohm**-bray may eh-**stah** moh-leh-**stahn**-doh
May I...?	¿Puedo...? **pweh**-doh
...join you	...acompañarle ah-kohm-pahn-**yar**-lay
...sit here	...sentarme aquí sehn-**tar**-may ah-**kee**
...wait here until he's gone	...esperar aquí hasta que se vaya ese hombre eh-spehr-**ar** ah-**kee ah**-stah kay say **bī**-ah **eh**-say **ohm**-bray

You Want to Be Alone

I want to be alone.	Me gustaría estar sola. may goo-stah-**ree**-ah eh-**star soh**-lah
I'm not interested.	No estoy interesada. noh **eh**-stoy een-teh-reh-**sah**-dah
I'm married.	Estoy casada. **eh**-stoy kah-**sah**-dah
I'm waiting for my husband.	Estoy esperando a mi marido. **eh**-stoy eh-spehr-**ahn**-doh ah mee mah-**ree**-doh
I'm a lesbian.	Soy lesbiana. soy lehs-bee-**ah**-nah
I have a contagious disease.	Tengo una enfermedad contagiosa. **tehn**-goh **oo**-nah ehn-fehr-meh-**dahd** kohn-tah-*hee*-**oh**-sah

SERVICES

hether you're getting a haircut, going to a spa, getting something fixed, or doing laundry, you'll find the phrases you need in this chapter.

HAIR AND BODY

At the Hair Salon

haircut	corte de pelo	**kor**-tay day **peh**-loh
Where is...?	¿Dónde hay...?	**dohn**-day ī
...a hair salon	...una peluquería	**oo**-nah peh-loo-keh-**ree**-ah
...a barber	...un barbero	oon bar-**beh**-roh
...the price list	...la lista de precios	lah **lee**-stah day **preh**-thee-ohs
I'd like...	Me gustaría...	may goo-stah-**ree**-ah
...a haircut.	...cortarme el pelo.	kor-**tar**-may ehl **peh**-loh
...a shampoo.	...un lavado.	oon lah-**vah**-doh
...highlights.	...ponerme mechas.	poh-**nehr**-may **meh**-chahs
...my hair colored.	...teñirme el pelo.	tehn-**yeer**-may ehl **peh**-loh
...a permanent.	...hacerme una permanente.	ah-**thehr**-may **oo**-nah pehr-mah-**nehn**-tay
...just a trim.	...que me cortara las puntas.	kay may kor-**tah**-rah lahs **poon**-tahs
How much?	¿Cuánto cuesta?	**kwahn**-toh **kweh**-stah
Cut about this much off.	Corte más o menos esto.	**kor**-tay mahs oh **meh**-nohs **eh**-stoh
Here. (gesturing)	Aquí.	ah-**kee**
Short.	Corto.	**kor**-toh
Shorter.	Más corto.	mahs **kor**-toh

Shave it all off.	Afeitelo todo. ah-**fay**-ee-teh-loh **toh**-doh
As long as possible.	Lo más largo posible. loh mahs **lar**-goh poh-**see**-blay
Longer.	Más largo. mahs **lar**-goh
(long) layers	capas (largas) **kah**-pahs (**lar**-gahs)
bangs	flequillo fleh-**kee**-yoh
Cut my bangs here.	Corte mi flequillo aquí. **kor**-tay mee fleh-**kee**-yoh ah-**kee**
front	en frente ehn **frehn**-tay
top	arriba ah-**ree**-bah
back	atrás ah-**trahs**
sides	lados **lah**-dohs
sideburns	patillas pah-**tee**-yahs
beard / moustache	barba / bigote **bar**-bah / bee-**goh**-tay
hair color	color de pelo koh-**lor** day **peh**-loh
blond / brown / **black / red**	rubio / castaño / negro / pelirrojo **roo**-bee-oh / kah-**stahn**-yoh / **neh**-groh / peh-lee-**roh**-hoh
Please touch up my **roots.**	Teñir un poco las raíces, por favor. tehn-**yeer** oon **poh**-koh lahs **rī**-thehs por fah-**bor**
I'd like my...	Me gustaría que me... may goo-stah-**ree**-ah kay may
...hair blow-dried.	...secara el pelo con el secador. seh-**kah**-rah ehl **peh**-loh kohn ehl seh-kah-**dor**
...hair styled.	...hiciera un peinado. ee-thee-**ehr**-ah oon pay-**nah**-doh
...hair straightened.	...alisara el pelo. ah-lee-**sah**-rah ehl **peh**-loh
...hair wavy.	...ondulara el pelo. ohn-doo-**lah**-rah ehl **peh**-loh

I want to look like I just got out of bed.	Quiero parecer como si me acabara de levantar. kee-**ehr**-oh pah-reh-**thehr koh**-moh see may ah-kah-**bah**-rah day leh-bahn-**tar**
hair gel	gel *hehl*
hairspray	laca **lah**-kah
It looks good.	Se ve muy bien. say bay **moo**-ee bee-**ehn**
A tip for you.	Una propina para usted. **oo**-nah proh-**pee**-nah **pah**-rah oo-**stehd**

At the Spa

spa	balneario bahl-neh-**ah**-ree-oh
spa treatment	tratamiento spa trah-tah-mee-**ehn**-toh spah
Where can I get a...?	¿Dónde puedo hacerme un / una...? **dohn**-day **pweh**-doh ah-**thehr**-may oon / **oo**-nah
I'd like a...	Me gustaría un / una... may goo-stah-**ree**-ah oon / **oo**-nah
...massage	...masaje mah-**sah**-hay
...manicure	...manicura mah-nee-**koo**-rah
...pedicure	...pedicura peh-dee-**koo**-rah
...facial	...tratamiento facial trah-tah-mee-**ehn**-toh fah-thee-**ahl**
...wax	...depilación con cera deh-pee-lah-thee-**ohn** kohn **theh**-rah
eyebrows	las cejas lahs **theh**-hahs
upper lip	el labio superior ehl **lah**-bee-yoh soo-pehr-ee-**or**
legs	las piernas lahs pee-**ehr**-nahs
bikini	las ingles lahs **een**-glehs
a Brazilian	un brasileño oon brah-see-**lehn**-yoh

Massage

massage	masaje mah-**sah**-hay
Where can I get a massage?	¿Dónde puedo conseguir un masaje? **dohn**-day **pweh**-doh kohn-seh-**geer** oon mah-**sah**-hay
30 minutes / 1 hour / 90 minutes	de treinta minutos / de una hora / de noventa minutos day **trayn**-tah mee-**noo**-tohs / day **oo**-nah **oh**-rah / day noh-**behn**-tah mee-**noo**-tohs
How much?	¿Cuánto cuesta? **kwahn**-toh **kweh**-stah
Spend more / less time on my...	Quiero que me trates más / menos... kee-**ehr**-oh kay may **trah**-tehs mahs / **meh**-nohs
...back.	...la espalda. lah eh-**spahl**-dah
...neck.	...el cuello. ehl **kweh**-yoh
...shoulders.	...los hombros. lohs **ohm**-brohs
...head.	...la cabeza. lah kah-**beh**-thah
...arms.	...los brazos. lohs **brah**-thohs
...hands.	...los manos. lohs **mah**-nohs
...legs.	...las piernas. lahs pee-**ehr**-nahs
...feet.	...los pies. lohs pee-**ays**
It hurts.	Me duele. may **dweh**-lay
Ouch!	¡Ay! ī
Light / Medium / Firm pressure.	Presión muy suave / no tan / fuerte. preh-see-**ohn** **moo**-ee **swah**-bay / noh tahn / **fwehr**-tay
Less / More pressure.	Menos / Más fuerte. **meh**-nohs / mahs **fwehr**-tay
Don't stop. / Stop.	No pares. / Para. noh **pah**-rehs / **pah**-rah
That feels good.	Eso se sienta bien. **eh**-soh say see-**ehn**-tah bee-**ehn**

REPAIRS

These handy lines can apply to various repairs, whether you tackle them yourself or go to a shop.

This doesn't work.	Esto no funciona. **eh**-stoh noh foon-thee-**oh**-nah
Can I borrow...?	Me puede prestar...? may **pweh**-day preh-**star**
I need a...	Necesito un / una... neh-theh-**see**-toh oon / **oo**-nah
screwdriver (Phillips / straight edge)	destornillador (Phillips / de punta plana) deh-stor-nee-yah-**dor** (**fee**-leeps / day **poon**-tah **plah**-nah)
pliers	alicates ah-lee-**kah**-tehs
wrench	llave inglesa **yah**-bay een-**gleh**-sah
hammer	martillo mar-**tee**-yoh
scissors	tijeras tee-**heh**-rahs
needle	aguja ah-**goo**-hah
thread	hilo **ee**-loh
string	cordel kor-**dehl**
duct tape	cinta adhesiva de tela **theen**-tah ah-deh-**see**-bah day **teh**-lah
Can you fix it?	¿Lo puede arreglar? loh **pweh**-day ah-reh-**glar**
Just do the essentials.	Haga sólo lo esencial. **ah**-gah **soh**-loh loh eh-sehn-thee-**ahl**
How much will it cost?	¿Cuánto costará? **kwahn**-toh koh-stah-**rah**
When will it be ready?	¿Cuándo estará listo? **kwahn**-doh eh-stah-**rah** **lee**-stoh
I need it by _____.	Lo necesito para _____. loh neh-theh-**see**-toh **pah**-rah _____
Without it, I'm lost.	Sin esto, estoy perdido[a]. seen **eh**-stoh **eh**-stoy pehr-**dee**-doh

LAUNDRY

Laundry Locator

Where is a...?	¿Dónde hay una...? **dohn**-day ī **oo**-nah
...full-service laundry	...lavandería lah-vahn-deh-**ree**-ah
...self-service laundry	...lavandería de autoservicio lah-vahn-deh-**ree**-ah day ow-toh-sehr-**bee**-thee-oh
Do you offer laundry service? (ask hotelier)	¿Tienen servicio de lavandería? tee-**ehn**-ehn sehr-**bee**-thee-oh day lah-vahn-deh-**ree**-ah
How much?	¿Cuánto cuesta? **kwahn**-toh **kweh**-stah
What time does this open / close?	¿A qué hora abren / cierran? ah kay **oh**-rah **ah**-brehn / thee-**ehr**-ahn

Full-Service Laundry

At some launderettes, you can pay extra to have the attendant wash, dry, and fold your clothes. Be sure to clearly communicate the time you will pick it up.

full-service laundry	lavandería lah-vahn-deh-**ree**-ah
Same-day service?	¿Sirven en el mismo día? **seer**-behn ehn ehl **mees**-moh **dee**-ah
By when do I need to drop off my clothes?	¿Para cuándo tengo que dejar mi ropa? **pah**-rah **kwahn**-doh **tehn**-goh kay deh-**har** mee **roh**-pah
When will my clothes be ready?	¿Cuándo estará lista mi ropa? **kwahn**-doh eh-stah-**rah** **lee**-stah mee **roh**-pah
Could I get them sooner?	¿Podría recogerla antes? poh-**dree**-ah reh-koh-**hehr**-lah **ahn**-tehs

Do you...?	¿Hay servicio de...? ī sehr-**bee**-thee-oh day
...dry them	...secado seh-**kah**-doh
...fold them	...doblado doh-**blah**-doh
...iron them	...planchado plahn-**chah**-doh
Please don't dry this.	No seque esto por favor. noh seh-**kay eh**-stoh por fah-**bor**
I'll come back...	Volveré... bohl-beh-**ray**
...later today.	...un poco más tarde. oon **poh**-koh mahs **tar**-day
...tomorrow.	...mañana. mahn-**yah**-nah
...at _____ o'clock.	...a las _____. ah lahs _____
This isn't mine.	Esto no es mío. **eh**-stoh noh ehs **mee**-oh
I'm missing a _____.	Me falta un / una _____. may **fahl**-tah oon / **oo**-nah _____

For lists of clothes and colors, see pages 220 and 225 in the Shopping chapter.

Self-Service Laundry

self-service laundry	lavandería de autoservicio lah-vahn-deh-**ree**-ah day ow-toh-sehr-**bee**-thee-oh
washer / dryer	lavadora / secadora lah-vah-**doh**-rah / seh-kah-**doh**-rah
soap	jabón hah-**bohn**
detergent	detergente deh-tehr-**hehn**-tay
softener	suavizante swah-bee-**thahn**-tay
stain remover	quitamanchas kee-tah-**mahn**-chahs
money	dinero dee-**nehr**-oh
token	ficha **fee**-chah
Help me, please.	Ayúdeme, por favor. ī-**yoo**-deh-may por fah-**bor**

Where do I pay?	¿Dónde pago? **dohn**-day **pah**-goh
I need change.	Necesito cambio. neh-theh-**see**-toh **kahm**-bee-oh
Where is the soap?	¿Dónde está el jabón? **dohn**-day eh-**stah** ehl hah-**bohn**
Where do I put the soap?	¿Dónde echo el jabón? **dohn**-day **eh**-choh ehl hah-**bohn**
This doesn't work.	Esto no funciona. **eh**-stoh noh foon-thee-**oh**-nah
How do I start this?	¿Cómo lo enciendo? **koh**-moh loh ehn-thee-**ehn**-doh
How long will it take?	¿Cuánto tardará? **kwahn**-toh tar-dar-**ah**
Are these yours?	¿Son suyos? sohn **soo**-yohs
This stinks.	Esto apesta. **eh**-stoh ah-**peh**-stah
Smells like...	Huele a... **weh**-lay ah
...springtime.	...primavera. pree-mah-**behr**-ah
...a locker room.	...vestidor. vehs-tee-**dor**
...cheese.	...queso. **keh**-soh

Don't begin a load too soon before closing time—or you might get evicted with a damp pile of partly washed laundry. Look for a sign telling you the last time you're allowed to start a load (*último lavado a las 20:00*), or what time the machines stop working, such as *Las lavadoras dejan de funcionar a las 21:00.* (The machines stop working at 9 p.m.)

Laundry Instructions Decoder

Many launderettes are unstaffed. Every launderette has clearly posted instructions, but they're not always in English. Use this decoder to figure things out.

instrucciones	instructions
lavadora	washer
ropa / prendas	clothes / garments
colada	load
lavar / secar	wash / dry
jabón / detergente	soap / detergent
suavizante	softener
lejía	bleach
líquido / polvo / pastillas	liquid / powder / pellets
cajetín	reservoir (for adding soap)
bajo su propia responsabilidad	at your own risk
meter (ropa) / introducir (dinero)	insert (clothes) / insert (money)
moneda / ficha	coin / token
monedero	coin slot
importe exacto	exact change required
no devuelve cambio	no change given
abrir / cerrar la puerta	open / close door
pulsar botón	press button
elegir / introducir	choose / enter
comenzar / programa	start / program
ropa blanca / color	whites / colors
ropa inarrugable	permanent press
ropa delicada	delicates
caliente / templado / frío	hot / warm / cold
en uso	in use
prelavado / ciclo principal de lavado	pre-wash / main wash cycle
centrifugado / aclarado	spin / rinse
secadora	dryer
por minuto de secadora	per minute of drying
vacío / sacar	empty / remove
terminado	finished

Wash Temperatures

When choosing your wash cycle, you might see a series of numbers, such as:

45° / 90° / 55 m	whites
45° / 60° / 50 m	colors
45° / 45° / 40 m	permanent press / mixed
– / 30° / 30 m	warm
– / 17° / 25 m	cold / delicates

The first two numbers are the temperatures in Celsius for the pre-wash cycle and the main-wash cycle; the third number shows how many minutes the load takes. (For a rough conversion from Celsius to Fahrenheit, double the number and add 30.)

You'll likely buy drying time in small units (5- or 10-minute increments) rather than a full cycle. The choice of temperatures are: *en bajo* (low and slow), *en medio* (medium), and *en alto* (high).

PERSONAL CARE
AND HEALTH

This chapter will help keep you supplied with toiletries and guide you in getting treatment if you're not feeling well. Along with words for ailments, body parts, and medications, you'll find sections on eye and ear care, dental needs, reproductive health, women, babies, allergies, mental health, disabilities, and various medical conditions. For medical emergencies, see page 250 in the Help! chapter.

PERSONAL CARE

aftershave lotion	after-shave "after-shave"
antiperspirant	antitranspirante ahn-tee-trahn-spee-**rahn**-tay
breath mints	caramelos refrescantes kah-rah-**meh**-lohs reh-frehs-**kahn**-tehs
comb	peine **pay**-nay
conditioner for hair	acondicionador ah-kohn-dee-thee-ohn-ah-**dor**
dental floss	seda dental **seh**-dah dehn-**tahl**
deodorant	desodorante deh-soh-doh-**rahn**-tay
face cleanser	limpiadora de cara leem-pee-ah-**doh**-rah day **kah**-rah
facial tissue	toallitas para la cara toh-ah-**yee**-tahs **pah**-rah lah **kah**-rah
fluoride rinse	enjuague bucal con fluoruro ehn-*hwah*-gay boo-**kahl** kohn floo-oh-**roo**-oh
hair dryer	secador de pelo seh-kah-**dor** day **peh**-loh
hairbrush	cepillo del pelo theh-**pee**-yoh dehl **peh**-loh
hand lotion	crema de manos **kreh**-mah day **mah**-nohs
hand sanitizer	desinfectante de manos deh-seen-fehk-**tahn**-tay day **mah**-nohs

lip balm	cacao de labios kah-**kah**-oh day **lah**-bee-ohs
lip gloss	brillo de labios **bree**-yoh day **lah**-bee-ohs
lipstick	pintalabios peen-tah-**lah**-bee-ohs
makeup	maquillaje mah-kee-**yah**-hay
mirror	espejo eh-**speh**-hoh
moisturizer...	crema hidratante... **kreh**-mah ee-drah-**tahn**-tay
...with sunblock	...con protector solar kohn proh-tehk-**tor** soh-**lar**
mouthwash	enjuague bucal ehn-**hwah**-gay boo-**kahl**
nail clipper	cortaúñas kor-tah-**oon**-yahs
nail file	lima de uñas **lee**-mah de **oon**-yahs
nail polish	esmalte de uñas eh-**smahl**-tay day **oon**-yahs
nail polish remover	quitaesmaltes kee-tah-eh-**smahl**-tehs
perfume	perfume pehr-**foo**-may
Q-tips (cotton swabs)	bastoncillos bah-stohn-**thee**-yohs
razor (disposable)	cuchilla de afeitar (desechable) koo-**chee**-yah day ah-fay-**tar** (deh-seh-**chah**-blay)
sanitary pads	compresas kohm-**preh**-sahs
scissors	tijeras tee-**hehr**-ahs
shampoo	champú chahm-**poo**
shaving cream	espuma de afeitar eh-**spoo**-mah day ah-fay-**tar**
soap	jabón hah-**bohn**
sunscreen	protección de sol / crema de sol proh-tehk-thee-**ohn** day sohl / **kreh**-mah day sohl
suntan lotion	crema bronceadora **kreh**-mah brohn-theh-ah-**doh**-rah

tampons	tampones	tahm-**poh**-nehs
tissues	pañuelos de papel pahn-yoo-**eh**-lohs day pah-**pehl**	
toilet paper	papel higiénico pah-**pehl** ee-hee-**ay**-nee-koh	
toothbrush	cepillo de dientes theh-**pee**-yoh day dee-**ehn**-tehs	
toothpaste	pasta de dientes **pah**-stah day dee-**ehn**-tehs	
tweezers	pinzas **peen**-thahs	

HEALTH

Throughout Europe, people with a health problem go first to the pharmacist, who can diagnose and prescribe remedies for most simple ailments. Pharmacists are usually friendly and speak English. If necessary, the pharmacist will send you to a doctor or a clinic.

Getting Help

Where is a...?	¿Dónde está un / una...? **dohn**-day eh-**stah** oon / **oo**-nah
...pharmacy (open 24 hours)	...farmacia (abierta las veinticuatro horas) far-**mah**-thee-ah (ah-bee-**ehr**-tah lahs bayn-tee-**kwah**-troh oh-**rahs**)
...clinic	...clínica **klee**-nee-kah
...hospital	...hospital oh-spee-**tahl**
I am sick.	Estoy enfermo[a]. eh-**stoy** ehn-**fehr**-moh
He / She is sick.	Él / Ella está enfermo[a]. ehl / **ay**-yah eh-**stah** ehn-**fehr**-moh
I need a doctor...	Necesito un médico... neh-theh-**see**-toh oon **may**-dee-koh

Key Phrases: Health

I am sick.	Estoy enfermo[a]. eh-**stoy** ehn-**fehr**-moh
I need a doctor (who speaks English).	Necesito un médico (que hable inglés). neh-theh-**see**-toh oon **may**-dee-koh (kay **ah**-blay een-**glays**)
pain	dolor doh-**lor**
It hurts here.	Me duele aquí. may **dweh**-lay ah-**kee**
medicine	medicina meh-dee-**thee**-nah
pharmacy	farmacia far-**mah**-thee-ah

We need a doctor...	Necesitamos un médico... neh-theh-see-**tah**-mohs oon **may**-dee-koh
...who speaks English.	...que hable inglés. kay **ah**-blay een-**glays**
Please call a doctor.	Por favor, llame a un médico. por fah-**bor yah**-may ah oon **may**-dee-koh
Could a doctor come here?	¿El médico podría venir aquí? ehl **may**-dee-koh poh-**dree**-ah beh-**neer** ah-**kee**
It's urgent.	Es urgente. ehs oor-**hehn**-tay
ambulance	ambulancia ahm-boo-**lahn**-thee-ah
health insurance	seguro médico seh-**goo**-roh **may**-dee-koh
Receipt, please.	Una factura, por favor. **oo**-nah fahk-**too**-rah por fah-**bor**

Ailments

I have...	Tengo... **tehn**-goh
He / She has...	Él / Ella tiene... ehl / **ay**-yah tee-**ehn**-ay
I need medicine for...	Necesito medicina para... neh-theh-**see**-toh meh-dee-**thee**-nah **pah**-rah
bee sting	una picadura de abeja **oo**-nah pee-kah-**doo**-rah day ah-**beh**-hah
bite(s) from...	picadura(s) de... pee-kah-**doo**-rah(s) day
...bedbugs	...las chinches lahs **cheen**-chehs
...a dog	...un perro oon **pehr**-oh
...mosquitoes	...los mosquitos lohs moh-**skee**-tohs
...a spider	...una araña **oo**-nah ah-**rahn**-yah
...a tick	...una garrapata **oo**-nah gah-rah-**pah**-tah
blisters	ampollas ahm-**poh**-yahs
body odor	olor corporal **oh**-lor kor-poh-**rahl**
burn	quemadura keh-mah-**doo**-rah
chapped lips	labios secos **lah**-bee-ohs **seh**-kohs
chest pains	dolor de pecho doh-**lor** day **peh**-choh
chills	escalofríos eh-skah-loh-**free**-ohs
a cold	un resfriado oon rehs-free-**ah**-doh
congestion	congestión kohn-heh-stee-**ohn**
constipation	estreñimiento eh-strehn-yee-mee-**ehn**-toh
cough	tos tohs
cramps...	calambres... kah-**lahm**-brehs
...muscle	...de músculo day **moo**-skoo-loh
...stomach	...de estómago day eh-**stoh**-mah-goh

diarrhea	diarrea dee-ah-**reh**-ah
dizziness	vértigo **behr**-tee-goh
earache	dolor de oído doh-**lor** day oh-**ee**-doh
eczema	eczema ehk-**theh**-mah
fever	fiebre fee-**eh**-bray
flu	gripe **gree**-pay
food poisoning	envenenamiento de comida ehn-behn-ehn-ah-mee-**ehn**-toh day koh-**mee**-dah
gas	gases **gah**-thehs
hay fever	fiebre del heno fee-**eh**-bray dehl **eh**-noh
headache	dolor de cabeza doh-**lor** day kah-**beh**-thah
heartburn	ardor de estómago ar-**dor** day eh-**stoh**-mah-goh
hemorrhoids	hemorroides eh-moh-**roy**-dehs
hot flashes	calores kah-**loh**-rehs
indigestion	indigestión een-dee-heh-stee-**ohn**
infection	infección een-fehk-thee-**ohn**
inflammation	inflamación een-flah-mah-thee-**ohn**
insomnia	insomnio een-**sohm**-nee-oh
lice	piojos pee-**oh**-hohs
lightheaded	mareado mah-reh-**ah**-doh
menstrual cramps	dolor de la menstruación doh-**lor** day lah mehn-stroo-ah-thee-**ohn**
migraine	jaqueca hah-**keh**-kah
motion sickness	mareo al viajar mah-**reh**-oh ahl bee-ah-**har**
nausea	náuseas **now**-see-ahs
numbness	dormidos dor-**mee**-dohs

pain	dolor doh-**lor**
pimples	granos **grah**-nohs
pneumonia	pulmonía pool-moh-**nee**-ah
pus	pus poos
rash	erupción eh-roop-thee-**ohn**
sinus problems	sinusitis see-noo-**see**-tees
sneezing	estornudos eh-stor-**noo**-dohs
sore throat	dolor de garganta doh-**lor** day gar-**gahn**-tah
splinter	astilla ah-**stee**-yah
stomachache	dolor de estómago doh-**lor** day eh-**stoh**-mah-goh
(bad) sunburn	quemaduras de sol (peligrosas) keh-mah-**doo**-rahs day sohl (peh-lee-**groh**-sahs)
swelling	hinchazón een-chah-**thohn**
tendinitis	tendinitis tehn-dee-**nee**-tees
toothache	dolor de muelas doh-**lor** day **mweh**-lahs
urinary tract infection	infección urinaria een-fehk-thee-**ohn** oo-ree-**nah**-ree-ah
urination (frequent / painful)	orinar (frequentemente / doloroso) oh-ree-**nar** (freh-kwehn-tah-**mehn**-tay / doh-loh-**roh**-soh)
vomiting	vomitar boh-mee-**tar**
warts	verrugas beh-**roo**-gahs
I'm going bald.	Me estoy quedando calvo. may **eh**-stoy keh-**dahn**-doh **kahl**-boh

For major illnesses, see "Medical Conditions" on page 292.

It Hurts

pain	dolor doh-**lor**
painful	doloroso doh-loh-**roh**-soh
hurts	duele **dweh**-lay
It hurts here.	Me duele aquí. may **dweh**-lay ah-**kee**
My _____ hurts. (body parts listed in next section)	Me duele el / la _____. may **dweh**-lay ehl / lah _____
aching	dolorido doh-loh-**ree**-doh
bleeding	sangrando sahn-**grahn**-doh
blocked	bloqueado bloh-keh-**ah**-doh
broken	roto **roh**-toh
bruised	amoratado ah-moh-rah-**tah**-doh
chafing	irritado ee-ree-**tah**-doh
cracked	agrietado ah-gree-eh-**tah**-doh
fractured	fracturado frahk-too-**rah**-doh
infected	infectado een-fehk-**tah**-doh
inflamed	inflamado een-flah-**mah**-doh
punctured (a rusty nail)	perforado (un clavo oxidado) pehr-foh-**rah**-doh (oon **klah**-boh ohk-see-**dah**-doh)
scraped	rasguñado rahs-goon-**yah**-doh
sore	dolorido doh-loh-**ree**-doh
sprained	tener un esguince teh-**nehr** oon ehs-**geen**-thay
swollen	hinchado een-**chah**-doh
weak	débil **day**-beel
diagnosis	diagonóstico dee-ahg-**noh**-stee-koh
What can I do?	¿Qué puedo hacer? kay **pweh**-doh ah-**thehr**
Is it serious?	¿Es serio? ehs **seh**-ree-oh
Is it contagious?	¿Es contagioso? ehs kohn-tah-hee-**oh**-soh

Body Parts

ankle	tobillo toh-**bee**-yoh
appendix	apéndice ah-**pehn**-dee-thay
arm	brazo **brah**-thoh
back	espalda eh-**spahl**-dah
bladder	vejiga beh-**hee**-gah
blood	sangre **sahn**-gray
body	cuerpo **kwehr**-poh
bone	hueso **weh**-soh
bowel movement	evacuación ee-bah-koo-ah-thee-**ohn**
brain	cerebro theh-**reh**-broh
breasts	pechos **peh**-chohs
chest	pecho **peh**-choh
ear	oído oh-**ee**-doh
elbow	codo **koh**-doh
eye	ojo oh-*hoh*
face	cara **kah**-rah
fingers	dedos **deh**-dohs
fingernail	uña **oon**-yah
foot	pie pee-**ay**
hand	mano **mah**-noh
head	cabeza kah-**beh**-thah
heart	corazón koh-rah-**thohn**
hip	cadera kah-**dehr**-ah
kidney	riñón reen-**yohn**
knee	rodilla roh-**dee**-yah
leg	pierna pee-**ehr**-nah
lips	labios **lah**-bee-ohs
liver	higado ee-**gah**-doh
lung	pulmón pool-**mohn**
mouth	boca **boh**-kah
muscles	músculos **moo**-skoo-lohs

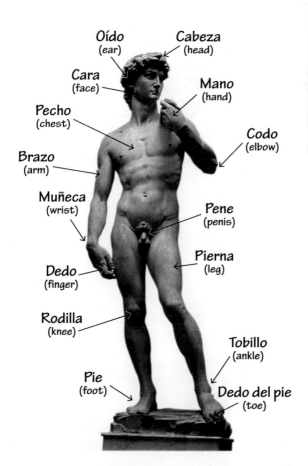

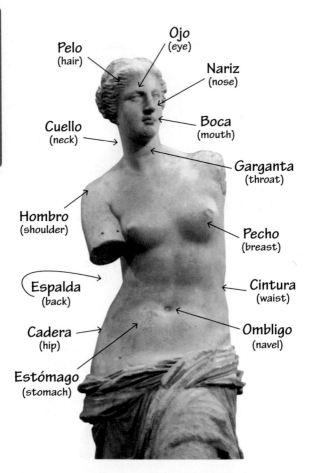

Pelo (hair)
Ojo (eye)
Nariz (nose)
Boca (mouth)
Cuello (neck)
Garganta (throat)
Hombro (shoulder)
Pecho (breast)
Espalda (back)
Cintura (waist)
Cadera (hip)
Ombligo (navel)
Estómago (stomach)

neck	cuello **kweh**-yoh
nose	nariz nah-**reeth**
ovary	ovario oh-**vah**-ree-oh
penis	pene **peh**-nay
poop	caca **kah**-kah
shoulder	hombro **ohm**-broh
skin	piel pee-**ehl**
stomach	estómago eh-**stoh**-mah-goh
teeth	dientes dee-**ehn**-tehs
testicles	testículos tehs-**tee**-koo-lohs
throat	garganta gar-**gahn**-tah
toes	dedos del pie **deh**-dohs dehl pee-**ay**
toenail	uña del dedo del pie **oon**-yah dehl **deh**-doh dehl pee-**ay**
tongue	lengua **lehn**-gwah
urine	orina oh-**ree**-nah
uterus	útero **oo**-teh-roh
vagina	vagina bah-**hee**-nah
waist	cintura theen-**too**-rah
wrist	muñeca moon-**yeh**-kah
right / left	derecho[a] / izquierdo[a] deh-**reh**-choh / eeth-kee-**ehr**-doh

First-Aid Kit and Medications

American name-brand medications are rare in Europe, but you'll find equally good local equivalents. Rather than looking for Sudafed, ask for an *anticongestivo* (decongestant). Instead of Nyquil, request a *medicina para un resfriado* (cold medicine). For prescription drugs, ask your doctor for the generic name (for example, atorvastatin instead of Lipitor), which is more likely to be understood internationally. If using a European thermometer, see page 422 for help with temperature conversions.

medicine	medicina	meh-dee-**thee**-nah
pill	pastilla	pah-**stee**-yah
prescription	receta	reh-**theh**-tah
refill	recambio	reh-**kahm**-bee-oh
pharmacy	farmacia	far-mah-**thee**-ah
antacid	antiácido	ahn-tee-**ah**-thee-doh
anti-anxiety medicine	tranquilizante	trahn-kee-lee-**thahn**-tay
antibiotic	antibiótico	ahn-tee-bee-**oh**-tee-koh
antihistamine (like Benadryl)	antihistamínico	ahn-tee-eest-ah-**meen**-ee-koh
aspirin	aspirina	ah-spee-**ree**-nah
non-aspirin substitute (like Tylenol)	paracetamol / Nolotil	pah-rah-theh-tah-**mohl** / noh-loh-**teel**
adult diapers (like Depends)	pañales para adultos	pahn-**yah**-lehs **pah**-rah ah-**dool**-tohs
bandage	venda	**behn**-dah
Band-Aids	tiritas	tee-**ree**-tahs
cold medicine	medicina para un resfriado	meh-dee-**thee**-nah **pah**-rah oon rehs-free-**ah**-doh
cough drops	caramelos para la tos	kah-rah-**meh**-lohs **pah**-rah lah tohs
decongestant (like Sudafed)	anticongestivo	ahn-tee-kohn-heh-**stee**-boh
diarrhea medicine	medicina para la diarrea	meh-dee-**thee**-nah **pah**-rah lah dee-ah-**reh**-ah
disinfectant	desinfectante	deh-seen-fehk-**tahn**-tay
first-aid cream	crema de primera ayuda	**kreh**-mah day pree-**mehr**-ah ah-**yoo**-dah
gauze / tape	gasa / esparadrapo	**gah**-sah / ehs-pah-rah-**drah**-poh

hemorrhoid medicine	crema antihemorroidal **kreh**-mah ahn-tee-eh-moh-roh-ee-**dahl**
hydrogen peroxide	peróxido de hidrógeno pehr-**ohk**-see-doh day ee-**droh**-heh-noh
ibuprofen	ibuprofeno ee-boo-proh-**feh**-noh
inhaler	inhalador een-ah-lah-**dor**
insulin	insulina een-soo-**lee**-nah
itch reliever	alivio del picor ah-**lee**-bee-oh dehl pee-**kor**
laxative	laxativo lahk-sah-**tee**-boh
lip balm	cacao de labios kah-**kah**-oh day **lah**-bee-ohs
moleskin (for blisters)	parches (para ampollas) **par**-chehs (**pah**-rah ahm-**poh**-yahs)
mosquito repellant	repelente para mosquitos reh-peh-**lehn**-tay **pah**-rah moh-**skee**-tohs
painkiller	analgésico ah-nahl-**hay**-see-koh
stomachache medicine	medicamento para el dolor del estómago meh-dee-kah-**mehn**-toh **pah**-rah ehl doh-**lor** dehl eh-**stoh**-mah-goh
support bandage	vendaje de apoyo behn-**dah**-hay day ah-**poh**-yoh
syringe	jeringuilla *h*ehr-een-**gee**-yah
tetanus shot	vacuna de tétano bah-**koo**-nah day **tay**-tah-noh
thermometer	termómetro tehr-**moh**-meh-troh
tweezers	pinzas peen-**thahs**
Vaseline	vaselina bah-seh-**lee**-nah
vitamins	vitaminas bee-tah-**mee**-nahs
Does it sting?	¿Arde? **ar**-day
Take one pill every _____ hours for _____ days.	Tome una pastilla cada _____ horas durante _____ días. **toh**-may **oo**-nah pah-**stee**-yah **kah**-dah _____ **oh**-rahs doo-**rahn**-tay _____ **dee**-ahs

SPECIFIC NEEDS

The Eyes Have It

optician	óptico	**ohp**-tee-koh
eye(s)	ojo(s)	**oh**-hoh(s)
eye drops (for inflammation)	colirio (para inflamación)	koh-**lee**-ree-oh (**pah**-rah een-flah-mah-thee-**ohn**)
artificial tears	lágrimas artificiales	**lah**-gree-mahs ar-tee-fee-thee-**ah**-lehs
glasses	gafas	**gah**-fahs
sunglasses	gafas de sol	**gah**-fahs day sohl
reading glasses	gafas para leer	**gah**-fahs **pah**-rah leh-**ehr**
glasses case	funda de gafas	**foon**-dah day **gah**-fahs
(broken) lens	cristal (roto)	kree-**stahl** (**roh**-toh)
repair	arreglar	ah-reh-**glar**
replacement	cambio	**kahm**-bee-oh
prescription	receta médica	reh-**theh**-tah **may**-dee-kah
contact lenses...	lentillas...	lehn-**tee**-yahs
...soft	...blandos	**blahn**-dohs
...hard	...duros	**doo**-rohs
cleaning solution	solución limpiadora	soh-loo-thee-**ohn** leem-pee-ah-**doh**-rah
soaking solution	solución	soh-loo-thee-**ohn**
all-purpose solution	solución para limpiar y guardar las lentillas	soh-loo-thee-**ohn pah**-rah leem-pee-**ar** ee gwar-**dar** lahs lehn-**tee**-yahs
contact lens case	estuche para lentillas	eh-**stoo**-chay **pah**-rah lehn-**tee**-yahs
I don't see well.	No veo bien.	noh **beh**-oh bee-**ehn**
nearsighted	miope	mee-**oh**-pay

| **farsighted** | hipermétrope ee-pehr-**may**-troh-pay |
| **20 / 20 vision** | vista perfecta **bee**-stah pehr-**fehk**-tah |

All Ears

ear(s)	oído(s) oh-**ee**-doh(s)
right / left	derecho / izquierdo deh-**reh**-choh / eeth-kee-**ehr**-doh
earache	dolor de oído doh-**lor** day oh-**ee**-doh
ear infection	infección del oído een-fehk-thee-**ohn** dehl oh-**ee**-doh
ear wax (removal)	cera en el oído (quitar) **theh**-rah ehn ehl oh-**ee**-doh (kee-**tar**)
I don't hear well.	No oigo bien. noh oh-**ee**-goh bee-**ehn**
hearing aid	audífono ow-**dee**-foh-noh
batteries	pilas **pee**-lahs

Tooth Trouble

dentist	dentista dehn-**tee**-stah
tooth / teeth	diente / dientes dee-**ehn**-tay / dee-**ehn**-tehs
toothache	dolor de muelas doh-**lor** day **mweh**-lahs
braces	aparatos ah-pah-**rah**-tohs
crown	corona koh-**roh**-nah
dentures	dentadura postiza dehn-tah-**doo**-rah poh-**stee**-thah
gums	encías ehn-**thee**-ahs
filling	empaste ehm-**pah**-stay
broken	roto **roh**-toh
cracked	fracturado frahk-too-**rah**-doh

The filling / tooth fell out.	El empaste / diente se me ha caído.
	ehl ehm-**pah**-stay / dee-**ehn**-tay say may ah kah-**ee**-doh
Ouch! That hurts!	¡Ay! ¡Eso duele! **ī** / **ay**-soh **dweh**-lay

Dental products (such as dental floss) appear in the "Personal Care" list at the beginning of this chapter.

On Intimate Terms

personal lubricant (like KY Jelly)	lubricante personal
	loo-bree-**kahn**-tay pehr-soh-**nahl**
contraceptives	anticonceptivos
	ahn-tee-kohn-thehp-**tee**-bohs
condoms	preservativos preh-sehr-bah-**tee**-bohs
birth-control pills	píldoras anti-conceptiva
	peel-doh-rahs
	ahn-**tee**-kohn-thehp-**tee**-bah
prescription refill	receta médica
	reh-**theh**-tah **may**-dee-kah
morning-after pill	la pildora del día después
	lah peel-**doh**-rah dehl **dee**-ah dehs-**pways**
herpes (inactive)	herpes (inactivo)
	ehr-pehs (een-ahk-**tee**-boh)
HIV / AIDS	VIH / SIDA **oo**-bay ee **ah**-chay / **see**-dah
STD (sexually transmitted disease)	ETS (enfermedad de transmisión sexual)
	ay tay **ehs**-ay (ehn-fehr-meh-**dahd** day trahns-mee-see-**ohn** sehks-oo-**ahl**)

For Women

menstruation	menstruación mehn-stroo-ah-thee-**ohn**
period	regla **reh**-glah
tampons	tampones tahm-**poh**-nehs

sanitary pads	compresas kohm-**preh**-sahs
I need medicine for...	Necesito medicina para... neh-theh-**see**-toh meh-dee-**thee**-nah **pah**-rah
...menstrual cramps.	...el dolor de la menstruación. ehl doh-**lor** day lah mehn-stroo-ah-thee-**ohn**
...a urinary tract infection.	...una infección urinaria. **oo**-nah een-fehk-thee-**ohn** oo-ree-**nah**-ree-ah
...a yeast infection.	...una infección de hongos. **oo**-nah een-fehk-thee-**ohn** day **ohn**-gohs
cranberry juice	zumo de arandanos rojos **thoo**-moh day ah-rahn-**dah**-nohs **roh**-hohs
I'd like to see a...	Me gustaría ver a una... may goo-stah-**ree**-ah behr ah **oo**-nah
...female doctor.	...médica. **may**-dee-kah
...female gynecologist.	...ginecóloga. hee-neh-**koh**-loh-gah
I've missed a period.	No me vino la regla. noh may **bee**-noh lah **reh**-glah
pregnancy test	prueba de embarazo proo-**eh**-bah day ehm-bah-**rah**-thoh
ultrasound	ecografía ee-koh-grah-**fee**-ah
I am / She is... pregnant.	Estoy / Está... embarazada. **eh**-stoy / eh-**stah** ehm-bah-rah-**thah**-dah
... _____ weeks / months	...de _____ semanas / meses day _____ seh-**mah**-nahs / **meh**-sehs
miscarriage	aborto espontáneo ah-**bor**-toh eh-spohn-**tahn**-eh-oh
abortion	aborto ah-**bor**-toh
menopause	menopausia meh-noh-**pow**-see-ah

For Babies

baby	bebé beh-**bay**
baby food	papilla de niños pah-**pee**-yah day **neen**-yohs
backpack to carry baby	mochila para llevar al bebé moh-**chee**-lah **pah**-rah yeh-**bar** ahl beh-**bay**
bib	babero bah-**beh**-roh
booster seat	silla elevadora **see**-yah eh-leh-bah-**doh**-rah
bottle	biberón bee-beh-**rohn**
breastfeeding	dando de mamar **dahn**-doh day mah-**mar**
Where can I breastfeed?	¿Dónde puedo dar de mamar? **dohn**-day **pweh**-doh dar day mah-**mar**
car seat	sillita para el coche see-**yee**-tah **pah**-rah ehl **koh**-chay
crib	cuna **koo**-nah
diapers	pañales pahn-**yah**-lehs
diaper wipes	toalletas húmedas (para bebés) toh-ah-**yeh**-tahs **oo**-meh-dahs (**pah**-rah beh-**bays**)
diaper ointment	pomada de pañal poh-**mah**-dah day pahn-**yahl**
formula...	leche maternizada... **leh**-chay mah-tehr-nee-**thah**-dah
...powdered	...en polvo ehn **pohl**-boh
...liquid	...líquida **lee**-kee-dah
...soy	...de soja day **soh**-hah
high chair	trona **troh**-nah
medication for...	medicación para... meh-dee-kah-thee-**ohn pah**-rah

...diaper rash	...el escozor del pañal ehl eh-skoh-**thor** dehl pahn-**yahl**
...ear infection	...infección del oído een-fehk-thee-**ohn** dehl oh-**ee**-doh
...teething	...le están saliendo los dientes lay eh-**stahn** sah-lee-**ehn**-doh lohs dee-**ehn**-tehs
nipple	pezón peh-**thohn**
pacifier	chupete choo-**peh**-tay
playpen	parque para niños **par**-kay **pah**-rah **neen**-yohs
stroller	carrecoche kah-reh-**koh**-chay
Is it safe for children?	¿Es seguro para los niños? ehs seh-**goo**-roh **pah**-rah lohs **neen**-yohs
He / She is ____ months / years old.	Él / Ella tiene ____ meses / años. ehl / **ay**-yah tee-**ehn**-ay ____ **meh**-sehs / **ahn**-yohs
Will you refrigerate this?	¿Podría refrigerarme esto? poh-**dree**-ah reh-free-hehr-**ar**-may **eh**-stoh
Will you warm... for a baby?	¿Podría calentar... para un bebé? poh-**dree**-ah kah-lehn-**tar**... **pah**-rah oon beh-**bay**
...this	...esto **eh**-stoh
...some water	...un poco de agua oon **poh**-koh day **ah**-gwah
...some milk	...un poco de leche oon **poh**-koh day **leh**-chay
Not too hot, please.	No demasiado caliente, por favor. noh deh-mah-see-**ah**-doh kah-lee-**ehn**- tay por fah-**bor**

Allergies

If you need to explain which specific food you're allergic to, look it up in this book's Menu Decoder.

I am allergic to...	Soy alérgico[a] a...
	soy ah-**lehr**-hee-koh ah
He / She is allergic to...	Él / Ella es alérgico[a] a...
	ehl / **ay**-yah ehs ah-**lehr**-hee-koh ah
lactose / dairy products	la lactosa / los lácteos
	lah lahk-**toh**-sah / lohs **lahk**-teh-ohs
nuts	frutos secos **froo**-tohs **seh**-kohs
penicillin	penicilina peh-nee-thee-**lee**-nah
pet fur	pelo de las mascotas
	peh-loh day lahs mahs-**koh**-tahs
pollen	polen **poh**-lehn
shellfish	mariscos mah-**ree**-skohs
sulfa	sulfamida sool-fah-**mee**-dah
wheat	trigo **tree**-goh
epipen	epipen "epipen"

Mental Health

anxiety	ansiedad ahn-see-eh-**dahd**
bipolar disorder	disorden bipolar
	dee-**sor**-dehn bee-poh-**lar**
confusion	confusión kohn-foo-see-**ohn**
depression	depresión deh-preh-see-**ohn**
panic attacks	ataques de pánico
	ah-**tah**-kehs day **pahn**-ee-koh
I feel suicidal.	Me siento suicido[a].
	may see-**ehn**-toh soo-ee-**thee**-doh

I need...	Necesito... neh-theh-**see**-toh
...medicine to calm down.	...un medicamento para tranquilizarme. oon meh-dee-kah-**mehn**-toh **pah**-rah trahn-keel-ee-**thar**-may
...to call home.	...llamar a casa. **yah**-mar ah **kah**-sah
...a psychologist.	...un psicólogo. oon see-**koh**-loh-goh
...a psychiatrist.	...un psiquiatra. oon see-kee-**ah**-trah

Disabilities

cane	bastón bah-**stohn**
disabled	descapacitado[a] deh-skah-pah-thee-**tah**-doh
elevator	ascensor ah-thehn-**sor**
ramp	rampa **rahm**-pah
stairs	escaleras eh-skah-**lehr**-ahs
walker	andador ahn-dah-**dor**
wheelchair	silla de ruedas **see**-yah day roo-**eh**-dahs
I am / He is / She is disabled.	Soy / Él es / Ella es descapacitado[a]. soy / ehl ehs / **ay**-yah ehs deh-skah-pah-thee-**tah**-doh
Stairs are difficult / impossible.	Las escaleras son difíciles / imposibles. lahs eh-skah-**lehr**-ahs sohn dee-**fee**-thee-lehs / eem-poh-**see**-blehs
Do you have a fully adapted entrance / room?	¿Tiene una entrada / habitación totalmente adaptada para descapacitados? tee-**ehn**-ay **oo**-nah ehn-**trah**-dah / ah-bee-tah-thee-**ohn** toh-tahl-**mehn**-tay ah-dahp-**tah**-dah **pah**-rah deh-skah-pah-thee-**tah**-dohs
Do you have an elevator?	¿Tiene un ascensor? tee-**ehn**-ay oon ah-thehn-**sor**

MEDICAL CONDITIONS

If you have a condition that's not listed here, find out the Spanish word and keep it handy.

I have...	Tengo... **tehn**-goh
He / She has...	Él / Ella tiene... ehl / **ay**-yah tee-**ehn**-ay
Alzheimer's disease	Alzheimer "Alzheimer"
arthritis	artritis ar-**tree**-tees
asthma	asma **ahs**-mah
cancer	cáncer **kahn**-thehr
cancer of the _____ (body parts listed earlier)	cáncer de _____ **kahn**-thehr day _____
leukemia	leucemia leh-oo-**thehm**-ee-ah
lymphoma	linfoma leen-**foh**-mah
I have been in remission for _____ months / years.	He estado en remisión durante _____ meses / años. ay eh-**stah**-doh ehn reh-mee-see-**ohn** doo-**rahn**-tay _____ **meh**-sehs / **ahn**-yohs
chronic pain	dolor crónico doh-**lor kroh**-nee-koh
diabetes	diabetes dee-ah-**beh**-tehs
epilepsy	epilepsia eh-pee-**lehp**-see-ah
heart condition	problemas de corazón proh-**bleh**-mahs day koh-rah-**thohn**
heart disease	cardiopatía kar-dee-oh-pah-**tee**-ah
heart attack	infarto een-**far**-toh
stroke	infarto cerebral een-**far**-toh theh-reh-**brahl**
I have a pacemaker.	Tengo un marcapasos. **tehn**-goh oon mar-kah-**pah**-sohs
high blood pressure	tensión alta tehn-thee-**ohn ahl**-tah
high cholesterol	colesterol alto koh-leh-**steh**-rohl **ahl**-toh

incontinence	incontinencia een-kohn-tee-**nehn**-thee-ah
multiple sclerosis	esclerosis múltiple eh-sklehr-**oh**-sees **mool**-tee-play
Aging sucks. ("Aging is a pain.")	Hacerse viejo es una lata. ah-**thehr**-say bee-**eh**-*h*oh ehs **oo**-nah **lah**-tah

CHATTING

When it comes time to connect with the locals, these phrases can help you strike up a conversation, talk to children, chat about the weather, or ignite a Spanish romance.

SMALL TALK

Introductions

My name is _____.	Me llamo _____. may **yah**-moh _____
What's your name?	¿Cómo se llama? **koh**-moh say **yah**-mah
Pleased to meet you.	Mucho gusto. moo-choh **goo**-stoh
This is _____.	Le presento _____. lay preh-**sehn**-toh _____
How are you?	¿Cómo está? **koh**-moh eh-**stah**
Very well, thanks.	Muy bien, gracias. **moo**-ee bee-**ehn grah**-thee-ahs
May I sit here?	¿Puedo sentarme aquí? **pweh**-doh sehn-**tar**-may ah-**kee**
May we sit here?	¿Podemos sentarnos aquí? poh-**deh**-mohs sehn-**tar**-nohs ah-**kee**

Key Phrases: Chatting

My name is _____.	Me llamo _____. may **yah**-moh _____
What's your name?	¿Cómo se llama? **koh**-moh say **yah**-mah
Where are you from?	¿De dónde es? day **dohn**-day ehs
I'm from _____.	Soy de _____. soy day _____
I like _____.	Me gusta _____. may **goo**-stah _____
Do you like _____?	¿Le gusta _____? lay **goo**-stah _____
I'm going to _____.	Voy a _____. boy ah _____
Where are you going?	¿A dónde va? ah **dohn**-day bah
Have a good trip!	¡Buen viaje! bwehn bee-**ah**-hay

Where are you from?	¿De dónde es?	day **dohn**-day ehs
What...?	¿Qué...?	kay
...city	...ciudad	thee-oo-**dahd**
...country	...país	pī-**ees**
...planet	...planeta	plah-**neh**-tah
I'm from...	Soy de...	soy day
...the United States.	....los Estados Unidos.	lohs eh-**stah**-dohs oo-**nee**-dohs
...Canada.	...Canadá.	kah-nah-**dah**
Where are you going?	¿A dónde vas?	ah **dohn**-day bahs
I'm going to _____.	Voy a _____.	boy ah _____
We're going to _____.	Vamos a _____.	**bah**-mohs ah _____

Nothing More than Feelings

I am / You are...	Estoy / Está...	**eh**-stoy / eh-**stah**
He is / She is...	Él / Ella está....	ehl / **ay**-yah eh-**stah**
...happy.	...feliz.	feh-**leeth**
...excited.	...emocionado[a].	eh-moh-thee-oh-**nah**-doh
...sad.	...triste.	**tree**-stay
...tired.	...cansado[a].	kahn-**sah**-doh
...angry.	...enfadado[a].	ehn-fah-**dah**-doh
...jealous.	...celoso[a].	theh-**loh**-soh
...frustrated.	...frustrado[a].	froo-**strah**-doh
I am...	Tengo...	**tehn**-goh
...hungry.	...hambre.	**ahm**-bray
...thirsty.	...sed.	sehd
...hot.	...calor.	kah-**lor**
...cold.	...frío.	**free**-oh
...homesick.	...morriña.	moh-**reen**-yah
...lucky.	...suerte.	**swehr**-tay

If you're *cansado*, you're tired. If you're *casado*, you're married. If you're both, you probably have *hijos* (children).

Who's Who

This is my...	Le presento a mí... lay preh-**sehn**-toh ah mee
friend (m / f)	amigo / amiga ah-**mee**-goh / ah-**mee**-gah
boyfriend / girlfriend	novio / novia **noh**-bee-oh / **noh**-bee-ah
husband / wife	marido / esposa mah-**ree**-doh / eh-**spoh**-sah
son / daughter	hijo / hija **ee**-hoh / **ee**-hah
brother / sister	hermano / hermana ehr-**mah**-noh / ehr-**mah**-nah
father / mother	padre / madre **pah**-dray / **mah**-dray
uncle / aunt	tío / tía **tee**-oh / **tee**-ah
nephew / niece	sobrino / sobrina soh-**bree**-noh / soh-**bree**-nah
cousin (m / f)	primo / prima **pree**-moh / **pree**-mah
grandpa / grandma	abuelo / abuela ah-**bweh**-loh / ah-**bweh**-lah
grandson / granddaughter	nieto / nieta nee-**eh**-toh / nee-**eh**-tah
great-_____	bis-_____ bees-_____

Family Matters

Are you...?	¿Está...? eh-**stah**
I am / We are...	Estoy / Estamos... eh-stoy / eh-**stah**-mohs
...married	...casado[a] kah-**sah**-doh

...engaged	...prometido[a] proh-meh-**tee**-doh	
We are friends.	Somos amigos / amigas. **soh**-mohs ah-**mee**-gohs / ah-**mee**-gahs	
We are partners ("a couple").	Somos una pareja. **soh**-mohs oo-nah pah-**reh**-hah	
Do you have...?	¿Tiene...? tee-**ehn**-ay	
I have / We have...	Tengo / Tenemos... **tehn**-goh / teh-**neh**-mohs	
...children	...hijos ee-**h**ohs	
...grandchildren	...nietos nee-**eh**-tohs	
...photos	...fotos **foh**-tohs	
boy / girl	niño / niña **neen**-yoh / **neen**-yah	
How many boys / girls?	¿Cuántos[as] niños / niñas? **kwahn**-tohs **neen**-yohs / **neen**-yahs	
Beautiful baby!	¡Que bebé más guapo[a]! kay beh-**bay** mahs **gwah**-poh	
Beautiful boy / girl!	¡Que niño / niña más guapo[a]! kay **neen**-yoh / **neen**-yah mahs **gwah**-poh	
Beautiful children!	¡Qué niños más guapos! kay **neen**-yohs mahs **gwah**-pohs	
How old is your child?	¿Cuántos años tiene su hijo[a]? **kwahn**-tohs **ahn**-yohs tee-**ehn**-ay soo **ee**-hoh	
age / ages	edad / edades **eh**-dahd / eh-**dah**-dehs	
grown-up	adulto ah-**dool**-toh	

Chatting with Children

What's your name?	¿Cómo te llamas? **koh**-moh tay **yah**-mahs
My name is _____.	Me llamo _____. may **yah**-moh _____
How old are you?	¿Cuántos años tienes? **kwahn**-tohs **ahn**-yohs tee-**ehn**-ehs

How old am I?	¿Cuántos años tengo? kwahn-tohs **ahn**-yohs **tehn**-goh
I'm _____ years old.	Tengo _____ años. **tehn**-goh _____ **ahn**-yohs
Do you have brothers and sisters?	¿Tienes hermanos? tee-**ehn**-ehs ehr-**mah**-nohs
Do you like school?	¿Te gusta la escuela? tay **goo**-stah lah eh-**skweh**-lah
What are you studying?	¿Qué estás estudiando? kay eh-**stahs** eh-stoo-dee-**ahn**-doh
What's your favorite subject?	¿Cúal es tu asignatura favorita? kwahl ehs too ah-seeg-nah-**too**-rah fah-boh-**ree**-tah
Will you teach me / us some Spanish words?	¿Me / Nos enseñas algunas palabras en español? may / nohs ehn-**sehn**-yahs ahl-**goo**-nahs pah-**lah**-brahs ehn eh-spahn-**yohl**
Do you have pets?	¿Tienes mascotas? tee-**ehn**-ehs mah-**skoh**-tahs
I have / We have a...	Tengo / Tenemos un... **tehn**-goh / teh-**neh**-mohs oon
...cat / dog / fish / bird.	...gato / perro / pez / pájaro. **gah**-toh / **pehr**-oh / pehth / **pah**-hah-roh
Gimme five.	Choca los cinco. **choh**-kah lohs **theen**-koh

Work

What is your occupation?	¿En qué trabaja? ehn kay trah-**bah**-hah
Do you like your work?	¿Le gusta su trabajo? lay **goo**-stah soo trah-**bah**-hoh
I am...	Estoy... eh-stoy

...retired.	...jubilado[a]. hoo-bee-**lah**-doh
...unemployed.	...en desempleado[a]. ehn dehs-ehm-pleh-**ah**-doh
I'm...	Soy... soy
...a student.	...estudiante. eh-stoo-dee-**ahn**-tay
...a professional traveler.	...de profesión viajero. day proh-feh-see-**ohn** bee-ah-**heh**-roh
I'm studying to work in...	Estudio para trabajar en... eh-**stoo**-dee-oh **pah**-rah trah-bah-**har** ehn
I work in...	Trabajo en... trah-**bah**-hoh ehn
I used to work in...	Solía trabajar en... soh-**lee**-ah trah-bah-**har** ehn
I want a job in...	Busco trabajo en... **boo**-skoh trah-**bah**-hoh ehn
accounting	contabilidad kohn-tah-bee-lee-**dahd**
the arts	el arte ehl **ar**-tay
banking	la banca lah **bahn**-kah
business	los negocios lohs neh-**goh**-thee-ohs
construction	la construcción lah kohn-strook-thee-**ohn**
education	la educación lah eh-doo-kah-thee-**ohn**
engineering	ingeniería een-heh-nee-ehr-**ee**-ah
a factory	una fábrica **oo**-nah **fah**-bree-kah
government	el gobierno ehl goh-bee-**ehr**-noh
information technology	informática een-for-**mah**-tee-kah
journalism	de periodista day peh-ree-oh-**dee**-stah
the legal profession	el mundo del derecho ehl **moon**-doh dehl deh-**reh**-choh
the medical field	la medicina lah meh-dee-**thee**-nah
the military	el ejército ehl eh-**hehr**-thee-toh

public relations	relaciones públicas reh-lah-thee-**oh**-nehs **poo**-blee-kahs
a restaurant	un restaurante oon reh-stoh-**rahn**-tay
the sciences	las ciencias lahs thee-**ehn**-thee-ahs
social services	servicios sociales sehr-**bee**-thee-ohs soh-thee-**ah**-lehs
the travel industry	el sector de viajes ehl sehk-**tor** day bee-**ah**-hehs

Travel Talk

I am / Are you...?	Estoy / ¿Está...? **eh**-stoy / eh-**stah**
...on vacation	...de vacaciones day bah-kah-thee-**oh**-nehs
...on business	...de negocios day neh-**goh**-thee-ohs
How long have you been traveling?	¿Cuánto tiempo hace que está viajando? **kwahn**-toh tee-**ehm**-poh **ah**-thay kay eh-**stah** bee-ah-**hahn**-doh
day(s) / week(s)	día(s) / semana(s) **dee**-ah(s) / seh-**mah**-nah(s)
month(s) / year(s)	mes(es) / año(s) meh(-sehs) / **ahn**-yoh(s)
When are you going home?	¿Cuándo vuelves a casa? **kwahn**-doh **bwehl**-behs ah **kah**-sah
This is my / our first time in _____.	Ésta es mi / nuestra primera vez en _____. **eh**-stah ehs mee / **nweh**-strah pree-**mehr**-ah behth ehn _____
It's (not) a tourist trap.	(No) es un timo turístico. (noh) ehs oon **tee**-moh too-**ree**-stee-koh
This is paradise.	Es un paraíso. ehs oon pah-rah-**ee**-soh
Spain is wonderful.	España es preciosa. eh-**spahn**-yah ehs preh-thee-**oh**-sah

The Spanish are friendly / rude.	Los españoles son amables / maleducados. lohs eh-spahn-**yoh**-lehs sohn ah-**mah**-blehs / mah-leh-doo-**kah**-dohs
What is your favorite...?	¿Cúal es su... favorito? kwahl ehs soo... fah-bor-**ee**-toh
...country	...país pī-**ees**
...place	...lugar loo-**gar**
...city	...ciudad thee-oo-**dahd**
My favorite is _____.	Mi favorito es _____. mee fah-bor-**ee**-toh ehs _____
I've / We've traveled to _____.	He / Hemos viajado a _____. ay / **eh**-mohs bee-ah-**hah**-doh ah _____
Next I'll go / we'll go to _____.	Después iré / iremos a _____. dehs-**pways** ee-**ray** / ee-**reh**-mohs ah _____
I'd / We'd like...	Me / Nos gustaría... may / nohs goo-stah-**ree**-ah
...to go to _____.	...ir a _____. eer ah _____
...to return to _____.	...volver a _____. bohl-**behr** ah _____
My / Our vacation is _____ days long.	Mis / Nuestras vacaciones son _____ días. mees / **nweh**-strahs bah-kah-thee-**oh**-nehs sohn _____ **dee**-ahs
Travel is enlightening.	Viajar es instructivo. bee-ah-**har** ehs een-strook-**tee**-boh
I wish all (American) politicians traveled.	Ojalá que todos los políticos (americanos) viajaran. oh-hah-**lah** kay **toh**-dohs lohs poh-**lee**-tee-kohs (ah-meh-ree-**kah**-nohs) bee-ah-**hah**-rahn
Have a good trip!	¡Buen viaje! bwehn bee-**ah**-hay
Keep on travelin'!	¡Siga viajando! **see**-gah bee-ah-**hahn**-doh

Spain

Bay

Atlantic Ocean

Ferrol • A Coruña

Santiago de Compostela • Lugo

Oviedo • Camillas •

G A L I C I A

C A N T A B R I A

• Pontevedra

• Ponferrada

León • Aguilar •

S. María •

• Benevente

100 Kilometers

100 Miles

• Braga

Porto DOURO VALLEY

Douro

Valladolid

• Aveiro

Guarda

Salamança S P A

Ciudad Rodrigo

Segovia •

Figueira da Foz • Coimbra

Piedranita • Ávila

PORTUGAL

• Plasencia

Madrid ®

Nazaré •

• Fátima

Tajo

Óbidos •

Tejo

Sintra • Portalegre

Toledo •

CASTILE-

Lisbon

Évora

• Trujillo

Setúbal •

Mérida •

L A

ALENTEJO

• Beja

EXTREMADURA

Alcarecejos •

• Jabugo

Linares •

A L G A R V E

Huelva

Sevilla •

Córdoba •

Jaén •

Salema • Lagos

Faro Tavira

A N D A L U C Í A

Jerez • Arcos

Granada •

Cádiz •

Ronda • Málaga

Nerja •

Vejer •

COSTA

Atlantic Ocean

Algeciras • DEL SOL

Tarifa •

GIBRALTAR (UK)

Tangier •

• Tétouan

MOROCCO

Europe

Staying in Touch

What is your...?	¿Cuál es su...? kwahl ehs soo
Here is my...	Aquí tiene mi... ah-**kee** tee-**ehn**-ay mee
...email address	...email "email"
...street address	...dirección dee-rehk-thee-**ohn**
...phone number	...número de teléfono **noo**-mehr-oh day teh-**lay**-foh-noh
I am / Are you on Facebook?	Estoy / ¿Está en Facebook? eh-stoy / eh-**stah** ehn "Facebook"

Weather

Is it going to rain...?	¿Va a llover...? bah ah **yoh**-behr
What will the weather be like...?	¿Qué tiempo va a hacer...? kay tee-**ehm**-poh bah ah ah-**thehr**
...today	...hoy oy
...tomorrow	...mañana mahn-**yah**-nah
cloudy	nublado noo-**blah**-doh
cold	frío **free**-oh
foggy	niebla nee-**eh**-blah
hot	caluroso kah-loo-**roh**-soh
muggy	húmedo **oo**-meh-doh
rainy	lluvioso yoo-bee-**oh**-soh
snowy	nevoso neh-**boh**-soh
stormy	tempestuoso tehm-pehs-too-**oh**-soh
sunny	soleado soh-leh-**ah**-doh
warm	cálido **kah**-lee-doh
windy	ventoso vehn-**toh**-soh
Like today?	¿Como hoy? **koh**-moh oy

Should I bring a jacket / an umbrella?	¿Debería llevar una chaqueta / un paraguas? deh-beh-**ree**-ah yeh-**bar** oo-nah chah-**keh**-tah / oon pah-**rah**-gwahs
It's raining buckets.	Llueve a cántaros. **yeh**-bay ah **kahn**-tah-rohs
A rainbow!	¡Un arco iris! oon **ar**-koh **ee**-rees

To figure out temperature conversions, see page 422.

Thanks a Million

Thank you very much.	Muchas gracias. **moo**-chahs **grah**-thee-ahs
This is great fun.	¡Qué divertido! kay dee-behr-**tee**-doh
You are...	Usted es... oo-**stehd** ehs
...kind.	...amable. ah-**mah**-blay
...wonderful.	...maravilloso[a]. mah-rah-bee-**yoh**-soh
...generous.	...generoso[a]. heh-neh-**roh**-soh
You've been a great help.	Me ha ayudado mucho. may ah ī-yoo-**dah**-doh **moo**-choh
I will remember / We will remember you...	Le recordaré / recordaremos... lay reh-kor-dah-**ray** / reh-kor-dah-**reh**-mohs
...always.	...siempre. see-**ehm**-pray
...till Tuesday.	...hasta el martes. **ah**-stah ehl **mar**-tehs

Responses for All Occasions

I / We like that.	Eso me / nos gusta. **eh**-soh may / nohs **goo**-stah
I / We like you.	Me / Nos cae bien. may / nohs **kah**-ay bee-**ehn**

I trust you.	Confío en usted. kohn-**fee**-oh ehn oo-**stehd**
I will miss you.	Le echaré de menos. lay eh-chah-**ray** day **meh**-nohs
That's great!	¡Qué bien! kay bee-**ehn**
Excellent!	¡Excelente! ehk-thehl-**ehn**-tay
What a nice place.	Que sitio más bonito. kay **seet**-yoh mahs boh-**nee**-toh
Perfect.	Perfecto. pehr-**fehk**-toh
Funny.	Divertido. dee-behr-**tee**-doh
Interesting.	Interesante. een-teh-reh-**sahn**-tay
I see.	Ya veo. yah **beh**-oh
Why not?	¿Por qué no? por kay noh
Really?	¿De verdad? day behr-**dahd**
Wow!	¡Vaya! **bī**-ah
Congratulations!	¡Felicidades! feh-lee-thee-**dah**-dehs
Well done!	¡Bien hecho! bee-**ehn eh**-choh
You're welcome.	De nada. day **nah**-dah
Bless you! (after sneeze)	¡Salud! sah-**lood**
What a pity!	¡Qué pena! kay **peh**-nah
That's life.	Así es la vida. ah-**see** ehs lah **bee**-dah
No problem.	No hay problema. noh ī proh-**bleh**-mah
OK.	De acuerdo. / Vale. day ah-**kwehr**-doh / **bah**-lay
I'll be right back.	Ahora vengo. ah-**oh**-rah **behn**-goh
I hope so.	Eso espero. **eh**-so eh-**spehr**-oh
I hope not.	Espero que no. eh-**spehr**-oh kay noh
This is the good life!	¡Esto sí que es vida! **eh**-stoh see kay ehs **bee**-dah
Have a good day!	¡Que tenga buen día! kay **tehn**-gah bwehn **dee**-ah

| Good luck! | ¡Mucha suerte! **moo**-chah **swehr**-tay |
| Let's go! | ¡Vámonos! **bah**-mah-nohs |

The Spanish say *La vida es corta. No corras.* (Life is short. Don't run.)

Favorite Things

What is your favorite...?	¿Cúal es su... favorito? kwahl ehs soo... fah-boh-**ree**-toh
My favorite... is ____.	Mi... favorito es ____. mee... fah-boh-**ree**-toh ehs ____
art	arte **ar**-tay
book	libro **lee**-broh
food	comida koh-**mee**-dah
hobby	pasatiempo pah-sah-tee-**ehm**-poh
ice cream	helado eh-**lah**-doh
movie	película peh-**lee**-koo-lah
music	música **moo**-see-kah
sport	deporte deh-**por**-tay
team	equipo eh-**kee**-poh
TV show	serie de televisión seh-**ree**-ay day teh-leh-bee-thee-**ohn**
vice	vicio **bee**-thee-oh
video game	videojuego bee-deh-oh-**hweh**-goh
Who is your favorite...?	¿Cúal es su... favorito? kwahl ehs soo... fah-boh-**ree**-toh
...actor	...actor ahk-**tor**
...singer	...cantante kahn-**tahn**-tay
...artist	...artista ar-**tee**-stah
...author	...autor ow-**tor**
...director	...director dee-rehk-**tor**
...athlete	...atleta aht-**leh**-tah

For sports words, see page 206.

GRUNTS AND CURSES, SMOKES AND TOKES

Conversing with Animals

rooster / cock-a-doodle-doo	gallo / cacarea **gah**-yoh / kah-kah-**reh**-ah
bird / tweet tweet	pájaro / pío pío **pah**-*h*ah-roh / **pee**-oh **pee**-oh
cat / meow	gato / miau **gah**-toh / **mee**-ow
dog / woof woof	perro / guau guau **pehr**-oh / gwow gwow
duck / quack quack	pato / cuac cuac **pah**-toh / kwah kwah
cow / moo	vaca / muu **bah**-kah / moo
pig / oink oink	cerdo / oink oink **thehr**-doh / (just snort)

Profanity

People make animal noises, too. These words will help you understand what the more colorful locals are saying.

Go to hell!	¡Vete a la mierda! **beh**-tay ah lah mee-**ehr**-dah
Damn it.	¡Mierda! mee-**ehr**-dah
breasts (colloq.)	tetas **teh**-tahs
woman's private parts (our C-word)	coño **kohn**-yoh
penis (colloq.)	polla **poh**-yah
drunkard	borracho[a] boh-**rah**-choh
our F-word	joder *h*oh-**dehr**
This sucks.	¡Qué putada! kay poo-**tah**-dah
Shit. / Bullshit.	Mierda. mee-**ehr**-dah

This is a piece of shit.	Esto es una mierda.
	eh-stoh ehs **oo**-nah mee-**ehr**-dah
Shove it up your ass.	Mételo en el culo.
	may-teh-loh ehn ehl **koo**-loh
Kiss my ass.	Bésame el culo.
	bay-sah-may ehl **koo**-loh
You are a...	Eres un / una... **eh**-rehs oon / **oo**-nah
Don't be a...	No seas un / una...
	noh **seh**-ahs oon / **oo**-nah
...asshole.	...gilipollas. hee-lee-**poh**-yahs
...bitch.	...zorra. **thoh**-rah
...son of a whore.	...hijo de puta. **ee**-hoh day **poo**-tah
...idiot.	...idiota. ee-dee-**oh**-tah
...jerk ("horned sheep").	...cabrón[a]. kah-**brohn**
...imbecile.	...imbécil. eem-**bay**-theel
...stupid.	...estúpido[a]. eh-**stoo**-pee-doh

Spaniards are not as shy about using profanity as Americans. Favorite insults include **hijo de puta** (son of a whore) and **cabrón** (literally a horned sheep; this implies that the insultee's spouse sleeps around). Even what we'd consider to be the most extreme curses (**joder, coño**) are used far more freely than their American counterparts, often even turning up around the dinner table in mixed company.

Sweet Curses

My goodness.	Dios mío. **dee**-ohs **mee**-oh
Goodness gracious.	Dios mío de mi corazón.
	dee-ohs **mee**-oh day mee koh-rah-**thohn**
Oh, my gosh!	¡Oh, Dios mío! oh **dee**-ohs **mee**-oh
Shoot! / Wow!	¡Vaya! **bī**-ah
Darn it!	¡Caray! kah-**rī**

Smokes and Tokes

Do you smoke?	¿Fuma?	**foo**-mah
Do you smoke pot?	¿Fumas maría?	**foo**-mahs mah-**ree**-ah
I (don't) smoke.	(No) fumo.	(noh) **foo**-moh
We (don't) smoke.	(No) fumamos.	(noh) foo-**mah**-mohs
I don't have any.	No tengo.	noh **tehn**-goh
lighter	mechero	meh-**cheh**-roh
cigarettes	cigarillos	thee-gah-**ree**-yohs
cigar	puro	**poo**-roh
marijuana	marihuana	mah-ree-**wah**-nah
hash	hachís	ah-**chees**
joint	porro	**poh**-roh
stoned	colocado[a]	koh-loh-**kah**-doh
Wow!	¡Vaya!	**bi**-ah

For drinking phrases, see page 157 in the Eating chapter.

A SPANISH ROMANCE

Words of Love

I / me / you / we	yo / mi / tú / nosotros	
	yoh / mee / too / noh-**soh**-trohs	
love	amor	ah-**mor**
kiss	beso	**beh**-soh
hug	abrazo	ah-**brah**-thoh
to flirt	coquetear	koh-keh-teh-**ar**
to cuddle	acurrucarse	ah-koo-roo-**kar**-say
to date	salir	sah-**leer**
to make love	hacer el amor	ah-**thehr** ehl ah-**mor**
single	soltero[a]	sohl-**tehr**-oh
married	casado[a]	kah-**sah**-doh
engaged	prometido[a]	pro-meh-**tee**-doh

anniversary	aniversario ah-nee-behr-**sah**-ree-oh
faithful	fiel fee-**ehl**
sexy	sexy "sexy"
cozy	acogedor ah-koh-**heh**-dor
romantic	romántico roh-**mahn**-tee-koh
honey	cariño[a] kah-**reen**-yoh
darling	querido[a] keh-**ree**-doh
my angel	mi ángel mee **ahn**-hehl
my love	mi amor mee ah-**mor**
my heaven	mi cielo mee thee-**eh**-loh

Ah, Amor

For words related to birth control and safe sex, see page 286.

What's the matter?	¿Qué te pasa? kay tay **pah**-sah
Nothing.	Nada. **nah**-dah
I am / Are you...?	Soy / ¿Eres...? soy / **eh**-rehs
...single	...soltero[a] sohl-**tehr**-oh
...straight	...heterosexual eh-teh-roh-sehk-soo-**ahl**
...gay	...gay "gay"
...bisexual	...bisexual bee-sehk-soo-**ahl**
...undecided	...indeciso[a] een-deh-**thee**-soh
...prudish	...prudente proo-**dehn**-tay
I have...	Tengo... **tehn**-goh
Do you have...?	¿Tienes...? tee-**ehn**-ehs
...a boyfriend	...un novio oon **noh**-bee-oh
...a girlfriend	...una novia **oo**-nah **noh**-bee-ah
We are on our honeymoon.	Estamos de luna de miel. eh-**stah**-mohs day **loo**-nah day mee-**ehl**
I'm married.	Estoy casado[a]. **eh**-stoy kah-**sah**-doh

I'm married, but...	Estoy casado[a], pero... **eh**-stoy kah-**sah**-doh **pehr**-oh
I'm not married.	No estoy casado[a]. noh **eh**-stoy kah-**sah**-doh
I'm adventurous.	Soy aventurero. soy ah-behn-too-**rehr**-oh
I'm lonely (tonight).	Me siento solo[a] (esta noche). may see-**ehn**-toh **soh**-loh (**eh**-stah **noh**-chay)
I'm rich and single.	Soy rico[a] y soltero[a]. soy **ree**-koh ee sohl-**tehr**-oh
Do you mind if I sit here?	¿Te importa si me siento aquí? tay eem-**por**-tah see may see-**ehn**-toh ah-**kee**
Would you like a drink?	¿Te gustaría tomar algo? tay goo-stah-**ree**-ah toh-**mar ahl**-goh
Will you go out with me?	¿Quieres salir conmigo? kee-**ehr**-ehs sah-**leer** kohn-**mee**-goh
Would you like to go out tonight for...?	¿Te gustaría salir esta noche para...? tay goo-stah-**ree**-ah sah-**leer eh**-stah **noh**-chay **pah**-rah
...a walk	...dar un paseo dar oon pah-**seh**-oh
...dinner	...cenar theh-**nar**
...a drink	...tomar algo toh-**mar ahl**-goh
Where can we go dancing?	¿Donde podemos ir a bailar? **dohn**-day poh-**deh**-mohs eer ah bī-**lar**
Do you want to dance?	¿Quieres bailar? kee-**ehr**-ehs bī-**lar**
Again?	¿Otra vez? **oh**-trah behth
Let's celebrate!	¡Vamos a celebrarlo! **bah**-mohs ah theh-leh-**brar**-loh
Let's just be friends.	Vamos a dejarlo como amigos. **bah**-mohs ah deh-**har**-loh **koh**-moh ah-**mee**-gohs

I have only safe sex.	Sólo practico sexo seguro. **soh**-loh prahk-**tee**-koh **sehk**-soh seh-**goo**-roh
Can I take you home?	¿Puedo acompañarte a casa? **pweh**-doh ah-kohm-pahn-**yar**-tay ah **kah**-sah
Kiss me.	Bésame. **bay**-sah-may
May I kiss you?	¿Puedo besarte? **pweh**-doh beh-**sar**-tay
Kiss me more.	Bésame más. **bay**-sah-may mahs
Can I see you again?	¿Te puedo volver a ver? tay **pweh**-doh bohl-**behr** ah behr
Your place or mine?	¿Tu casa o la mía? too **kah**-sah oh lah **mee**-ah
You are my most beautiful souvenir.	Tú eres mi mejor recuerdo. too **eh**-rehs mee meh-**hor** reh-**kwehr**-doh
Oh my God!	¡Dios mío! **dee**-ohs **mee**-oh
I love you.	Te quiero. tay kee-**ehr**-oh
Darling, will you marry me?	¿Querida, te casás conmigo? keh-**ree**-dah tay kah-**sahs** kohn-**mee**-goh

DICTIONARY

SPANISH / ENGLISH

A

a to; at
¿A quién? To whom?
a través through
abajo down; below
abanico fan (handheld)
abierto open
abogado[a] lawyer
abono de tren railpass
abordar to board
abordo aboard; on board
aborto abortion
abrazar to hug
abrazo hug
abrelatas can opener
abrigo coat; overcoat
abril April
abrir to open
abstracto abstract
abuela grandmother
abuelo grandfather
aburrido bored; boring
abusar to abuse
abuso abuse
acabar de to have just done something; to run out of; to finish; to end
acantilado cliff
acercarse to come closer
accesible accessible
acceso access
acesso a Internet Internet access
acceso de silla de ruedas wheelchair-accessible

accidente accident
aceite oil
aceptar to accept
acondicionador conditioner (hair)
aconsejar to advise
acostarse to go to bed
acuario aquarium
acuerdo, de agree; OK
adaptador eléctrico electrical adapter
adelante forward (direction, position)
además besides
adentro inside
adiós goodbye
aduana customs
adulto adult
aeropuerto airport
afeita shave
afeitadora electric shaver
afeitar to shave
África Africa
agencia de viajes travel agency
agosto August
agotado exhausted; sold out
agradecer to thank
agresivo agressive
agrio sour
agua water
agua con gas carbonated water
agua del grifo tap water
agua mineral mineral water
agua potable drinkable water

Spanish Dictionary Rules

Here are a few tips for using this dictionary:

- Remember that all Spanish nouns, even inanimate objects, have a grammatical **gender** (masculine or feminine). In general, words ending in *o* relate to males or masculine words, while those ending in *a* are for females or feminine words (though many exceptions exist). Because casual visitors aren't expected to get this perfect— and because it's often possible to guess correctly—I have not listed the gender for each noun.

- To make words **plural**, just add *s* (if it ends in a vowel) or *es* (if it ends in a consonant).

- **Nouns** that can describe either a man or a woman (such as professions) are listed in the dictionary like this: ***médico[a].*** A male doctor is ***un médico,*** while a female doctor is ***una médica.***

- **Adjectives** must match their nouns. For simplicity, I've listed all adjectives with the masculine ending, usually *o.* To change it to feminine, just swap the *o* for an *a.* (A handsome man is ***guapo,*** while an attractive woman is ***guapa.***) Adjectives ending in *e* don't change with the gender (a man or a woman can both be ***inteligente***). Adjectives should also match whether the noun is singular or plural: Smart women are ***mujeres inteligentes.***

- Verbs are listed in their infinitive form (ending in *ar, er,* or *ir*). This loosely translates to the English form "to ____" (for example, ***hablar*** is "to talk"). To use a verb correctly in a sentence, you'll have to conjugate it (for example, if ***hablar*** is "to talk," then ***hablo*** means "I talk"). For examples of conjugated verbs, see page 410.

- Most food terms are not included in the Dictionary but rather in my Menu Decoder, starting on page 163.

agua no potable undrinkable water

agua sin gas non-carbonated water

aguja needle

agujero hole

ahora now

ahorrar to save (money)

aire air

aire acondicionado air-conditioning

al natural plain (food)

ala wing

albergue hostel

albergue de juventud youth hostel

albornoz bathrobe

alcazaba Moorish castle

alcázar Moorish fortress / palace

alcohol alcohol

aldea tiny village

alegría happiness

alemán German

Alemania Germany

alergias allergies

alérgico allergic

alfiler pin

alfombra carpet; rug

algo something; anything

algodón cotton

alguien / alguna persona someone; anyone

algún lugar, en somewhere

alguno some; any

alicates pliers

aliento breath

alimentación nourishment

alimento food; nutrition

allá (allí) there

allá, más farther

almohada pillow

almorzar to eat lunch

almuerzo lunch

alrededor de around

alquilar to rent

altar altar

alto tall; high

amable friendly; kind; helpful

amanecer sunrise

amante lover

amar to love

amargo bitter

amarillo yellow

ambiente ambience; scene; setting

ambos both

ambulancia ambulance

amigable friendly

amigo[a] friend

amistad friendship

ampolla blister

amor love

analgésico painkiller

anaranjado orange (color)

ancho wide; loose-fitting

andar to walk

andén platform (train)

anillo ring

animal animal

animal doméstico pet

aniversario anniversary

anual annual; yearly

año year

Año Nuevo, día de New Year's Day

antepasado[a] ancestor

antes beforehand; before

antes de before (an event, an activity)

antiácido antacid

antibiótico antibiotic

anticonceptivo contraceptive

anticuarios antiques shop

antigüedades antiques

antiguo ancient

antipático mean (not nice)

antitranspirante antiperspirant

anunciar to announce

anuncio announcement; sign (placard)

anuncios news

apagar to turn off (lights, devices)

aparato machine

aparcamiento parking lot

aparcar to park

apartamento apartment

aparte separate (another)

apellido last name

apenas barely; hardly

apestar to stink

apestoso stinky

apodo nickname

aprender to learn

apurarse to hurry

apretado tight

aproximadamente approximately

apuntar to point; to take notes

apuntes notes

aquí (acá) here

araña spider

árbol tree

arco iris rainbow

ardor de estómago heartburn

área para jugar playground

armario closet

arquitecto[a] architect

arquitectura architecture

arreglar to repair; to fix

arriba up

arriba, de upstairs

arroba "at" sign (@)

arroyo stream

arroz rice

arte art

artesanía crafts

artificial artificial

artista artist

artístico artistic

artritis arthritis

asado roasted; cooked

ascensor elevator

asegurado insured

aseo toilet

asequible affordable

asiento seat

asistir (a) to attend (an event)

asistencia attendance

asma asthma

aspirina aspirin

asqueroso inedible

astilla splinter (sliver)

atar to tie

atascado stuck

atención attention

atención, prestar to pay attention
atender (a) to assist; to attend (to)
aterrizaje landing (airplane)
aterrizar to land
atleta athlete
atractivo attractive
atrás back (position)
atrás, hacia backwards
atravesar to go through
atún tuna
audioguía audioguide
auriculares earbuds; headphones
ausencia absence
ausente absent
auténtico authentic; genuine
autobús city bus
autocar long-distance bus
automático automatic
autopista expressway
autor[a] author
autoridad authority
autorizado authorized
autorizar to authorize
autorretrato self-portrait
autoservicio self-service
auto-stop, hacer to hitchhike
autovía expressway
AVE high-speed train
ave poultry
avenida avenue
aventurero adventurous
averiado breakdown; out of service
avión plane

ayer yesterday
ayuda help
ayudar to help
ayunar to fast
ayuntamiento town hall
azúcar sugar
azul blue
azulejo Moorish blue tile

B

babero bib
bailar to dance
baile dance
baile folclórico folk dancing
bajar to lower; to go down
bajar de peso to lose weight
bajo low; short (height); bass (instrument, music)
balcón balcony
balneario spa
baloncesto basketball
bañador swim trunks
bañarse to bathe
banco bank
bandera flag
bañera bathtub
baño bathroom; bath
bar bar; pub
bar deportivo sports bar
barato cheap
barba beard
barbería barber shop
barbero barber
barca de pedales paddleboat
barco boat; ship
barco de remo rowboat
barco de vela sailboat

barra de labios lipstick
base para la cara foundation (makeup)
¡Basta! Enough!
bastante enough; sufficient
bastardo bastard
bastoncillos cotton swabs (Q-tips)
basura trash
basurero trash can
batería battery; drums
bebé baby
beber to drink
bebida beverage; drink
béisbol baseball
Bélgica Belgium
besar to kiss
beso kiss
biberón baby bottle
Biblia Bible
biblioteca library
bicho bug (insect)
bicicleta bicycle
bicicleta de montaña mountain bike
bicicleta, montar en to ride a bike
bien well (well-being, manner)
bienestar well-being
bienvenido welcome
bigote moustache
bilingüe bilingual
billete ticket; bill (money)
blanco white
bloqueado locked (mobile phone)
blusa blouse
boca mouth

bocadillo sandwich (on baguette)
bocado bite (of food)
boda wedding
bodega cellar
bol bowl
bolígrafo pen
bollería pastries
bollo pastry
bolsa bag; purse
bolsa de cremallera zip-lock bag
bolsa de plástica plastic bag
bolsillo pocket
bomba de aire pump
bomberos fire department
bombilla lightbulb
bonito pretty; beautiful
borracho drunk
borrador eraser; rough draft
borrar to erase; to delete
bosque forest
botas boots
bote can
botella bottle
botón button
bragas panties
brazalete bracelet
brazo arm
breve brief; concise
brevemente briefly
brillante bright
broche brooch
broma joke
bromear to joke
bronce bronze
bronceado suntan
bronceador tanning lotion; bronzer (makeup)

B

broncearse to suntan
bronquitis bronchitis
bueno good
buenos días good day; hello
bufanda scarf
bujías sparkplugs
bulevar boulevard
buscar to look for; to search for
búsqueda search
buzón mailbox
buzón de voz voicemail

C

caballero gentleman, knight
caballo horse
caballo, montar a to ride a horse
cabello hair
cabeza head
cabeza, dolor de headache
cabina telefónica phone booth
cable cable
cable Ethernet Ethernet cable
cable USB USB cable
caca poop
cacao de labios lip balm
cada each; every
cadena chain; link
caderas hips
caducidad expiration (food)
caducir to expire (food)
caer to fall
café coffee
café de Internet Internet café
cafetería coffee shop
caja box
cajera cashier

cajero automático cash machine; ATM
calabozo dungeon
calambres cramps
calcetines socks
cálculo renal kidney stone
calendario calendar
calentar to heat
calidad quality
caliente warm; hot
calle street
callejón lane
calma calm
calmar to calm
calor heat
calor, tener to be hot
calores hot flashes
caloría calorie
calvo bald
calzoncillo slip
calzoncillos underpants
cama bed
cama de matrimonio double bed
cama individual single bed
cámara camera
cámara de vídeo video camera
cámara digital digital camera
camarera waitress
camarero waiter
camas vacancy
camas, dos twin beds
cambiar to change; to exchange; to transfer
cambio change; exchange; transfer
caminar to walk; to hike
caminata walk; hike

caminata, dar una to take a hike
camino way; street
camión truck
camisa shirt
camiseta t-shirt
camisón nightgown
campana bell
campeón champion
campeonato championship
camping camping; campsite
campo countryside; field
Canadá Canada
canal channel; canal
canasta basket
cancelar to cancel
canción song
candela candle
canoa canoe
cansado tired
cantante singer
cantar to sing
cantidad quantity; amount
cantina bar (pub)
capilla chapel
capitán captain
cara face
caramelo candy
caramelo para la tos cough drop
caramelo refrescante breath mint
caravana camper (R.V.)
cargador charger
cargador de pilas battery charger
cargar to charge
cariñoso affectionate
carne meat

carné membership card
carné de alberguista membership card (hostel)
carne de vaca beef
carrecoche stroller
carretera road
carretera de peaje toll road
carro de equipaje luggage cart
carta letter; menu
carta postal postcard
cartel poster
cartera wallet
carterista pickpocket
casa house
casa, hecho en homemade
casado married
casarse (con) to get married (to)
cascada waterfall
casco helmet
casco antiguo old town
casero homemade
casilleros lockers
castillo castle
casualidad, por by accident; by chance
catedral cathedral
católico Catholic
catre cot
caza hunt
cazar to hunt
ceja eyebrow
celebración celebration
celebrar to celebrate
celebridad celebrity
celos jealousy
celos, tener to be jealous
celoso jealous

cena dinner
cenar to eat dinner
cenicero ashtray
centro center; middle; downtown
centro comercial shopping mall
cepillarse to brush
cepillo brush; hairbrush
cepillo de dientes toothbrush
cerámica ceramic
cerca near
cerebro brain
cerdo pig; pork
cerillas matches
cero zero
cerrado closed
cerradura lock
cerrar to lock; to close
cerveza beer
chaleco vest
champú shampoo
chance chance
chanquetas flip-flops
chaqueta jacket
charcutería delicatessen
cheque check
cheque de viajero traveler's check
chica girl
chicle gum
chico boy; guy
chinches bedbugs
China China
chino Chinese
chip chip (cell phone)
chiste joke
chistes, hacer to make jokes
chistoso funny (amusing)

chocolate chocolate
chorizo sausage (slightly spicy)
chupete pacifier
churrigueresco Spanish Baroque
cielo sky; heaven
cien hundred
ciencia science
científico[a] scientist; scientific
cigarrillo cigarette
cinco five
cine cinema
cinta adhesiva tape
cintura waist
cinturón belt
circo circus
círculo circle
cirugía surgery
cita appointment
ciudad city
ciudadano[a] citizen
claro clear
clase class; kind (type)
clase primera first class
clase segunda second class
clásico classical
claustro cloister
clave clue; key
clave, número PIN code
clima climate
clínica medical clinic
clip paper clip
club club
club nocturno nightclub
cobre copper
coche car; train car
coche cama sleeper (train)
coche comedor dining car (train)

cocido cooked; boiled; baked; roasted

cocina kitchen; kitchenette

cocinar to cook

código PIN PIN code

código postal zip code

codo elbow

coger to take; to catch; to pick up (get)

coincidencia coincidence

colegio high school

colgar to hang; to hang up (phone)

colina hill

colirio eye drops (for inflammation)

collar necklace

colocado stoned

color color

color de pelo hair color

colorar to color

colorete blush (makeup)

coma comma; coma

comedia comedy

comenzar to begin; to start

comer to eat

comezón itch

cómico comical; funny

comida food; meal; lunch

comida rápida fast food

comienzo start; beginning

comienzo, al at the start; at/in the beginning

como like; as

¿Cómo? How?

como quiera whatever (expression)

cómodo cozy; comfortable

compañero companion; partner

compañía company

compartir to share; to split

competición competition

competir to compete

complacer to please

completo complete; no vacancy

complicado complicated

comportamiento behavior

comprar to buy

compras shopping

compras, ir de to go shopping

comprender to understand

comprensión comprehension

compresas sanitary pads

comprometido engaged

compromiso commitment; engagement

computadora computer

común common

comunidad community

con with

concha shell

concierto concert

concurso contest

conducir to drive

conductor driver; conductor

conectar to connect

conejo rabbit

consejo advice

conexión connection; transfer (tranportation)

conexión, hacer to transfer (transportation)

confianza confidence

confianza, tener to be confident

C

confiar (en) to confide (in); to trust (in)
confirmación de reserva reservation confirmation
confirmar to confirm
congestión congestion (sinus)
conocer to know; to be familiar with (a place)
conocer a to be familiar with (a person)
conocido known
conocido, bien well-known
conociminento knowledge
conservador[a] conservative
conservante preservative
construcción construction
construir to build
contador[a] accountant
contagioso contagious
contento happy
contestar to answer
convertidor converter (voltage)
continuar to continue
copa cup; drink (alcohol)
copia copy
copiar y pegar to copy and paste
coqueta flirt (f)
coquetear to flirt
Corán Koran
corazón heart
corbata tie (clothing)
corcho cork
cordero lamb
cordón string
cordón para ropa clothesline
cordones shoelaces
coro choir

corrección correction
correcto right (correct)
corregir to correct
correo mail
correo electrónico email
correr to run
corrida de toros bullfight
corrupción corruption
cortauñas nail clipper
corte de pelo haircut
cortina curtain
corto short (length)
cosa thing
cosa, alguna something
costa coast
costar to cost
costumbre custom; tradition
crédito credit
crédito, tarjeta de credit card
creencia belief
creer (en) to believe (in)
crema cream
crema bronceadora suntan lotion
crema de manos hand lotion
crema de primera ayuda first-aid cream
crema de sol sunscreen
cremallera zipper
cripta crypt
cristiano[a] Christian
crucero cruise; cruise ship
crudo raw; undercooked
cruz cross
cuaderno notebook
cuadro square (shape); painting; frame

¿Cuál[es]? Which?; Which one[s]?

cualquier cosa anything; whatever

cualquier parte, en anywhere

cualquiera whichever; either

cuando when (conjunction)

¿Cuándo? When?

cuando sea anytime; whenever

¿Cuánto[a]? How much?

¿Cuántos[as]? Hom many?

cuarta parte quarter (¼)

cuarto room (building); quarter (¼)

cuatribanda quad-band

cuatro four

cubierta cover (protection)

cubista Cubist

cubrir to cover

cucaracha cockroach

cuchara spoon

cuchilla de afeitar razor (disposable)

cuchillo knife

cuello neck

cuenta bill (payment)

cuerda rope

cuero leather

cuerpo body

cuesta abajo downhill

cuesta arriba uphill

cueva cave

cuidado caution

cuidado, tener to be careful

cuidadoso careful; cautious

culpa guilt

culpable guilty

cumpleaños birthday

cuna crib

cuñada sister-in-law

cuñado brother-in-law

cuota fee

cúpula dome

cuyo whose

D

dama lady; woman

dando de mamar breastfeeding

dar to give

dar a luz to give birth

dar de comer to feed

dar de mamar to breastfeed

dar un paseo to stroll; to go on an outing

dar una caminata to hike

darse cuenta de to realize

darse la mano to shake hands

dársena platform; stall (at bus station)

de of; from; about

de acuerdo agree

de arriba upstairs

de ida one way (ticket)

de ida y vuelta round trip

¿De quién? Whose?

de repente suddenly

debajo de under

débil weak

débito, tarjeta de debit card

decir to say; to tell

declarar to declare (customs)

dejar to leave behind; to let

dejar caer to drop

dedo finger

D

dedo del pie toe
delgado slender
delicado delicate
delicioso delicious
demasiado too (adv); too much
demasiados too many
democracia democracy
dentición teething (baby)
dentista dentist
dentro de inside of
departamento department;
  apartment
deporte sport
depósito deposit
depósito de gasolina gas tank
derecha right (direction)
derecho straight (ahead)
desafortunadamente
  unfortunately
desafortunado unfortunate
desastre disaster
desayunar to eat breakfast
desayuno breakfast
desbloqueado unlocked (phone)
desbloquear to unlock (phone)
descafeinado decaffeinated
descansar to rest
descanso rest (break)
descolgar to pick up (phone)
descongestionante decongestant
desconocido[a] stranger
  (person); unknown
descuento discount
desde since
desear to desire; to wish
deseo desire; wish
desesperado desperate

desierto desert
desinfectante disinfectant
desinfectante de manos hand
  sanitizer
desnudo naked; nude
desodorante deodorant
desorden disorder
despacio slow
despegar to take off (airplane)
despertador alarm clock
despertarse to wake up
después afterwards
después de after (an event, an
  action)
destino destination
destornillador screwdriver
desvío detour
detergente laundry detergent
detrás de behind
devolución return; refund
devolver to return (something)
día day
diablo devil
diabético diabetic
diamante diamond
diapositiva slide (photo;
  PowerPoint)
diariamente daily
diario newspaper; daily
diarrea diarrhea
diccionario dictionary
diciembre December
diferente different
diente tooth
dieta diet
dieta, estar a to be on a diet
diez ten

difícil difficult; hard
dificultad trouble
dinero money
dios god
diosa goodness
dirección address; direction
dirección de email (correo electrónico) email address
dirección única one way (street)
directo direct
director manager; director; principal
dirigir to direct; to guide; to lead
disco disc
disco compacto CD (compact disc)
disco duro hard drive
discoteca discotheque; nightclub
discriminación discrimination
discriminar to discriminate
disculpa apology
disculpar to forgive; to excuse
disculpe excuse me
discurso presentation (talk)
discusión discussion
discutir to discuss
disfrutar to enjoy
disponible available; free
distancia distance
distante distant
distinto distinct; different
diversión fun (n)
divertido fun (adj); entertaining
divertirse to have fun
divorciado divorced
doble double
docena dozen

doctor[a] doctor (title)
doler to hurt; to ache
dolor pain; ache
dolor de cabeza headache
dolor de estómago stomachache
dolor de garganta sore throat
dolor de la menstruación menstrual cramp
dolor de muelas toothache
dolor de oído earache
dolor de pecho chest pain
dolorido sore
doméstico domestic
domicilio address
domingo Sunday
donde where (conjunction)
¿Dónde? Where?
donde sea wherever
dormido asleep; numb
dormir to sleep
dormirse to fall asleep
dormitorio dormitory; bedroom
dos camas twin beds
dos two
dos, los both
drama drama
dramático dramatic
droga drug (illegal)
ducha shower
ducharse to take a shower
duda doubt
dudar to doubt
dueño[a] owner
dulce sweet; candy
durar to last
duro hard; strong

E

DICTIONARY

Spanish / English

echar de menos to miss (someone)
economía economy
económico economical
edad age
edificio building
educación education
educar to educate
efectivo effective; cash
efectivo, en in cash
ejemplo example
ejemplo, por for example
ejercicio exercise
ejercicio, hacer to exercise
ejército military
el the (m, singular)
él he
ella she
ellas they (f)
ellos they (m)
embajada embassy
embarazada pregnant
embarazo pregnancy
embarazoso embarrassing
embarcarse to board
embargo, sin however; nevertheless
embarque boarding (transportation)
emborracharse to get drunk
emergencia emergency
emocionado excited
empezar to start
empleado[a] employee; employed
empleador[a] employer

emplear to employ
empleo employment; job
empleo modo de instructions for use
empleo sin unemployed
empujar to push
en in; on; at; into
en todas partes everywhere
en vez de instead of
encajar en to fit (in, into)
encaje lace
encantar to love; to delight
encendedor lighter (n)
encender to light; to turn on (lights, devices); to light up (smoking)
enchufar to plug in (outlet)
enchufe electrical outlet; plug
encierro bull run
encima de above; over
encoger to shrink
encontrar to find; to encounter; to meet
enemigo[a] enemy
enero January
enfadado mad; angry
enfermedad disease; illness
enfermero[a] nurse
enfermo sick
enfrente de in front of
enjuague bucal mouthwash; fluoride rinse
enlace connection (train); link (Internet)
enojado mad; angry
enrojecer to blush (to turn red)
ensalada salad

enseñar to teach; to show
ensuciar to dirty; to stain
entender to understand
entonces then; so
entrada entrance; cover charge
entrada al metro subway entrance
entrante appetizer; hors d'œuvre
entrar to enter
entre between
entremés appetizer; hors d'œuvre
entrenar to train; to practice
entrepierna crotch
entretenamiento entertainment
entretener to entertain
entretenido entertaining
envenenamiento de comida food poisoning
enviar to send
envolver to wrap
envuelto wrapped
epilepsia epilepsy
época era; time (period)
equipaje baggage
equipaje de mano carry-on luggage
equipo team
error mistake
erupción rash
es is
escalera de mano ladder
escaleras stairs
escalofríos chills
escandaloso scandalous
Escandinavia Scandinavia

escaparse to escape
escena scene
esconder to hide
escondido hidden
escozor del pañal diaper rash
escribir to write
escribir a máquina to type
escritor[a] writer
escritorio desk
escuchar to listen
escuela school
escuela primaria primary / elementary school
escuela secundaria secondary school
escultor[a] sculptor
escultura sculpture
esmalte de uñas nail polish
eso that (thing)
espalda back (anatomy)
España Spain
español Spanish
especia spice (seasoning)
especial special
especial del día special of the day (food)
especialidad specialty
especialmente especially
espectáculo show; spectacle
espejo mirror
esperanza hope
esperar to hope; to wait
esposo[a] spouse
espuma de afeitar shaving cream
esquí skiing
esquí acuático waterskiing

esquiar to ski
esquina corner (street)
esta noche tonight
estacas de tienda tent pegs
estación station; season
estación de autobuses bus station
estación de metro subway station
estación de tren train station
estado state
Estados Unidos (EEUU) United States (US)
estampilla stamp
estar to be; to feel
este east
estilo style
estirarse to stretch
esto this
estómago stomach
estómago, dolor de stomachache
estornudar to sneeze
estornudo sneeze
estrecho narrow
estrella star (in sky)
estreñimiento constipation
estudiante student
estúpido stupid; idiot
ETS (enfermedad de transmisión sexual) STD (sexually transmitted disease)
Europa Europe
europeo European
exactamente exactly
exacto exact; exactly
examen exam; test

examinar to examine; to test
excelente excellent
excepción exception
excepto except
experto[a] expert
expiración expiration
expirar to expire
explicación explanation
explicar to explain
exposición exhibition
exprés express; fast
expresar to express
expresión expression
extranjero[a] foreigner; foreign
extranjero, al abroad (travel)
extraño[a] stranger (n); strange
extensión extension

F

fábrica factory
fachada facade
fácil easy
fácilmente easily
factura formal written receipt
facturación, hora de check-in time
facturar el equipaje baggage check; to check in baggage
falda skirt
falso false
faltar to miss or lack something
familia family
familiar familiar; familial
famoso famous
fantasía fantasy
fantástico fantastic
farmacia pharmacy

faro lighthouse; headlight
favor favor
favor, por please
favorito favorite
febrero February
fecha date
felicidad happiness
felicidades congratulations
felicitaciones greetings
feliz happy
femenino feminine; female
feo ugly
ferretería hardware store
ferrocarril railway
festival festival
festivo holiday
ficha token; chip (cell phone)
fichero file (computer)
fiebre fever
fiebre del heno hay fever
fiesta party
fiesta, hacer to party
fila line (queue)
fin end
fin de semana weekend
fin, por finally
final final; ending
fino fine (thin; refined)
fiordo fjord
firma signature
firmar to sign (name)
flash flash (camera)
flequillo bangs (hair)
flor flower
florero vase
floristería flower market
fonda inn

fondo bottom; back; background
fondo, sin bottomless
footing jogging
forma form (shape, type)
formal formal
formar to form
foso moat
foto photo; picture
foto, sacar / hacer un to take
    a photo
fotocopia photocopy
fotocopias photocopy shop
fotografía photograph;
    photography
fotógrafo[a] photographer
frágil fragile
francés French
Francia France
frecuencia frequency
frecuencia, con frequently
frecuentemente frequently
frecuente frequent
frenos brakes
frente front; forehead
fresco fresh; cool (temperature)
frío cold
frío, tener to be cold
frito fried
frontera border
frustrado frustrated
frustrar to frustrate
fruta fruit
frutos secos nuts
fuego fire
fuego artificiales fireworks
fuente fountain
fuerte strong

fumador smoker
fumar to smoke; smoking
funda de gafas (eye)glasses case
furgoneta van
fusibles fuses
fútbol soccer
fútbol americano American football
futuro future

G

gafas glasses (eye)
gafas de sol sunglasses
gafas para leer reading glasses
galería gallery
galería de arte art gallery
ganador[a] winner
ganar to earn; to win
ganas de, tener to feel like doing something
ganga deal; bargain (n)
garaje garage
garantía guarantee
garganta throat
garganta, dolor de sore throat
garrafa carafe
garrapata tick (insect)
gas gas (vapor)
gasa gauze
gaseoso fizzy
gases gas (stomach)
gasóleo diesel
gasolina gasoline
gasolina sin plomo unleaded gasoline
gasolinera gas station
gastar to spend; to waste

gato cat
gay gay (homosexual)
gel hair gel
gemelos twins
genial great; cool
genio genius
generoso generous
gente people
gerente[a] manager
gimnasia gymnastics
gimnasio fitness club
ginecólogo[a] gynecologist
glorieta roundabout
gobierno government
gordo fat
gorro cap
gótico Gothic
gracia grace
gracias thank you
gracioso gracious
gramática grammar
Gran Bretaña Great Britain
gran great; grand
grande big
gran almacén department store
granja farm
granjero[a] farmer
grapa staple (for papers)
grapadora stapler
grasa fat; grease
grasoso greasy
gratis free
Grecia Greece
griego Greek
grifo faucet
gripe flu
gris gray

grúa tow truck
grueso thick
grupo group
grupo de música band
guantes gloves
guapo handsome; good-looking
guardar to keep; to save
 (computer)
¡Guau! Wow!
guerra war
guía guide; guidebook
guia del ocio event guide
guitarra guitar
gustar to like; to be pleasing

H

habitación room
habitaciónes rooms (vacancy
 sign)
hábito habit
hablar to talk; to speak
hacer to make; to do
hachís hash (drug)
hambre hunger
hambre, tener to be hungry
harina flour
hasta until
hecho a mano handmade
hecho en casa homemade
helado ice cream
Hemoal Preparation H
hemorroides hemorrhoids
herida injury; wound
herido injured
herir to injure
hermana sister; sibling
hermano brother; sibling

hermoso handsome; beautiful
hervido boiled
hervir to boil
hidratante moisturizer
hidroplano hydrofoil
hielo ice
hierba grass; herb
hija daughter
hijo son
hilo thread
hincha fan (enthusiast)
hinchar to swell
hinchazón swelling
hipermétrope farsightedness
 (vision)
historia history; story
hola hello; hi
Holanda Netherlands
holgado loose-fitting
hombre man; male (n)
hombros shoulder
honesto honest
hongos en los pies athlete's foot
hora hour; time (specific)
hora de cierre curfew (hotel,
 hostel); closing time
hora de facturación check-in
 time
hora de llegada arrival time
hora de salida departure time;
 check-out time
horario timetable; schedule
horas de apertura opening
 hours
horneado baked
hornear to bake
horno oven

hostaría inn
hoy today
hoy en día nowadays
huelga strike
huevo egg
húmedo muggy; humid
humilde humble
humano human
humano, ser human being
humo smoke

I

ibuprofeno ibuprofen
ida y vuelta, de round trip
ida, de one way (ticket)
idea idea
idea, ni no idea
iglesia church
ilegal illegal
ilógico illogical
iluminar to illuminate; to light up
imperdible safety pin
imperfecto imperfect; flawed
impermeable raincoat
importado imported
importante important
imposible impossible
impresionista Impressionist
impreso form (document)
imprimir to print
impuesto tax
incluido included
incluir to include
inconsciente unconscious
incorrecto incorrect
increíble incredible
independiente independent

indigestión indigestion
industria industry
infanta infant; princess
infante infant; prince
infección infection
infección urinaria urinary tract
  infection
infierno hell
inflamación inflammation
información information
información telefónica directory
  assistance
informar to inform
ingeniero[a] engineer
ingeniería engineering
ingnorante ignorant
ignorar to ignore
igual equal; same
igualmente equally
Inglaterra England
inglés English
injusticia injustice
inmediatamente immediately
inmediato immediate
inmigración immigration
inmigrante immigrant
inocente innocent
insecto insect
insolación sunstroke
inspección inspection
instante instant
instrucciones instructions
  (directions)
insultar to insult
insulto insult
inteligente intelligent
intención intention

intentar to try; to intend
interesante interesting
interior inside
intermitente turn signal
intersección intersection
intestinos intestines
inútil useless
investigación investigation; research
investigar to investigate; to research
invierno winter
invitación invitation
invitado[a] guest
invitar to invite; to treat (to pay for)
ir to go
irse to leave
Irlanda Ireland
isla island
islámico Islamic
islamista Islamist
Italia Italy
italiano Italian
IVA (impuesto al valor agregado) VAT (Value-Added Tax)
izquierda left (direction)

J

jabón soap
¡Jaja! Haha!
jamás never; ever
jamón ham
jaqueca migraine
jardín garden
jardín infantil kindergarten

jardinería gardening
jefe[a] boss
joven young; teenager
jóvenes youths
joya jewel; jewelry
joyería jewelry; jewelry shop
jubilado[a] senior citizen
judío[a] Jewish
juego game
jueves Thursday
jugar to play (sports, games)
juguete toy
juguetería toy store
juicio judgment
julio July
junio June
juntos together
justicia justice
justo fair; just
juventud youth (era)
juzgar to judge

K

kiosco newsstand
kilo kilogram (about 2 pounds)
kilometraje mileage (in kilometers)
kilómetro kilometer (about .6 miles)

L

la the (f, singular); it
labio lip
laca hairspray
lactosa lactose
lado side
lado de, al next to; beside

ladrón thief
lago lake
lágrima tear (crying)
lágrimas artificiales eye drops
lámpara lamp
lana wool
lápiz pencil
lápiz de ojos eyeliner
largo long
las the (f, plural)
lástima pity
latón brass
lavabo sink
lavadora washer
lavandería launderette (full service)
lavandería de autoservicio launderette (self-service)
lavar to wash
lavar a mano to handwash
laxativo laxative
leche milk; baby formula
leer to read
leer, gafas para reading glasses
lejos far
lejos, más farther
lejos de far from
lengua tongue; language
lenguaje language
lentillas contact lenses
lentamente slowly
lento slow
lesbiana lesbian
letrero sign (placard)
levantar to lift; to raise
levantarse to get up; to rise
liberación freedom

liberal liberal
liberar to liberate; to unlock (phone)
libre free (liberated); available; vacant
libre de impuestos duty free
librería book shop
libro book
líder leader
liderazgo leadership
ligero light (weight)
ligón flirt (m)
lima de uñas nail file
límite de velocidad speed limit
limón lemon
limonada lemonade
limpiadora de cara face cleanser
limpiaparabrisas windshield wipers
limpiar to clean
limpio clean
lindo pretty
línea line
linea aérea airline
lino linen
linterna flashlight
líquido liquid
líquido de insectos insect repellant
líquido de transmisión transmission fluid
lista list
listo ready; clever; smart
litera berth (train); bunk beds
litro liter
llama flame
llamada phone call

llamada gratuita toll-free call
llamada internacional
  international call
llamada nacional domestic call
llamar to call; to phone
llamarse to be called (thing); to
  call oneself (name)
llave key
llegadas arrivals
llegar to arrive
llegar a tiempo to arrive on time
llegar con retraso to arrive late
llegar temprano to arrive early
llenar to fill
lleno full
llevar to carry; to bring; to wear
llevar, para take-out (food)
llorar to cry
llover to rain
lluvia rain
lo it
lo siento sorry; excuse me
local local
loco crazy
locutorio cheap long-distance
  call shop
los the (m, plural)
lubricante personal personal
  lubricant
luces de atrás taillights
lucha fight
lucha libre wrestling
luchar to fight
lugar place; position
lujo luxury
lujoso luxurious
luna moon

luna de miel honeymoon
lunes Monday
luz light (illumination)
luz del sol sunshine

M

machine máquina
macho macho
madera wood
madre mother
maduro ripe
magnífico great
maja young woman
majo nice
maleducado rude
malentender to misunderstand
malentendido misunderstanding;
  misunderstood
maleta suitcase
maletas, hacer las to pack
  suitcase
mal bad; evil (n); badly
malo bad; evil (adj)
maltratado mistreated
maltratar to mistreat
mama breast
mamá mom
mandar to send; to mail
manejar to manage; to handle
mañana morning; tomorrow
mañana, pasado day after
  tomorrow
manch spot; stain
manchar to stain; to dirty
mandíbula jaw
mangas sleeves
manicura manicure

M

manifestación public demonstration
mano hand
mano, a by hand
mano, darse la to shake hands
mano, equipaje de carry-on luggage
mano, hecho a handmade
manta blanket
mantel tablecloth
mantener to maintain
mantequilla butter
manzana apple
mapa map
maquillaje makeup
maquillarse to put on makeup
mar sea
marcha gear
mareado dizzy; lightheaded
mareo al viajar motion sickness
marido husband
marihuana marjuana
mármol marble (material)
marrón brown
Marruecos Morocco
martes Tuesday
marzo March
más more
más, el / la most
más de more than (numbers)
más que more than
más... que more... than
más tarde later
masaje massage
mascota pet
masticar to chew
masculino male (adj); masculine

matar to kill
matrimonio marriage
máximo maximum
mayo May
me me (indirect / direct object)
mecánico[a] mechanic; mechanical
media ración half portion (food)
mediano medium
medianoche midnight
medias nylons (panty hose)
medicina medicine
medicina para el resfriado cold medicine
medicina para la diarrea diarrhea medicine
médico[a] doctor
medio half; medium
medio ambiente environment (nature)
mediodía noon
medios media
mejor better
mejor, lo / la the best
mejor que better than
memoria memory
memoria, tarjeta de memory card
menos less; minus; except
menos de less than (numbers)
menos que less than
menos... que less... than
mensaje de texto (SMS) text message
menstruación menstruation
menstruación, dolor de la menstrual cramps

mente mind (brain)
mentir to lie
mentira lie
menú menu
mercado market
mercado al aire libre open-air market
merced mercy
merienda afternoon snack
mes month
mesa table
meta goal
meter to pack
método method
método anticonceptivo birth control
metro subway; meter (about 1 yard)
mezclado mixed
mezclar to mix
mezquita mosque
mi my
mí me
miedo fear
miedo, tener to be afraid
miedoso afraid
miel honey
miércoles Wednesday
mil thousand
milla mile
millaje mileage (in miles)
mínimo minimum
ministro minister
ministro, primer prime minister
minusválido handicapped
minutos minutes
mío mine

miope nearsighted
mirador viewpoint
mirando browsing
mirar to watch; to look at
misa Mass
misa, servicio church service
mismo same
mitad half (1/2)
mixto mixed
mochila backpack
moda fashion
modo method; means
modos, de todos anyway(s)
modernista Art Nouveau
moderno modern
mojado wet
molestar to disturb; to bother
molino windmill
moluscos shellfish; mollusks
momento moment; time (period)
monarquía monarchy
monasterio monastery
moneda coin
monja nun
monje monk
mono cute
monopatín skateboard
montaña mountain
montar to mount; to ride
montar a caballo to ride a horse
montar en bicicleta to ride a bike
monumento monument
morado purple
morder to bite
moreno brunette
morir to die

moriscos Moors (baptized after Reconquest)
moro Moorish
moros Moors (general)
morriña homesickness
mosca fly (insect)
mostrar to show
moto motorcycle
motocicleta motor scooter
motor engine
moverse to move (motion)
moviemiento movement
móvil mobile phone
mozárabe Christian under Moorish rule (Mozarab)
muchacha girl
muchacho guy
mucho much; a lot
muchos many; a lot
mudéjar Gothic-Islamic (post-Reconquest Moorish)
muebles furniture
muelas, dolor de toothache
muerte death
muerto dead
mujer woman; wife; female
multa fine (penalty)
multitud crowd
mundo world
muñeca wrist; doll
músculo muscle
museo museum
música music
música en vivo live music
músico[a] musician
muslo thigh
musulmán[a] Muslim

muy very

N

nación nation
nacional national
nacionalidad nationality
nacido born
nacimiento birth
nada nothing
nadar to swim
nadie nobody; no one
nalgas buttocks
naranja orange (fruit)
narcótico narcotic; drug
nariz nose
naturaleza nature
naturalmente naturally
Navidad Christmas
necesario necessary
necesidad need (necessity)
necesitar to need
negocio business
negro black
nene[a] darling; honey
nervioso nervous
nevar to snow
ni... ni neither... nor
nieble fog
nieta granddaughter
nieto grandson
nietos grandchildren
nieve snow
nilón nylon (material)
niñera babysitter
ninguna parte nowhere
ninguno none; not one
niño[a] child

niños children
no no; not
noche night
noche, esta tonight
Nochebuena Christmas Eve
Nochevieja New Year's Eve
noches, buenas good evening; good night
Nolotil non-aspirin substitute
nombre name
nombre, segundo middle name
norma policy
norma de cancelación cancellation policy
normal normal; regular
norte north
nosotros[as] we; us
nota note (message)
noticias news
novia girlfrind; fiancée
noviembre November
novio boyfriend; fiancé
nuboso cloudy
nuestro[a] our
nueve nine
nuevo new
número number
número clave PIN code
número de móvil mobile-phone number
número de teléfono telephone number
nunca never

O

o or
obedecer to obey

obispo bishop
obra work (of art, theater)
obra de teatro play
obra maestra masterpiece
océano ocean
ocho eight
ocio entertainment
octubre October
ocupado occupied; busy
odiar to hate
odio hate; hatred
oeste west
oferta special offer
oferta, última final offer
oficial official
oficialmente officially
oficina office
oficina de objetos perdidos lost-and-found office
oficio occupation
ofrecer to offer
oído ear
oído, dolor de earache
oír to hear
ojo eye
ola wave (water)
oler to smell; to stink
Olimpiada Olympics
olla pot; kettle
olor smell; odor
olvidar to forget
ondulado wavy
operación operation
operar to operate
oprimir to press
oportunidad opportunity; chance
óptico optician

O

optimista optimistic
ordenador computer
órgano organ
oro gold
orzuelo sty (eyelid inflammation)
oscuro dark
otoño autumn; fall
otra vez again
otro other; another

P

padre father
padres parents
pagar to pay
página page
página web website
país country
paja drinking straw
pájaro bird
palabra word
palacio palace
palillo toothpick
pan bread
panadería bakery
pañal diaper
panorámica scenic
pantalla screen
pantalones pants
pantalones cortos shorts
pañuelos (de papel) facial tissue
papa potato
papá dad
Papa, El the Pope
Papá Noel Santa Claus
papel paper
papel, hoja de sheet of paper
papel higiénico toilet paper

papelería office supplies store
papilla de niños baby food
paquete package
par pair; couple
para for; in order to
para llevar take-out (food)
¿Para quién? For whom?
parada stop (in route)
parada de autobús bus stop
paraíso paradise
parador fancy historic hotel
paraguas umbrella
parar to stop
parches para ampollas moleskin (for blisters)
parecer to seem; to look like
parecido similar
pared wall
pared fortificada fortified wall
pareja couple; partner
parque park
parque de atracciones amusement park
parque para niños playpen
parquímetro parking meter
parte part (n)
parte nueva new town
partido game; match; political party
pasado past
pasado mañana day after tomorrow
pasaje passage
pasajero[a] passenger
pasaporte passport
pasatiempo hobby
Pascua Easter

pasear to stroll
paseo stroll; outing
paseo, dar un to go for a stroll or outing
pasillo aisle
paso step (footstep; dance move)
pasta de dientes toothpaste
pastel pastry; cake
pastelería pastry shop
patinar to skate
patinaje skating
patines Rollerblades
pato duck
pavo turkey (meat)
pavo real peacock
paz peace
peaje toll
peatón pedestrian
pecar to sin
pecado sin
pecho chest; breast
pecho, dolor de chest pain
pedazo piece
pedicura pedicure
pedir to order (food); to ask for
pedir prestado to borrow
pegar to paste
peinarse to comb
peine comb
pelea fight
pelea de gallos cockfight
pelearse con to fight with
película movie
peligro danger
peligroso dangerous
pelirrojo redheaded
pelo hair

pelota ball; creep
peltre pewter
peluquería hair salon
peluquero[a] hairstylist
pendientes earrings
pendrive flash drive
pene penis
pensamiento thought
pensar to think; to plan
pensión inexpensive hotel
peor worse
peor..., el/la the worst...
peor, lo/la the worst
peor que worse than
pequeño small; little
percha coat hanger
perdedor[a] loser
perder to lose
perdido lost; missing
perdón pardon; excuse me; forgiveness
perdonar to pardon; to excuse; to forgive
perfecto perfect
periódico newspaper
período period (of time)
permanente permanent
pero but
perra bitch
perro dog
persona person
pertenencias belongings
pesado heavy
pesar to weigh
pescado fish (food)
pescar to fish
pesimista pessimist; pessimistic

peso weight
peso, bajar de to lose weight
peso, subir de to gain weight
peso máximo weight limit
pestaña eyelash
pez fish (live)
picadura bug bite
picante spicy; hot
picnic, hacer to picnic
pie foot
piel skin
pierna leg
pijamas pajamas
píldora pill
píldora anticonceptiva birth control pill
pincho snack
pintar to paint
pintor[a] painter
pintura painting; paint
pinzas clothes pins; tweezers
piojos lice
piscina swimming pool
piso floor; apartment; flat
pista runway (airport)
pistola gun
plan plan
planear to plan
plano floor plan
planta plant; story (floor)
planta baja ground floor
plástico plastic
plata silver
plateresco Plateresque (frilly late Gothic)
plato plate; dish; serving
plato hondo bowl

plato principal main dish
plato, primer first course
plato, segundo second course; main dish
playa beach
playa nudista nude beach
plaza square (town); place, seat, spot (train, bus, restaurant)
plaza del toros bullring
plomo lead
plomo, sin unleaded
población population
pobre poor
pobrecito[a] poor thing
poco few; little
poco, un a little; a little bit
poder can (to be able to)
poderoso powerful
podrido rotten
policía police; police officer
poliester polyester
político politician; political
póliza policy
pollo chicken
polución pollution
polvos powder; dust
polvos de talco talcum powder
polvos para la cara face powder
pomada de pañal diaper ointment
poner to put; to place; to set
ponerse a régimen to be on a diet
poquito very little
poquito, un a very little bit
por for; by; by means of; through; along; per

por ciento percent
por favor please
¿Por qué? Why?
porcelana porcelain
porcentaje percentage
porción portion; ration; serving
porque because
porro joint (marijuana)
portarse to behave (properly)
portátil laptop
posada inn
poseer to own
posible possible
posiblemente likely
postre dessert
práctica practice
practicar to practice
práctico practical
precedente precedent; preceding
precio price
precioso charming; lovely; cute
prefijo area code; prefix
preferencia preference
preferido preferred; favorite
preferir to prefer
pregunta question
preguntar to ask a question
prendas garments
prescripción prescription
presentar to present
presente present (time, attendance)
preservativo condom
presidente[a] president
presión pressure (tension)
presión, cerveza a draught beer
prensa press (media)

preocupado worried
preocuparse to worry
prestar to lend
prestar atención to pay attention
primavera spring (season)
primera clase first class
primero first
primeros auxilios first aid
primo[a] cousin
princesa princess
principal main
príncipe prince
principio beginning; start; principle
principio, al at/in the beginning; at the start
privado private
probablemente probably
probar to try; to taste; to test
problema problem
problemas de corazón heart condition
producir to produce
producto product
productos lácteos dairy products
profesión profession
profesor[a] teacher
programa program
prohibido forbidden
prohibir to prohibit; to forbid
promesa promise
prometer to promise
prometido engaged (to be married)
pronto soon

P

pronunciación pronunciation
pronunciar to pronounce
propina tip
prosperar to prosper
prostituta prostitute
protección de sol sunscreen
proteger to protect
protestante Protestant
próximo next
proyecto project ; plan
prudente prudish
prueba quiz; test; try; taste
prueba de embarazo pregnancy test
publicidad publicity
público public; audience
pueblo town; village
pueblo serrano hill town
puente bridge
puenting bungee jumping
puerta door
puerto harbor; port
pues so; then; well
puesta de sol sunset
puesto job
pulga flea
pulgar thumb
pulmones lungs
pulmonía pneumonia
púlpito pulpit
pulsera bracelet
pulso pulse
punto dot (computer); point (decimal); period (punctuation)
puntual on time

Q

que that; which; who
¿Qué? What?; Which?
¡Qué asco! Yuck!; How disgusting!
queda, toque de curfew (general)
quedar to stay
quedarse to fit (clothes)
queja complaint
quejarse to complain; to whine
quejido whine; whining
quemadura burn; sunburn
quemarse to get burned; to sunburn
querer to want; to love
querer decir to mean
querido dear (affection, letter salutation)
quesería cheese shop
queso cheese
quien who (conjunction)
¿Quién? Who?
quienquiera whoever
quiosco newsstand
quitaesmaltes nail polish remover
quitamanchas stain remover
quizás maybe; perhaps

R

rabia rabies
rabo tail
ración ration; portion; serving
racional rational; logical
racismo racism
racista racist

radiador radiator
radicales radicals
rápidamente quickly
rápido fast; quick; express
rastro flea market
rayos x X-ray
razón reason; point
razón, tener to be right
realizar to achieve
rebajas sale
recado message
recambio refill; replacement
recargar to top up (mobile-
   phone time); to recharge
recepcionista receptionist
receta recipe
receta médica prescription
recibir to receive
recibo receipt
recién recently
reciente recent
reclamar el equipaje to claim
   baggage; baggage claim
recomendación recommendation
recomendar to recommend
recordar to remember; to recall;
   to remind
recorte trim (hair)
recto straight (ahead)
recuerdo memory; souvenir;
   reminder
red network
reembolsar to refund
reembolso refund
refrescante refreshing
refresco soft drink; refreshment
refugiado refugee

regalar to gift
regalo gift
régimen diet
régimen, ponerse a to be on
   a diet
regresar to return; to go back
regla rule (law); ruler (measure);
   period (menstruation)
reina queen
reinar to rule
reino kingdom
reír to laugh
reírse de to make fun of
relajación relaxation
relajarse to relax
reliquia relic
reloj clock; watch
renacimiento Renaissance
repasar to review; to inspect
repaso review
repente, de suddenly
repetir to repeat
reproductor de MP3 MP3 player
República Checa Czech Republic
requerir to require
requerido required
requisito requirement
resbaladizo slippery
reserva reservation
reservado reserved
reservar to reserve
resfriado cold (illness)
residencia real royal residence
resolver to solve; to resolve
respetar to respect
respeto respect
respirar to breathe

R

respiración breathing
responder to respond; to answer
respuesta answer
restaurante restaurant
resto rest (remainder)
retirado withdrawl
retirar to withdraw
retiro withdrawl
retrasar to delay
retraso delay
retraso, con delayed; late
  (transportation)
revés, al inside-out; upside-
  down; backwards; reverse side
revisar to review; to check
revisión inspection; review;
  correction
revista magazine
rey king
ría sea inlet; fjord
rico rich; tasty
rincón corner (walls)
río river
risa laugh; laughter
rizado curly
robado stolen
robar to rob; to steal
robo robbery; theft
robusto sturdy
roca rock; stone
rodaja slice
rodilla knee
rojo red
románico Romanesque
romántico Romantic (style);
  romantic (love)
romper to break

roncar to snore
ropa clothes; clothing
ropa delicada delicates
ropa interior underwear
rosa pink
roto broken
rubio blond
rueda tire; wheel
rueda pinchada flat tire
ruido noise
ruidoso loud
ruinas ruins
Rusia Russia
ruso Russian
ruta route

S

sábado Saturday
sábana sheet
saber to know
sabiduría wisdom
sabio wise
sabor flavor; taste
sabroso tasty
sacacorchos corkscrew
sacerdote priest
saco de dormir sleeping bag
sagrado sacred
sal salt
sala hall (big room); living room
sala de espera waiting room
salado salty
saldo calling time (mobile phone)
salida exit; departure
salida de emergencia
  emergency exit
salidas departures

salir to leave; to depart
saltar to jump
salud health
¡Salud! Cheers!; Bless you! (sneeze)
saludable healthy
salvaje wild
sandalias sandals
sangrando bleeding
sangre blood
sangriento bloody
sano healthy
santo[a] saint; holy
sarna scabies
sazonar to season; to flavor
secador de pelo hair dryer
secadora dryer (clothes)
secar to dry
seco dry
secretario[a] secretary
secreto secret
sed thirst
sed, tener to be thirsty
seda silk
seda dental dental floss
sediento thirsty
seguir to follow; to continue
segunda clase second class
segundo second (time, order)
segundo nombre middle name
segundo plato second course; main course (food)
seguro safe; secure; sure; insurance
seguro médico health insurance
seis six
sello stamp

semáforo stoplight
semana week
semanal weekly
semejante similar
semilla seed
seña sign (gesture)
seña, lengua de sign language
señal sign (street)
sencillo simple
senderismo hiking
sendo trail
sentarse to sit
sentido sense
sentido de humor sense of humor
sentimiento feeling
sentir to sense
sentirse to feel (emotion, illness)
Señor (Sr.) Mr.
señor sir
Señora (Sra.) Mrs.
señora lady
Señorita (Srta.) Miss
señorita young lady
septiembre September
ser to be (permanent state)
ser humano human being
serio serious
serio, en seriously
servicio service
servicio de canguro babysitting service
servicios toilets
servilleta napkin
sexo sex
shuttle shuttle bus
si if

sí yes
SIDA AIDS
siempre always
siesta siesta; nap
siete seven
siglo century
significar to mean
signo sign; symbol
siguiente next; following
silencio silence
silla chair; seat
silla de ruedas wheelchair
silla elevadora booster seat
sillita para el coche car seat (child)
simbólico symbolic
simbolizar to symbolize
símbolo symbol
similar similar
simpático nice
sin without
sinagoga synagogue
sinceramente sincerely
sincero sincere
sintético synthetic
sinusitis sinus problems
SMS text message
snowboard, hacer to go snowboarding
sobre on; about; envelope
sobrina niece
sobrino nephew
soja soy
sol sun
sol, tomar el to sunbathe
solamente only
soldado soldier

soleado sunny
solo alone
sólo only
soltero single
solucíon solution (contacts)
sombra shade; shadow
sombra de ojos eye shadow
sombrero hat
soñar to dream
soñoliento sleepy
sonreír to smile
sonrisa smile
sopa soup
sorprender to surprise
sorpresa surprise
sortija ring (jewelry)
soso bland
sótano basement
su his; her; your (formal); their
suave soft; smooth; cool (slang)
subir to go up; to get on
subir de peso to gain weight
subraya underscore (_); underline
subrayar to underscore; to underline
subtítulos subtitles
sucio dirty
sudado sweaty
sudor sweat
suelo ground (earth); floor
sueño dream
sueño, tener to be sleepy
suerte luck
suerte, tener to be lucky
suéter sweater
suficiente enough

sufrimiento suffering
sufrir to suffer
Suiza Switzerland
sujetador bra
supermercado grocery store; supermarket
suplemento supplement
suprimir to delete (computer); to erase
sur south
surfear to surf
surfista surfer
suyo his; hers; yours (formal); theirs

T

taberna bar; pub
tabla board
tabla de surf surfboard
tableta tablet computer
tal such
tal vez maybe; perhaps
Talgo type of high-speed train
talla size
también also; too
tampoco neither
tampón tampon
tan so (very)
tan... como as... as
tanto so much
tantos so many
tapa appetizer; bar snack; cover (lid)
tapatear to eat tapas
tapón stopper; sink plug; plug (general)
tapón de oidos earplugs

taquilla cashier (at sights)
tarde late; afternoon; evening
tarde, más later
tardes, buenas good afternoon; good evening
tarjeta card
tarjeta de crédito credit card
tarjeta de débito debit card
tarjeta de embarque boarding pass
tarjeta de memoria memory card
tarjeta de visita business card
tarjeta SIM SIM card
tarjeta telefónica telephone card
tasca bar; pub
tatuaje tattoo
taxímetro taxi meter
taza cup
te you (direct / indirect object)
té tea
teatro theater
teatro, obra de play (theater)
techo roof
teclado keyboard
tejido cloth
tele TV
telefonista operator
teléfono telephone
teléfono móvil mobile phone
televisión television
temer to fear
temperatura temperature
templado lukewarm
temporal temporary
temprano early

tenedor fork
tener to have
tenis tennis
tensión tension; pressure
tensión alta high blood pressure
tensión baja low blood pressure
terciopelo velvet
terminado finished; done; over
terminar to finish; to end
termómetro thermometer
temporada season (time period)
terraza terrace
terrorista terrorist
tesoro treasury
testículos testicles
ti you (prep. pronoun)
tía aunt
tibio lukewarm
tiempo time; weather
tiempo, a on time
tienda store; shop
tienda de campaña tent
tienda de dulces sweets shop
tienda de fotos camera shop
tienda de informática computer store
tienda de móviles mobile-phone (cell-phone) shop
tienda de ropa clothing boutique
tienda de vinos wine shop
tierno tender
tierra earth; land; soil
tijeras scissors
timbre stamp
tímido shy
timo turístico tourist trap
tío uncle; guy (slang)

tipo type; guy (slang)
tirador handle (n)
tirar to pull; to throw
tirita Band-Aid
toalla towel
toalla pequeña washcloth
toalletas húmedas (para bebés) baby wipes
toallitas para la cara facial tissue
tobillo ankle
tocar to touch; to feel; to play (music, instrument)
todavía still; yet
todo every (all); everything
todos everybody
tomar to take; to eat; to drink
tomar el sol to sunbathe
tonto silly; stupid
toque touch (physical contact)
toque de queda curfew
Torá Torah
tormenta storm
toro bull
toros, corrida de bullfight
toros, plaza del bullring
torre tower
torta cake; pie
tortilla omelette
tos cough
toser to cough
tostado toasted
tour guiado guided tour
trabajar to work
trabajo job; work
tradición tradition; custom
tradicional traditional

tradicionalmente traditionally
traducción translation
traducir to translate
traer to bring
tráfico traffic
tragar to swallow
tragedia tragedy
trago stiff drink
traje suit
traje de baño swim suit
tranquilo quiet; calm; tranquil
transbordador ferry
transbordo transfer (transportation)
transbordo, hacer un to transfer (transportation)
transferirse to stream (computer)
transportar to transport
transporte transportation
tratamiento treatment
tratar to treat (to behave)
través, a through
tren train
tren nocturno overnight train
tres three
triángulo triangle; tri-band
trigo wheat
trípode tripod
triste sad
tristeza sadness
trona high chair
tu your (informal)
tú you (informal)
tubo de respiración snorkel
túnel tunnel
turista tourist

Turquía Turkey
tuyo yours (informal)

U

últimamente lately
último last; final
uña fingernail
una vez once
Unión Europea (UE) European Union (EU)
universidad university
uno one
uretra urethra
urgencias emergency room
urgente urgent
usar to use
usted (Ud.) you (formal)
ustedes (Uds.) you (formal, plural)
usuario username
útero uterus
útil useful

V

vaca cow
vacaciones vacation
vacaciones, ir de to vacation
vacío empty
vagón train car
vale OK
valer to be worth
validar to validate
válido valid
valle valley
valor worth; value; courage
vaqueros jeans
vaselina Vaseline

vaso glass
váter toilet (fixture)
¡Vaya! Wow!; Well!
vegetariano vegetarian
vegija bladder
vela candle
velocidad speed
venda bandage
vendaje de apoyo support bandage
vender to sell
vendo for sale
venir to come
venta inn
venta, en on sale
ventana window
ventilador fan (machine)
ventilador, correa del fan belt
ventoso windy
ver to see
verano summer
verdad truth
verdadero true; real
verde green
verdura vegetable
vergüenza shame
vergüenza, tener to be ashamed (embarrassed)
verificar to check; to make sure
verruga wart
vértigo dizziness
vestido dress (clothing)
vez time (occurrence)
vez de, en instead of
vez, otra again
vez, una once

vía track (train)
viajar to travel
viaje trip; tour
viajero[a] traveler
vida life
vídeo video
videocámara video camera
videojuego video game
viejo old
viento wind
viernes Friday
vigilar to watch over; to look after
viñedo vineyard
vino wine
vino blanco white wine
vino tinto red wine
violación rape
violar to rape; to violate
violencia violence
visita visit
visitar to visit
vista view
vitamina vitamin
viuda widow
viudo widower
vivir to live
vivo alive
vivo, en live
volar to fly
volver to return; to go back
vomitar to vomit
vosotros[as] you (informal, plural)
voz voice
voz alta, en aloud; out loud

vuelo flight
vuelta, de ida y round trip
vuestro your; yours (informal, plural)

Y

y and
ya already
yo I
yodo iodine

yoga, hacer to do yoga
yogur yogurt

Z

zapatillas slippers
zapatillas de tenis tennis shoes
zapatos shoes
zona Wi-Fi Wi-Fi hotspot
zumo juice

ENGLISH / SPANISH

A

a lot mucho
aboard abordo
abortion aborto
about de; sobre
above encima
abroad al extranjero
absence ausencia
absent ausente
abstract abstracto
abuse (n) abuso
abuse (v) abusar
accept aceptar
access acceso
accessible accesible
accident accidente
accident, by por casualidad
accountant contador
ache (n) dolor
ache (v) doler
achieve realizar
adapter, electrical adaptador
  eléctrico
address dirección; domicilio
adult adulto
adventurous aventurero
advice consejo
advise aconsejar
affectionate cariñoso
affordable asequible
afraid miedoso
(to be) afraid tener miedo
Africa África
after después de
afternoon tarde

afterwards después
again otra vez
age edad
aggressive agresivo
agree de acuerdo
AIDS SIDA
air aire
air-conditioning aire
  acondicionado
airline línea aérea
airport aeropuerto
aisle pasillo
alarm clock despertador
alcohol alcohol
allergic alérgico
allergies alergias
allow permitir
allowed permitido
alone solo
along por
aloud en voz alta
already ya
altar altar
always siempre
ambience ambiente
ambulance ambulancia
America América; Estados
  Unidos
American americano;
  estadounidense
amount cantidad
ancestor antepasado[a]
ancient antiguo
and y
angel ángel

angry enfadado; enojado
animal animal
ankle tobillo
anniversary aniversario
announce anunciar
announcement anuncio
annual anual
another otro
answer (n) respuesta
answer (phone) (v) contestar
answer (question) (v) contestar;
  responder
antacid antiácido
antibiotic antibiótico
antiperspirant antitranspirante
antiques antigüedades
antiques shop tienda de
  antigüedades
any alguno
anybody alguien
anyone alguna persona
anything algo; cualquier cosa
anytime cuando sea
anyway de todos modos
anywhere en cualquier parte
apartment piso; departamento;
  apartamento
apology disculpa
appetizer tapa; aperitivo;
  entrante; entremés
appointment cita
approximately aproximadamente
April abril
aquarium acuario
architect arquitecto
architecture arquitectura
area code prefijo

arm brazo
around alrededor de
arrivals llegadas
arrive llegar
arrive early llegar temprano
arrive late llegar con retraso
arrive on time llegar a tiempo
art arte
art gallery galería de arte
Art Nouveau modernista
arthritis artritis
artificial artificial
artist artista
artistic artístico
as como
as... as tan... como
(to be) ashamed tener
  vergüenza
ashtray cenicero
ask preguntar
ask for pedir
asleep dormido
(to fall) asleep dormirse
aspirin aspirina
assist atender
asthma asma
at a; en
"at" sign (@) arroba
athlete atleta
athlete's foot hongos en los pies
attend (an event) asistir a
attend to atender a
attendance asistencia
attention atención
(to pay) attention prestar
  atención
ATM cajero automático

A

attractive atractivo
audience público
audioguide audioguía
August agosto
aunt tía
author autor[a]
authority autoridad
authorize autorizar
automatic automático
autumn otoño
available disponible; libre
avenue avenida

B

baby bebé; niño[a]
baby bottle biberón
baby food papilla de niños
baby formula leche
babysitter niñera
babysitting service servicio de
   canguro
back (anatomy) espalda
back (position) atrás
backpack mochila
backward hacia atrás
bad mal (n); malo (adj)
badly mal
bag bolsa
bag, plastic bolsa de plástica
bag, zip-lock bolsa de
   cremallera
baggage equipaje
baggage check facturar el
   equipaje
baggage claim reclamar el
   equipaje
bake hornear

baked horneado; cocido
bakery panadería
balcony balcón
bald calvo
ball pelota
band (musical) grupo de música
bandage venda
bandage, support vendaje de
   apoyo
Band-Aid tirita
bangs (hair) flequillo
bank banco
bar taberna; tasca; bar; cantina;
   pub
bar, sports bar deportivo
barber barbero
barber shop barbería
barely apenas
Baroque, Spanish
   churrigueresco
baseball béisbol
basement sótano
basket canasta
basketball baloncesto
bass (music) bajo
bastard bastardo
bath baño
bathe bañarse
bathrobe albornoz
bathroom baño
bathtub bañera
battery batería; pila
battery charger cargador de
   pilas
be (permanent state) ser
be (temporary state) estar
beach playa

beach, nude playa nudista
beard barba
beautiful bonito; hermoso
because porque
bed cama
bed, double cama de matrimonio
bed, single cama individual
(go to) bed acostarse
bedbugs chinches
bedroom habitación
beds, twin dos camas
bedsheet sábana
beef carne de vaca
beer cerveza
beer, draught cerveza a presión
before (an event, activity)
  antes de
before / beforehand antes
begin comenzar; empezar
beginning principio
(at / in the) beginning al
  principio
behave (properly) portarse
behavior comportamiento
behind detrás de
Belgium Bélgica
belief creencia
believe (in) creer (en)
bell campana
belongings pertenencias
below abajo
belt cinturón
berth (train) litera
beside al lado de
besides además
(the) best lo / la mejor
better mejor

better than mejor que
between entre
beverage bebida
bib babero
Bible Biblia
bicycle bicicleta
big grande
bilingual bilingüe
bill (money) billete
bill (payment) cuenta
bird pájaro
birth (n) nacimiento
(to give) birth dar a luz
birth control método
  anticonceptivo
birth control pill píldora
  anticonceptiva
birthday cumpleaños
bishop obispo
bitch perra
bite (of food) bocado
bite (v) morder
bitter amargo
black negro
bladder vegija
bland soso
blanket manta
bleeding sangrando
Bless you! (sneeze) ¡Salud!
blisters ampollas
block (street) manzana
blond rubio
blood sangre
blood pressure, low tensión baja
blood pressure, high tensión
  alta
bloody sangriento

blouse blusa
blue azul
blue tile (Moorish) azulejo
blush (makeup) colorete
blush (v) enrojecer
board (n) tabla
board (v) abordar; embarcarse
boarding (process) embarque
boarding pass tarjeta de
  embarque
boat barco
body cuerpo
boil hervir
boiled hervido; cocido
book libro
book shop librería
booster seat silla elevadora
boots botas
border frontera
bored / boring aburrido
born (v) nacer
borrow pedir prestado
boss jefe[a]
both ambos; los dos
bother molestar
bottle botella
bottom fondo
bottomless sin fondo
boulevard bulevar
boutique, clothing tienda de
  ropa
bowl bol; plato hondo
box caja
boy chico
boyfriend novio
bra sujetador
bracelet brazalete; pulsera

brain cerebro
brakes frenos
brass latón
bread pan
break (rest) descanso
break (v) romper
breakdown averiado
breakfast desayuno
(to eat) breakfast desayunar
breast pecho; mama
breastfeed dar de mamar
breastfeeding dando de mamar
breath aliento
breathing respiración
breathe respirar
breath mints caramelos
  refrescantes
bridge puente
brief breve
briefly brevemente
bright brillante
bring llevar; traer
Britain Gran Bretaña
broken roto
bronchitis bronquitis
bronze bronce
bronzer (makeup) bronceador
brooch broche
brother hermano
brother-in-law cuñado
brown marrón
browsing mirando
brunette moreno
brush (n) cepillo
brush (v) cepillarse
bug (insect) bicho
bug bites picaduras

build construir
building edificio
bulb, light bombilla
bull toro
bull run encierro
bullfight corrida de toros
bullring plaza del toros
bunk beds litera
burn (n) quemadura
(to get) burned quemarse
bus / city bus autobús
bus, long-distance autocar
bus station estación de autobuses
bus stop parada de autobús
business negocio
business card tarjeta de visita
busy ocupado
but pero
butter mantequilla
buttocks nalgas
button botón
buy comprar
by (train, car, etc.) en
by / by means of por

C

cable cable
cable, Ethernet cable Ethernet
cable, USB cable USB
cake pastel
calendar calendario
call (phone) llamada
call, domestic llamada nacional
call, international llamada internacional
call, toll-free llamada gratuita

call (v) llamar
(to be) called (thing) llamarse
calling time (mobile phone) saldo
calm (adj) tranquilo
calm (v) calmar
calorie caloría
camera cámara
camera, digital cámara digital
camera, video cámara de video
camera shop tienda de fotos
camper caravana
camping camping
campsite camping
can (n) bote
can (to be able to) poder
can opener abrelatas
Canada Canadá
Canadian canadiense
canal canal
cancel cancelar
cancellation policy norma de cancelación
candle candela; vela
candy caramelo; dulce
canoe canoa
cap gorro
captain capitán
car coche
car (train) vagón; coche
car, dining (train) coche comedor
car, sleeper (train) coche cama
car seat (child) sillita para el coche
carafe garrafa
card tarjeta

card, credit tarjeta de crédito
card, debit tarjeta de débito
card, hostel membership carné de albuerguista
card, membership carné
card, phone tarjeta telefónica
careful cuidadoso
(to be) careful tener cuidado
carpet alfombra
carry llevar
carry-on luggage equipaje de mano
cash efectivo
cash machine (ATM) cajero automático
cashier cajera
cashier (at sights) taquilla
castle castillo
castle (Moorish) alcazaba
cat gato
catch (v) coger
cathedral catedral
Catholic católico[a]
caution cuidado
cautious cuidadoso
(to be) cautious tener cuidado
cave cueva
CD CD; disco compacto
celebrate celebrar
celebration celebración
celebrity celebridad
cell phone móvil
cell-phone shop tienda de móviles
cellar bodega
center centro
century siglo

ceramic cerámica
chain cadena
chair silla
champion campeón
championship campeonato
chance chance; oportunidad
chance, by por casualidad
change (n) cambio
change (v) cambiar
chapel capilla
charge cargar
charger cargador
charming precioso
cheap barato
check cheque
check (make sure) verificar
check-in (baggage) facturar el equipaje
check-in (hotel) hacer el check-in
check-out (hotel) hacer el check-out
Cheers! ¡Salud!
cheese queso
cheese shop quesería
chest pecho
chest pains dolor de pecho
chew masticar
chicken pollo
child niño[a]
children niños
chills escalofríos
China China
Chinese chino
chip (cell phone) ficha; chip
chocolate chocolate
choir coro

Christian cristiano[a]
Christmas Navidad
Christmas Day día de Navidad
Chrismas Eve Nochebuena
church iglesia
church service misa; servicio
cigarette cigarrillo
cinema cine
circle círculo
circus circo
citizen ciudadano[a]
city ciudad
class clase
class, first primera clase
class, second segunda clase
classical clásico
clean (adj) limpio
clean (v) limpiar
clear claro
clever listo
cliff acantilado
climate clima
clinic (medical) clínica
clock reloj
clock, alarm despertador
cloister claustro
close (v) cerrar
closed cerrado
closet armario
cloth tejido
clothes ropa
clothes dryer secadora
clothesline cordón para ropa
clothing boutique tienda de
  ropa
cloudy nuboso
club club

club, night club; discoteca
clue clave
coast costa
coat abrigo
coat hanger percha
cockfight pelea de gallos
cockroach cucaracha
coffee café
coffee, decaf café descafeinado
coffee shop cafetería
coincidence coincidencia
coins monedas
cold (temperature) frío
cold (illness) resfriado
(to be) cold tener frío
cold medicine medicina para el
  resfriado
color (n) color
color (v) colorar
coma coma
comb (n) peine
comb (v) peinarse
come venir
come closer acercarse
comedy comedia
comfortable cómodo
comical cómico
comma coma
commitment compromiso
common común
community communidad
companion compañero
compete competir
competition competición
complain quejarse
complaint queja
complicated complicado

comprehension comprensión
computer ordenador; computadora
computer store tienda de informática
concert concierto
conditioner (hair) acondicionador
condom preservativo
conductor conductor
confide (in) confiar (en)
confidence confianza
(to be) confident tener confianza
confirm confirmar
congestion (sinus) congestión
congratulations felicidades
connect conectar
connection (electrical, Internet) conexión
connection (train) enlace; conexión
conservative conservador
constipation estreñimiento
construct construir
construction construcción
contact lenses lentillas
contagious contagioso
contest (n) concurso
continue continuar; seguir
contraceptives anticonceptivos
contraseña password
control (n) control
control (v) controlar
converter (voltage) convertidor
cook cocinar
cooked cocido

cool (slang) genial; suave
cool (temperature) fresco
copper cobre
copy copia
copy and paste copiar y pegar
copy shop fotocopias
cork corcho
corkscrew sacacorchos
corner (street) esquina
corner (wall) rincón
corridor pasillo
corruption corrupción
cost (n) precio
cost (v) costar
cot catre
cotton algodón
couch sofá
cough (n) tos
cough (v) toser
cough drops caramelos para la tos
count (v) contar
country país
countryside campo
courage valor
course (food) plato
course, first primer plato
course, main plato principal; segundo plato
course, second segundo plato
cousin primo[a]
cover (n) cubierta; tapa
cover (v) cubrir
cover charge entrada
cow vaca
cozy cómodo
crafts artesanía

cramps calambres
cramps, menstrual dolor de la menstruación
crazy loco
cream crema
cream, first-aid crema de primera ayuda
credit card tarjeta de crédito
creep pelota
crib cuna
cross cruz
crotch entrepierna
crowd (n) multitud
cruise / cruise ship crucero
cry llorar
crypt cripta
Cubist cubista
cup taza
curfew (general) toque de queda
curfew (hotel, hostel) hora de cierre
curly rizado
curtain cortina
custom (n) costumbre; tradición
customs aduana
cut (n) corte
cut (v) cortar
cute precioso; mono
Czech Republic República Checa

D

dad papá
daily diario; diariamente
dairy products productos lácteos
dance (n) baile
dance (v) bailar

dance step paso
danger peligro
dangerous peligroso
dark oscuro
darling nene[a]
date (n) fecha
daughter hija
day día
day after tomorrow pasado mañana
dead muerto
deal (good value) ganga
dear (affection, informal letter salutation) querido
death muerte
debit card tarjeta de débito
decaffeinated; decaf descafeinado
December diciembre
declare (customs) declarar
decongestant descongestinante
delay (n) retraso
delay (v) retrasar
delayed con retraso
delete borrar (writing); suprimir (computer)
delicate delicado
delicates (clothing) ropa delicada
delicatessen charcutería
delicious delicioso
democracy democracia
demonstration (public) manifestación
dental floss seda dental
dentist dentista
deodorant desodorante

depart salir
department departamento
department store gran almacén
departures salidas
deposit (n) depósito
desert desierto
desire (n) deseo
desire (v) desear
desk escritorio
desperate desesperado
dessert postre
destination destino
detergent detergente
detour desvío
devil diablo
diabetes diabetes
diabetic diabético[a]
diamond diamante
diaper pañal
diaper ointment pomada de
  pañal
diaper rash escozor del pañal
diaper wipes toalletas húmedas
  (para bebés)
diarrhea diarrea
diarrhea medicine medicina
  para la diarrea
dictionary diccionario
die morir
(to be on a) diet estar a dieta;
  ponerse a régimen
diesel gasóleo; diesel
difficult difícil
digital digital
digital camera cámara digital
dining car (train) coche
  comedor

dinner cena
(to eat) dinner cenar
direct directo
direction dirección
director director
directory assistance
  información telefónica
dirty (adj) sucio
dirty (v) ensuciar; manchar
disaster desastre
discount descuento
disorder desorden
discriminate discriminar
discrimination discriminación
discuss discutir
discussion discusión
disease enfermedad
dish plato
dish, main plato prinicipal;
  segundo plato
disinfectant desinfectante
disc disco
distance distancia
distant distante
distinct distinto
disturb molestar
divorced divorciado
dizziness vértigo
dizzy mareado
do hacer
doctor médico
doctor (title) doctor[a]
dog perro
doll muñeca
dome cúpula
domestic doméstico

domestic phone call llamada nacional

done terminado

door puerta

dormitory dormitorio

dot (computer) punto

double doble

doubt (n) duda

doubt (v) dudar

down abajo

(to go) down bajar

downhill cuesta abajo

download bajar

downtown centro

dozen docena

drama drama

dramatic dramático

dream (n) sueño

dream (v) soñar

dress (clothing) vestido

drink (alcohol) copa

drink (beverage) bebida

drink (soft drink) refresco

drink (v) beber; tomar

drive conducir

driver conductor

drop dejar caer

drug (illegal) droga; narcótico

drug (medicine) medicina

drugstore farmacia

drunk borracho

(to get) drunk emborracharse

drums batería

dry (adj) seco

dry (v) secar

duck pato

dungeon calabozo

dust polvo

duty free libre de impuestos

DVD DVD; disco de vídeo digital

E

each cada

ear oído

earache dolor de oído

earbuds auriculares

early temprano

earn ganar

earplugs tapón de oidos

earrings pendientes

earth tierra

east este

Easter Pascua

easy fácil

easily facilmente

eat comer; tomar

eat breakfast desayunar

eat dinner cenar

eat lunch almorzar

eat tapas tapatear

ebook reader kindle

economical económico

economy economía

eczema eczema

educate educar

education educación

effective efectivo

egg huevo

eight ocho

either (one) cualquiera

elbow codo

electrical adapter adaptador eléctrico

electrical outlet enchufe
elevator ascensor
email email; correo electrónico
email address dirección de email
(to be) embarrassed tener
  vergüenza
embarrassing embarazoso
embassy embajada
emergency emergencia
emergency exit salida de
  emergencia
emergency room urgencias
employ emplear
employee / employed
  empleado[a]
empty vacío
encounter encontrar
end (n) fin
end (v) terminar
ending final
enemy enemigo[a]
engaged comprometido
engagement compromiso
engine motor
engineer ingeniero[a]
engineering ingeniería
England Inglaterra
English inglés
enjoy disfrutar
enough suficiente; bastante
Enough! ¡Basta!
enter entrar
entertain entretener
entertaining entretenido
entertainment entretenamiento;
  ocio
entrance entrada

envelope sobre
environment (nature) medio
  ambiente
epilepsy epilepsia
equal igual
equally igualmente
era época; tiempo
erase (computer) suprimir
erase (writing) borrar
eraser borrador
escape escapar
Ethernet cable cable Ethernet
euro euro
Europe Europa
European europeo
European Union (EU) Unión
  Europea (UE)
evening la tarde
event guide guía del ocio
ever jamás
every (all) todo
every (each) cada
everybody todos
everything todo
everywhere en todas partes
evil (adj) malo
evil (n) mal
exact exacto
exactly exactamente; exacto
exam examen
examine examinar
example ejemplo
(for) example por ejemplo
excellent excelente
except excepto
exception excepción
exchange (n) cambio

exchange (v) cambiar
excited emocionado
excuse (v) disculpar; perdonar
excuse me lo siento; perdón;
  disculpe
exercise (n) ejercicio
exercise (v) hacer exercicios
exhausted agotado
exhibition exposición
exit salida
exit, emergency salida de
  emergencia
expensive caro
expert experto[a]
expiration (food) caducidad
expiration (validity) expiración
expire (food) caducir
expire (validity) expirar
explain explicar
explanation explicación
express (adj) rápido; exprés
express (v) expresar
expression expresión
extension extensión
extra extra
eye ojo
eyebrow ceja
eyelash pestaña
eye drops (artificial
  tears) lágrimas artificiales
eye drops (for
  inflammation) colirio
eye shadow sombra de ojos
eyeliner lápiz de ojos

F

facade fachada

face cara
face cleanser limpiadora de cara
face powder polvos para la cara
facial tissue pañuelos (de
  papel); toallitas para la cara
factory fábrica
fair (just) justo
fall (autumn) otoño
fall (v) caer
false falso
familiar familiar
(to be) familiar with (a
  place) conocer
(to be) familiar with (a
  person) conocer a
family familia
famous famoso
fan (enthusiast) hincha
fan (handheld) abanico
fan (machine) ventilador
fantastic fantástico
far lejos
far from lejos de
farm granja
farmer granjero[a]
farsighted hipermétrope
farther más lejos; más allá
fashion moda
fast rápido
fast (v) ayunar
fast food comida rápida
fat (overweight) gordo
fat (grease) grasa
father padre
faucet grifo
favor (n) favor
favorite favorito; preferido

fax   fax
fear (n)   miedo
fear (v)   temer
February   febrero
fee   cuota
feed   dar de comer
feel (emotion, illness)   estar; sentirse
feel (by touch)   tocar
feel like doing (something)   tener ganas de
feeling   sentimiento
female (adj)   femenino
female (n)   mujer
feminine   femenino
ferry   transbordador
festival   festival
fever   fiebre
few   poco
fiancé   novio
fiancée   novia
field   campo
fight (n)   lucha; pelea
fight (v)   luchar
fight with   pelearse con
file (computer)   fichero
fill   llenar
final   final; último
finally   por fin
fine (good)   bueno
fine (penalty)   multa
fine (thin; refined)   fino
finger   dedo
fingernail   uña
finish   terminar; acabar
finished   terminado
fire   fuego

fire department   bomberos
fireworks   fuegos artificiales
first   primero
first aid   primeros auxilios
first class   primera clase
first-aid cream   crema de primera ayuda
fish (live)   pez
fish (food)   pescado
fish (v)   pescar
fit (clothes)   quedarse
fit (in, into)   encajar (en)
fit (space)   caber
fitness club   gimnasio
five   cinco
fix   arreglar
fizzy   gaseoso
fjord   fiordo; ría
flag   bandera
flame   llama
flash (camera)   flash
flash drive   pendrive
flashlight   linterna
flat (apartment)   piso
flavor (n)   sabor
flawed   imperfecto
flea   pulga
flea market   rastro
flight   vuelo
flip-flops   chanquetas
flirt (f)   coqueta
flirt (m)   ligón
flirt (v)   coquetear
floor   piso; suelo
floor plan   plano
floss, dental   seda dental
flour   harina

flower flor
flower market floristería
flu gripe
fluoride rinse enjuague bucal
fly (n) mosca
fly (v) volar
fog niebla
folk dancing baile folclórico
follow seguir
following siguiente
food comida; alimento
food poisoning envenenamiento
  de comida
foot pie
football (soccer) fútbol
football, American fútbol
  americano
for para; por
forbid prohibir
forbidden prohibido
forehead frente
foreign extranjero
foreigner extranjero[a]
forest bosque
forget olvidar
forgive disculpar; perdonar
forgiveness perdón
fork tenedor
form (document) impreso
form (shape, type) forma
form (v) formar
formal formal
formula (for baby) leche
fortress (Moorish) alcázar
forward adelante
foundation (makeup) base para
  la cara

fountain fuente
four cuatro
fragile frágil
frame cuadro
France Francia
free (available) disponible; libre
free (no cost) gratis
free (v) liberar
freedom liberación
French francés
frequency frecuencia
frequent frecuente
frequently frecuentemente; con
  frecuencia
fresh fresco
Friday viernes
fried frito
friend amigo[a]
friendly amable; amigable
friendship amistad
Frisbee frisbee
from de
front frente
(in) front of enfrente de
fruit fruta
frustrate frustrar
frustrated frustrado
fry freír
full lleno
fun (adj)) divertido
fun (n) diversión
(to have) fun divertirse
(to make) fun of reírse de
funeral funeral
funny (amusing) chistoso
funny (comical) cómico
furniture muebles

fuse (n) fusible
F
future futuro

G

gain weight subir de peso
gallery galería
game juego
game (sports) partido
garage garaje
garden jardín
gardening jardinería
garments prendas
gas (stomach) gases
gas (vapor) gas
gas station gasolinera
gas tank depósito de gasolina
gasoline gasolina
gauze gasa
gay gay; homosexual
gears marchas
generous generoso
genious genio[a]
gentleman caballero
genuine auténtico
German alemán
Germany Alemania
get (pick up) coger
get on subir
get up levantarse
gift (n) regalo
gift (v) regalar
girl chica; muchacha
girlfriend novia
give dar
glass vaso
glasses (eye) gafas
glasses case funda de gafas

globalization globalización
gloves guantes
gluten gluten
gluten-free sin gluten
go ir
Go away! ¡Déjeme!
go back volver; regresar
go down bajar
go through atravesar
go up subir
God Dios
gold oro
golf golf
good bueno
good-looking guapo
good day buenos días
goodbye adiós
good night buenas noches
good afternoon buenas tardes
good evening buenas tardes;
  buenas noches
good morning buenos días
Gothic gótico
Gothic-Islamic (post-
  Reconquest Moorish) mudéjar
government gobierno
grammar gramática
grandchildren nietos
granddaughter nieta
grandfather abuelo
grandmother abuela
grandson nieto
grace gracia
gracious gracioso
grass hierba
gray gris
grease (fat) grasa

greasy (dirty) grasoso
great magnífico; genial
Great Britain Gran Bretaña
Greece Grecia
Greek griego
green verde
grocery store supermercado
ground (earth) suelo
ground floor planta baja
group grupo
guarantee garantía
guest invitado[a]
guide (n) guía; director
guide (v) dirigir
guidebook guía
guided tour tour guiado
guilt culpa
guilty culpable
guitar guitarra
gum chicle
gun pistola
guy chico; muchacho; tipo; tío
gymnastics gimnasia
gynecologist ginecólogo[a]

H

habit hábito
Haha! ¡Jaja!
hair pelo; cabello
hair color color de pelo
hair dryer secador de pelo
hair gel gel
hair salon peluquería
hairstylist peluquero[a]
hairbrush cepillo
haircut corte de pelo
hairspray laca

half mitad; medio
half portion (food) media ración
hall (big room) sala
hall (passage) pasillo
ham jamón
hand mano
hand lotion crema de manos
hand sanitizer desinfectante de manos
handicapped minusvalido[a]
handicrafts artesanía
handle tirador
handle (manage) manejar
handsome guapo; hermoso
handwash lavar a mano
hang colgar
hang up (phone) colgar
happiness alegría
happy feliz, contento
harbor puerto
hard (difficult) difícil
hard (strong) duro
hard drive disco duro
hardly apenas
hardware store ferretería
hash (drug) hachís
hat sombrero
hate / hatred odio
hate odiar
have tener
have just done (something) acabar
hay fever fiebre del heno
he él
head cabeza
headache dolor de cabeza
headlights faros

headphones auriculares
health salud
health insurance seguro médico
healthy sano
hear oír
heart corazón
heart condition problemas de corazón
heartburn ardor de estómago
heat (n) calor
heat (v) calentar
heaven cielo
heavy pesado
hell infierno
hello hola; buenos días
helmet casco
help (n) ayuda
help (v) ayudar
helpful amable
hemorrhoids hemorroides
hepatitis hepatitis
her su
herb yierba
hers suyo
here aquí; acá
hi hola
hide (v) esconder
hidden escondido
high alto
high blood pressure tensión alta
high chair trona
highway autopista
hike (n) caminata
hike (v) caminar; dar una caminata
hiking senderismo
hiking map mapa de senderismo

hill colina
hill town pueblo serrano
hips caderas
his su; suyo
history historia
hitchhike hacer auto-stop
hobby pasatiempo
hockey hockey
hole agujero
holiday festivo
holy santo
homemade hecho en casa; casero
homepage inicio
homesick morriña
honest honesto
honey (food) miel
honey (darling) nene[a]
honeymoon luna de miel
hope (n) esperanza
hope (v) esperar
horrible horrible
hors d'œuvre entrante; entremés; tapa
horse caballo
horseback riding montar a caballo
hospital hospital
hostel albergue
hot (spicy) picante
hot (temperature) caliente
(to be) hot tener calor
hot flashes calores
hotel hotel
hotel, inexpensive pensión
hotel, historic parador
hour hora

house casa
How? ¿Cómo?
however (nevertheless) sin embargo
How many? ¿Cuántos[as]?
How much? ¿Cuánto[a]?
hug (n) abrazo
hug (v) abrazar
human humano
human being ser humano
humble humilde
humid húmedo
humor humor
humor, sense of sentido de humor
hundred cien
hunt (n) caza
hunt (v) cazar
hunger hambre
(to be) hungry tener hambre
hurry (v) apurarse
hurt (v) doler
husband marido
hydrofoil hidroplano
hyphen (-) guión

I

I yo
ibuprofen ibuprofeno
ice hielo
ice cream helado
idea idea
ideal ideal
idiot idiota
if si
ignorant ignorante

ignore ignorar
ill enfermo
illegal ilegal
illness enfermedad
illogical ilógico
illuminate iluminar
immediate inmediato
immediately inmediatamente
immigrant inmigrante
immigration inmigración
imperfect imperfecto
important importante
imported importado
impossible imposible
Impressionist impresionista
in en
in order to para
include incluir
included incluido
incorrect incorrecto
incredible increíble
independent independiente
indigestion indigestión
industry industria
inedible asqueroso
infant infante[a]
infection infección
inflammation inflamación
inform informar
informal informal
information información
injure herir
injured herido
injury herida
injustice injusticia
innocent inocente

I

insect insecto
insect repellant líquido de insectos
inside interior; adentro
inside-out al revés
inside of dentro de
inspect repasar
inspection inspección; revisión
instant instante
instead of en vez de
instructions (directions) instrucciones
instructions for use modo de empleo
insult (n) insulto
insult (v) insultar
insurance seguro
insurance, health seguro médico
insured asegurado
intelligent inteligente
intend intentar
intention intención
interesting interesante
international internacional
international call llamada internacional
Internet Internet
Internet access acceso a Internet
Internet café café de Internet
intersection intersección
intestines intestinos
into en
investigate investigar
investigation investigación
invite invitar

invitation invitación
iodine yodo
Ireland Irlanda
is es
Islam Islam
Islamic islámico
Islamist islamista
island isla
Italian italiano
Italy Italia
itch comezón
itch reliever alivio del picor

J

jacket chaqueta
January enero
jaw mandíbula
jealous celoso
(to be) jealous tener celos
jealousy celos
jeans vaqueros
jewel joya
jewelry joya; joyería
jewelry shop joyería
Jewish judío[a]
job trabajo; empleo; puesto
jogging footing
joint (marijuana) porro
joke (n) broma; chiste
joke (v) bromear; hacer chistes
journey viaje
judge (v) juzgar
judgment juicio
juice zumo
July julio
jump saltar
June junio

K

kayak kayak
keep (v) guardar
kettle olla
key (clue) clave
key (lock) llave
keyboard teclado
kidney stone cálculo renal
kill matar
kilogram (about 2 lbs.) kilo
kilometer (about .6 mile) kilómetro
kind (nice) amable
kind (type) clase
kindergarten jardín infantil
king rey
kiss (n) beso
kiss (v) besar
kitchen / kitchenette cocina
knee rodilla
knife cuchillo
knight caballero
know (someone) conocer a
know (a place, something) conocer
know (info, how to) saber
knowledge conocimiento
known conocido
Koran Corán

L

lace (fabric) encaje
lactose lactosa
lactose intolerant intolerante a la lactosa
ladder escalera de mano
ladies señoras
lake lago
lamb cordero
lamp lámpara
land (earth, soil) tierra
land (v) aterrizar
landing (plane) aterrizaje
lane (street) callejón
language lengua; lenguaje
laptop portátil
large grande
last (adj) último
last (v) durar
late tarde
late (transportation) con retraso
later más tarde
lately últimamente
laugh (v) reír
laugh / laughter risa
launderette (full service) lavandería
launderette (self-service) lavandería de autoservicio
laundry soap detergente
lawyer abogado[a]
laxative laxativo
lazy perezoso
lead (v) dirigir
leader líder
leadership liderazgo
learn (v) aprender
leather cuero
leave (v) salir; irse
leave behind dejar
left (direction) izquierda
leg pierna
legal legal

lemon limón
lemonade limonada
lend (v) prestar
lenses, contact lentillas
lesbian lesbiana
less menos
less than menos que
less than (numbers) menos de
less... than menos... que
let (allow) dejar
letter carta
liberal liberal
liberate liberar
library biblioteca
lice piojos
lie (fib) (v) mentir
life vida
lift (v) levantar
light (illumination) luz
light (weight) ligero
light (v) encender
light up (illuminate) iluminar
light up (smoking) encender
lightbulb bombilla
lighter encendedor
lightheaded mareado
lighthouse faro
like (as) como
like (v) gustar
line (n) línea
line (queue) fila
linen lino
link (chain) cadena
link (Internet) enlace
lip labio
lip balm cacao de labios
lipstick barra de labios

liquid líquido
list lista
listen (v) escuchar
liter litro
little (small, short) pequeño
little poco
little bit, a un poco
little, very poquito
live (adj) en vivo
live (v) vivir
local local
lock (n) cerradura
lock (v) cerrar
locked cerrado
locked (phone) bloqueado
lockers casilleros
logical lógico; racional
long largo
look after vigilar
look at mirar
look for buscar
look like parecer
loose-fitting holgado; ancho
lose perder
lose weight bajar de peso
loser perdedor[a]
lost perdido
lost and found oficina de ojetos
    perdidos
lotion, hand crema de manos
loud ruidoso
loud, out en voz alta
love (n) amor
love (v) amar; querer
love (something) encantar
lovely precioso
lover amante

low bajo
lower (v) bajar
luck suerte
(to be) lucky tener suerte
luggage equipaje
luggage, carry-on equipaje de mano
luggage cart carro de equipaje
lukewarm templado; tibio
lunch almuerzo; comida
(to eat) lunch almorzar; comer
lungs pulmones
luxurious lujoso
luxury lujo

M

machine máquina; aparato
macho macho
mad (angry) enfadado; enojado
magazine revista
mail (n) correo
mail (v) mandar
mailbox buzón
main principal
main course (food) segundo plato
maintain mantener
make (v) hacer
makeup maquillaje
male (adj) masculino
mall (shopping) centro comercial
man hombre
manage manejar
manager director[a]; gerente[a]
manicure manicura
many muchos

many, too demasiados
map mapa
marble (material) mármol
March marzo
marijuana marihuana
market mercado
market, flea rastro
market, flower floristería
market, open-air mercado al aire libre
marriage matrimonio
married casado
(to get) married (to) casarse (con)
mascara máscara
masculine masculino
Mass misa
massage masaje
masterpiece obra maestra
match (sports) partido
matches cerillas
material material
maximum máximo
May mayo
maybe tal vez; quizás
me me (indirect / direct object); mí (personal pronoun)
meal comida
mean (not nice) antipático
mean (v) significar; querer decir
means (method) modo
meat carne
mechanic / mechanical mecánico[a]
media medios
medicine medicina

medicine, cold medicina para el resfriado
medicine, non-aspirin substitute Nolotil
medieval medieval
medium (size) mediano
meet encontrar
membership card carné
membership card (hostel) carné de alberguista
memory memoria
memory (souvenir) recuerdo
memory card tarjeta de memoria
men hombres
menstrual cramps dolor de la menstruación
menstruation menstruación
menu carta; menú
mercy merced
message recado
metal metal
meter (about 1 yard) metro
meter, taxi taxímetro
method modo
middle centro
midnight medianoche
migraine jaqueca
military ejército
mile milla
mileage (in kilometers) kilometraje
mileage (in miles) millaje
milk leche
mind (brain) mente
mine (adj) mío
minimum mínimo

minus menos
minutes minutos
mirror espejo
Miss Señorita
miss (someone) echar de menos
miss (lack) faltar
missing (lost) perdido
mistake error
mistreat maltratar
mistreated maltratado
misunderstand malentender
misunderstanding malentendido
mix (v) mezclar
mixed mixto; mezclado
moat foso
mobile phone móvil
mobile-phone number número de móvil
mobile-phone shop tienda de móviles
modern moderno
moisturizer hidratante
moleskin for blisters parches para ampollas
mollusk molusco
mom mamá
moment momento
monastery monasterio
Monday lunes
money dinero
monk monje
month mes
monument monumento
moon luna
Moorish Moros
Moorish blue tile azulejo
Moorish castle alcazaba

Moorish fortress/palace alcázar
Moors moros
more más
more than más que
more than (numbers) más de
more... than más... que
morning mañana
morning-after pill la pildora del día después
Morocco Marruecos
mosque mezquita
mosquito mosquito
most el / la más
mother madre
motion sickness mareo al viajar
motor scooter motocicleta
motorcycle moto
mount (v) montar
mountain montaña
mountain bike bicicleta de montaña
moustache bigote
mouth boca
mouthwash enjuague bucal
move (motion) moverse
movement movimiento
movie película
MP3 player reproductor de MP3
Mr. Señor
Mrs. Señora
much mucho
much, too demasiado
muggy húmedo
mural mural
muscle músculo
museum museo
music música

music, live música en vivo
musician músico[a]
Muslim musulmán[a]
my mi

N

nail (finger) uña
nail clipper corta uñas
nail file lima de uñas
nail polish esmalte de uñas
nail polish remover quitaesmaltes
naked desnudo
name nombre
name (last) apellido
name (middle) segundo nombre
nap siesta
napkin servilleta
narcotic narcótico
narrow estrecho
nation nación
national nacional
nationality nacionalidad
natural natural
naturally naturalmente
nature naturaleza
nausea náusea
near cerca
nearsighted miope
necessary necesario
neck cuello
necklace collar
need (n) necesidad
need (v) necesitar
needle aguja
neither tampoco
neither... nor ni... ni

nephew   sobrino
nervous   nervioso
Netherlands   Holanda
network   red
never   nunca; jamás
new   nuevo
new town   parte nueva
New Year's Day   día de Año Nuevo
New Year's Eve   Nochevieja
news   noticias; anuncios
newspaper   periódico; diario
newsstand   kiosco; quiosco
next   siguiente; próximo
next to   al lado de
nice   majo; simpático; amable
nickname   apodo
niece   sobrina
night   noche
nightclub   club nocturno; discoteca
nightgown   camisón
nine   nueve
no   no
no one   nadie
no idea   ni idea
no vacancy   completo
nobody   nadie
noisy   ruidoso
non-aspirin substitute   Nolotil
non-smoking   no fumadores
none   ninguno
noon   mediodía
normal   normal
north   norte
nose   nariz
not   no

note (message)   nota
notes (observations)   apuntes
notebook   cuaderno
nothing   nada
November   noviembre
now   ahora
nowadays   hoy en día
nowhere   ninguna parte
nude   desnudo
numb   dormido
number   número
numbness   dormido
nun   monja
nurse   enfermero[a]
nutrition   alimentación
nuts   frutos secos
nylon (material)   nilón
nylons (panty hose)   medias

O

obey   obedecer
occupation   oficio
occupied   ocupado
ocean   océano
October   octubre
odor   olor
of   de
offer (n)   oferta
offer (v)   ofrecer
offer, last   última oferta
office   oficina
office supplies store   papelería
official   oficial
officially   oficialmente
oil   aceite
OK   OK; de acuerdo; vale
old   viejo

old town casco antiguo
olive aceituna
Olympics Olimpíada
on sobre; en
on time puntual
once una vez
one uno
one way (street) dirección única
one way (ticket) de ida
only sólo; solamente
open (adj) abierto
open (v) abrir
open-air market mercado al aire libre
opening hours horas de apertura
opera ópera
operate operar
operation operación
operator telefonista
opinion opinión
opportunity oportunidad
optician óptico
optimist / optimistic optimista
or o
orange (color) anaranjado
orange (fruit) naranja
order (n) orden
order (food) (v) pedir
order, in en orden
organ órgano
original original
other otro
our nuestro
outing paseo
outing, to go on an dar un paseo
outlet (plug) enchufe
outside fuera

oven horno
over (finished) terminado
over (above) encima de
overcoat abrigo
overcooked muy hecho
overnight train tren nocturno
overweight gordo
own (v) poseer
owner dueño[a]

P

pacifier chupete
pack (v) meter
pack the suitcases hacer las maletas
package paquete
paddleboat barca de pedales
page página
pail cubo
pain dolor
painkiller analgésico
pains, chest dolor de pecho
paint (v) pintar
painter pintor[a]
painting pintura; cuadro
pair par; pareja
pajamas pijamas
palace palacio
palace (Moorish) alcázar
panties bragas
pants pantalones
paper papel
paper, sheet of hoja de papel
paper clip clip
paradise paraíso
pardon perdón
parents padres

park (n) parque
park (v) aparcar
parking lot aparcamiento
parking meter parquímetro
party (celebration) fiesta
party (political) partido
party (v) hacer fiesta
partner compañero; pareja
passage pasaje
passenger pasajero[a]
passport pasaporte
password contraseña
past pasado
pastries bollería
pastry bollo; pastel
pastry shop pastelería
pay pagar
pay attention prestar atención
peace paz
peacock pavo real
pedestrian peatón
pedicure pedicura
pen bolígrafo
pencil lápiz
penis pene
people gente
percent por ciento
percentage porcentaje
perfect (ideal) perfecto
perfume perfume
period (of time) período
period (punctuation) punto
period (woman's) regla
permanent permanente
person persona
personal lubricant lubricante
    personal

pessimist / pessimistic
    pesimista
pet (n) mascota; animal
    doméstico
pewter peltre
pharmacy farmacia
phone (n) teléfono
phone (v) llamar
phone booth cabina telefónica
phone call llamada telefónica
phone, mobile teléfono móvil
photo foto
(take a) photo sacar / hacer
    un foto
photograph (v) fotografear
photographer fotógrafo[a]
photocopy fotocopia
photocopy shop fotocopias
piano piano
pick up (get) coger
pick up (phone) descolgar
pickpocket carterista
picnic (n) picnic
picnic (v) hacer picnic
picture (painting) pintura
picture (photo) foto
piece pedazo
pig cerdo
pill píldora
pill, birth control píldora
    anticonceptiva
pillow almohada
pin alfiler
PIN code código; número clave
pink rosa
pity lástima
pizza pizza

place (position) lugar
place (site) sitio; plaza
place (v) poner
plain (food) al natural
plan (n) plan
plan (v) pensar; planear
plane avión
plant planta
plastic plástico
plastic bag bolsa de plástica
plate plato
Plateresque (frilly late Gothic) plateresco
platform (train) andén
platform (bus) dársena
play (theater) obra de teatro
play (music, instrument) tocar
play (sports, games) jugar
playground área para jugar
playpen parque para niños
please por favor
please (make happy) complacer
(to be) pleasing gustar
pliers alicates
plug (for blocking a hole) tapón
plug (outlet) enchufe
plug in enchufar
pneumonia pulmonía
pocket bolsillo
point (n) punto
point (reason) razón
point (v) apuntar
police / police officer policía
policy póliza; norma
policy, cancellation norma de cancelación
political político

politician político
pollution polución
polyester poliester
poop caca
poor pobre
poor thing pobrecito[a]
Pope, the el Papa
popular popular
population población
porcelain porcelana
pork cerdo
portion ración
portrait retrato
Portugal Portugal
possible posible
possibly posiblemente
postcard carta postal
poster cartel
poultry ave
powder polvos
power poder
powerful poderoso
practical práctico
practice (n) práctica
practice (v) practicar
precious precioso
prefer preferir
preference preferencia
preferred preferido
pregnancy embarazo
pregnancy test prueba de embarazo
pregnant embarazada
Preparation H Hemoal
prescription prescripción; receta médica
present (gift) regalo

present (time, attendance) presente
present (v) presentar
presentation (talk) discurso
preservative conservante
president presidente[a]
press (media) prensa
press (v) oprimir
pressure presión; tensión
pretty bonito; lindo
price precio
priest sacerdote
prince príncipe; infante
princess princesa; infanta
principal director
principle principio
print (v) imprimir
private privado
problem problema
produce (fruits and vegetables) frutas y verduras
produce producir
product producto
profession profesión
program programa
prohibited prohibido
project (plan) proyecto
promise (n) promesa
promise (v) prometer
pronounce pronunciar
pronunciation pronunciación
prosper prosperar
prostitute prostituta
protect proteger
Protestant protestante
prudish prudente
public público

publicity publicidad
pull tirar
pulpit púlpito
pulse pulso
pump (n) bomba de aire
punctual puntual
purple morado
purse bolsa
push empujar
put poner

Q

Q-tips (cotton swabs) bastoncillos
quad-band cuatribanda
quality calidad
quantity cantidad
quarter (¼) cuarta parte; cuarto
queen reina
question pregunta
(to ask a) question preguntar
quick rápido
quickly rápidamente
quiet tranquilo

R

R.V. caravana
rabbit conejo
rabies rabia
racism racismo
racist racista
radiator radiador
radicals radicales
radio radio
railpass abono de tren
railway ferrocarril
rain (n) lluvia

rain (v) llover
rainbow arco iris
raincoat impermeable
raise levantar
rape (n) violación
rape (v) violar
rash erupción
rash, diaper escozor del pañal
ration ración; portion
rational racional; lógico
raw crudo
razor (disposable) cuchilla de afeitar
read leer
reading glasses gafas para leer
ready listo
real real; auténtico; verdadero
realize darse cuenta de
receipt recibo
receive recibir
recent reciente
recently recién
receptionist recepcionista
recharge recargar
recipe receta
recommend recomendar
recommendation recomendación
red rojo
redheaded pelirrojo
refill (replacement) recambio
refreshing refrescante
refreshment (soft drink) refresco
refugees refugiados
refund (n) reembolso; devolución
refund (v) reembolsar
regular normal

relax relajarse
relaxation relajación
relic reliquia
religion religión
remember recordar
remind recordar
reminder recuerdo
remove quitar
Renaissance Renacimiento
rent (v) alquilar
repair (v) arreglar
repeat repita
require requerer
required requerido
requirement requisito
research (n) investigación
research (v) investigar
reservation reserva
reservation confirmation confirmación de reserva
reserve reservar
reserved reservado
resolve resolver
respect (n) respeto
respect (v) respetar
rest (break) descanso
rest (remainder) resto
rest (v) descansar
restaurant restaurante
return (for refund) devolución
return (go back) volver; regresar
return (something) devolver
review (n) repaso; revisión
review (v) repasar; revisar
rice arroz
rich rico
right (correct) correcto

right (direction) derecha
(to be) right tener razón
ring (jewelry) sortija, anillo
ripe maduro
rise levantarse
river río
road carretera
rob robar
robbed robado
robbery robo
rock (stone) roca
Rollerblades patines
Romanesque románico
romantic romántico
Romantic romántico
roof techo
room (building) habitación; cuarto
room (space) espacio
rope cuerda
rotten podrido
rough draft borrador
roundabout glorieta
round trip ida y vuelta
route ruta
rowboat barco de remo
royal residence residencia real
rucksack mochila
rude maleducado
rule (n) regla
rule (v) reinar
ruler (measure) regla
rug alfombra
ruins ruinas
run correr
run out of acabar de
runway (airport) pista

Russia Rusia
Russian ruso

S

sad triste
safe seguro
safety pin imperdible
sailboat barco de vela
saint santo[a]
salad ensalada
sale rebajas
sale, for vendo
sale, on en venta
salt sal
salty salado
same mismo; igual
sandals sandalias
sandwich bocadillo
sanitary pads compresas
Santa Claus Papá Noel
Saturday sábado
sausage (slightly spicy) chorizo
sausage (mild) salchicón
save (computer) guardar
save (money) ahorrar
say decir
scabies sarna
scandalous escandaloso
Scandinavia Escandinavia
scarf bufanda
scene escena; ambiente
scenic panorámica
school colegio
school, primary escuela primaria
school, secondary escuela secundaria

schedule (timetable) horario
science ciencia
scientist / scientific científico[a]
scissors tijeras
screen pantalla
screwdriver destornillador
sculptor escultor[a]
sculpture escultura
sea mar
seafood marisco
search (n) búsqueda
search (v) buscar
season (time period) temporada; estación
season (food) sazonar
seasoning especia
seat asiento, plaza; silla
second segundo
second class segunda clase
secret secreto
secretary secretario[a]
see ver
seed semilla
seem parecer
self-portrait autorretrato
self-service autoservicio
sell vender
send enviar; mandar
senior citizen jubilado[a]
sense (n) sentido
sense (v) sentir
sensible sensible
separate (another) aparte
September septiembre
serious serio
seriously en serio

serve servir
service servicio
service, church misa, servicio
serving porción; ración
set (v) poner
setting escena; ambiente
seven siete
sex sexo
sexy sexy
shade sombra
shadow sombra
shake hands darse la mano
share (v) compartir
shame (n) vergüenza
shampoo (n) champú
shave (n) afeita
shave (v) afeitar
shaver (electric) afeitadora
shaving cream espuma de afeitar
she ella
sheet (bed) sábana
sheet (paper) hoja de papel
shell concha
shellfish marisco
ship (boat) barco
ship (cruise ship) crucero
ship (v) enviar
shirt camisa
shoelaces cordones
shoes zapatos
shoes, tennis zapatillas de tenis
shop (n) tienda
shop (v) ir de compras
shop, antique anticuarios
shop, barber barbería
shop, camera tienda de fotos

shop, cell phone tienda de móviles
shop, coffee cafetería
shop, jewelry joyería
shop, pastry pastelería
shop, photocopy fotocopias
shop, souvenir tienda de souvenirs
shop, sweets tienda de dulces
shop, wine tienda de vinos
shopping compras
shopping mall centro comercial
short (height) bajo
short (length) corto
shorts pantalones cortos
shoulder hombros
show (spectacle) espectáculo
show (v) enseñar; mostrar
shower (n) ducha
shower (v) ducharse
shrink encoger
shuttle bus shuttle
shy tímido
sibling hermano[a]
sick enfermo
sickness enfermedad
side lado
siesta siesta; nap
sign (placard) anuncio; letrero
sign (gesture) seña
sign (street) señal
sign (symbol) signo
sign (v) firmar
sign language lengua de señas
signature firma
silence silencio
silk seda

silly tonto
silver plata
SIM card tarjeta SIM
similar similar; parecido
simple sencillo
sin (n) pecado
sin (v) pecar
since desde
sincere sincero
sincerely sinceramente
sing cantar
singer cantante
single soltero[a]
sink lavabo
sink stopper tapón
sinus problems sinusitis
sir señor
sister hermana
sister-in-law cuñada
sit sentarse
six seis
size talla
skate (v) patinar
skates (Rollerblades) patines
skateboard (n) monopatín
skating patinaje
ski (v) esquiar
skiing esquí
skin piel
skirt falda
sky cielo
sleep dormir
sleeper (train) coche cama
sleeping bag saco de dormir
sleepy soñoliento
(to be) sleepy tener sueño
sleeves mangas

slender delgado
slice rodaja; loncha
slide (photo, PowerPoint)
  diapositiva
slip calzoncillo
slippers zapatillas
slippery resbaladizo
slow despacio; lento
slowly lentamente
small pequeño
smartphone smartphone
smell (n) olor
smell (v) oler
smile (n) sonrisa
smile (v) sonreír
smoke (n) humo
smoke (v) fumar
smoker fumador
smoking fumar
smooth suave
snack pincho; tapa
snack, afternoon merienda
sneeze (n) estornudo
sneeze (v) estornudar
snore roncar
snorkel tubo de respiración
snow (n) nieve
snow (v) nevar
(to go) snowboarding hacer
  snowboard
so (interjection) pues; entonces
so (very) tan
so much tanto
so many tantos
soap jabón
soap, laundry detergente
soccer fútbol

socks calcetines
sofa sofá
soft suave
soil (earth, land) tierra
sold out agotado
soldier soldado
solution solucíon
solve resolver
some alguno
someone alguien; alguna
  persona
something algo; alguna cosa
somewhere en algún lugar
son hijo
song canción
soon pronto
sore dolorido
sore throat dolor de garganta
sorry lo siento
soup sopa
sour agrio
south sur
souvenir shop tienda de
  souvenirs
soy soja
spa balneario
space (room) espacio
space (spot, place) plaza; sitio
Spain España
Spanish español
sparkplugs bujías
speak hablar
special especial
special of the day (food)
  especial del día
special offer oferta
specialty especialidad

spectacle (show) espectáculo
speed velocidad
speed limit límite de velocidad
spend gastar
spice (seasoning) especia
spice up (season) sazonar
spicy picante
spider araña
splinter (sliver) astilla
split (share) compartir
spoon cuchara
sport deporte
sports bar bar deportivo
spot (space, place) sitio; plaza
spot (stain) mancha
spouse esposo[a]
spring (season) primavera
square (shape) cuadro; cuadrado
square (town) plaza
stain (n) mancha
stain (v) ensuciar
stain remover quitamanchas
stairs escaleras
stall (bus station) dársena
stamp sello; estampilla; timbre
staple (for papers) grapa
stapler grapadora
star estrella
start (n) comienzo; principio
start (v) comenzar; empezar
start, at the al comienzo; al principio
state estado
station estación
station, bus estación de autobuses

station, subway estación de metro
station, train estación de tren
stay (v) quedar
STD (sexually transmitted disease) ETS (enfermedad de transmisión sexual)
steal robar
step (footstep, dance move) paso
stiff drink trago
stink (v) apestar
stinky apestoso
still (as before, even) todavía
stolen robado
stomach estómago
stomachache dolor de estómago
stoned colocado
stop (in route) parada
stop, bus parada de autobús
stop (v) parar
stoplight semáforo
stopper, sink tapón
store tienda
store, clothing tienda de ropa
store, computer tienda de informática
store, department gran almacén
store, hardware ferretería
store, office supplies papelería
store, toy juguetería
storm tormenta
story (floor) planta
story (tale) historia
straight (ahead) recto; derecho
strange extraño

stranger (person) desconocido[a]; extraño[a]

straw, drinking paja

stream (water) arroyo

stream (computer) transferirse

street calle

strenuous difícil

strep throat infección de garganta

stretch estirarse

strike huelga

string cordón

stroll (n) paseo

stroll (v) pasear; dar un paseo

stroller carrecoche

strong fuerte

stuck atascado

student estudiante

stupid estúpido; tonto

sturdy robusto

sty (eyelid inflammation) orzuelo

style estilo

subtitles subtítulos

subway metro

subway entrance entrada al metro

subway exit salida de metro

subway map mapa

subway station estación de metro

subway stop parada

such tal

suddenly de repente

suffer sufrir

suffering sufrimiento

sufficient suficiente; bastante

sugar azúcar

suitcase maleta

summer verano

sun sol

sunbathe tomar el sol

sunburn (n) quemadura

sunburn (v) quemarse

Sunday domingo

sunglasses gafas de sol

sunny soleado

sunrise amanecer

sunscreen protección de sol; crema de sol

sunset puesta de sol

sunshine luz del sol

sunstroke insolación

suntan (n) bronceado

suntan (v) broncearse

suntan lotion crema bronceadora

supermarket supermercado

supplement suplemento

sure seguro

surf (v) surfear

surfboard tabla de surf

surfer surfista

surgery cirugía

surprise (n) sorpresa

surprise (v) sorprender

symbol símbolo; signo

symbolic simbólico

symbolize simbolizar

swallow tragar

sweat (n) sudor

sweat (v) sudar

sweaty sudado

sweater suéter

sweet dulce
sweets shop tienda de dulces
swell hinchar
swelling hinchazón
swim nadar
swim suit traje de baño
swim trunks bañador
swimming pool piscina
Switzerland Suiza
synagogue sinagoga
synthetic sintético

T

table mesa
tablecloth mantel
tablet computer tableta
tail rabo
taillights luces de atrás
take tomar
take off (airplane) despegar
take off (clothes) quitarse
take-out (food) para llevar
talcum powder polvos de talco
talk hablar
tall alto
tampon tampón
tanning lotion bronceador
tape cinta adhesiva
taste (n) sabor
taste (v) probar
tasty sabroso; rico
tattoo tatuaje
tax impuesto
taxi meter taxímetro
tea té
teach enseñar
teacher profesor[a]

team equipo
tear (crying) lágrima
teenager joven
teeth dientes
teething (baby) dentición
telephone teléfono
telephone book guía de
  teléfonos
telephone card tarjeta telefónica
telephone number número de
  teléfono
television televisión
tell decir
temperature temperatura
temporary temporal
ten diez
tender tierno
tendinitis tendinitis
tennis tenis
tennis shoes zapatillas de tenis
tent tienda de campaña
tent pegs estacas de tienda
terminal terminal
terrace terraza
terrible terrible
terrorist terrorista
test (n) examen; prueba
test (v) examinar; probar
testicles testículos
text message SMS; mensaje
  de texto
thank agradecer
thanks gracias
that (thing) eso
that (conjunction) que
the (singular) el; la
the (plural) los; las

theater teatro
theft robo
their su
theirs suyo
thermometer termómetro
then entonces; pues
there allá; allí
there is / are hay
they ellos (m); ellas (f)
thick grueso
thief ladrón
thigh muslo
thin delgado
thing cosa
think pensar
thirsty sediento
this esto
thought pensamiento
thousand mil
thread hilo
three tres
throat garganta
throat, sore garganta, dolor de
through a través; por
throw tirar
thumb pulgar
Thursday jueves
tick (insect) garrapata
ticket billete
tie (clothing) corbata
tie (something) atar
tight apretado
time tiempo
time (occurrence) vez
time (period) momento; época; tiempo
time (specific) hora

time, arrival hora de llegada
time, check-in hora de facturación
time, closing hora de cierre
time, departure hora de salida
time, on puntual; a tiempo
timetable horario
tip (gratuity) propina
tire (wheel) rueda
tire, flat rueda pinchada
tired cansado
tissue, facial pañuelos (de papel); toallitas para la cara
to a
toasted tostado
today hoy
toe dedo del pie
together juntos
toilet (fixture) váter
toilets aseos; servicios
toilet paper papel higiénico
token ficha
toll peaje
toll-free call llamada gratuita
toll road carretera de peaje
tomorrow mañana
tomorrow, day after pasado mañana
tonight esta noche
tongue lengua
too (also) también
too many demasiados
too much demasiado
tooth diente
toothache dolor de muelas
toothbrush cepillo de dientes
toothpaste pasta de dientes

toothpick palillo
Torah Torá
total total
touch tocar
tour viaje; tour
tour, guided tour guiado
tourist turista
tourist trap timo turístico
tow truck grúa
towel toalla
tower torre
town pueblo
town hall ayuntamiento
toy juguete
toy store juguetería
track (train) vía
tradition tradición
traditional tradicional
traditionally tradicionalmente
traffic tráfico
tragedy tragedia
trail sendo
train tren
train, high-speed Talgo; AVE
train (to practice) entrenar
train car vagón; coche
train station estación de tren
tranquil tranquilo
transfer (transportation) transbordo; conexión
transfer (v) cambiar; hacer conexión; hacer un transbordo
translate traducir
translation traducción
transmission fluid líquido de transmisión
transport (v) transportar

transportation transporte
trash basura
trashcan basurero
travel (v) viajar
travel agency agencia de viajes
traveler viajero[a]
traveler's check cheque de viajero
treasury tesoro
treat (v) tratar
treat (to pay for) invitar
treatment tratamiento
tree árbol
tri-band tribanda
triangle triángulo
trim (hair) recorte
trip viaje
tripod trípode
trouble dificultad
truck camión
true verdadero
trust confianza
trust (in) confiar (en)
truth verdad
try (attempt) intentar; tratar de
try (taste) probar
T-shirt camiseta
Tuesday martes
tuna atún
tunnel túnel
turkey (meat) pavo
Turkey Turquía
turn off (lights, devices) apagar
turn on (lights, devices) encender
turn signal intermitente
tweezers pinzas

twin beds dos camas
twins gemelos
two dos
type (n) tipo
type (v) escribir a máquina

U

ugly feo
umbrella paraguas
uncle tío
unconscious inconsciente
under debajo
undercooked crudo
underline (n) subraya
underline (v) subrayar
underpants calzoncillos
underscore (_) subraya
underscore (v) subrayar
understand entender;
  comprender
unemployed sin empleo
unfortunate desafortunado
unfortunately desafor-
  tunadamente
unknown desconocido
United States (US) Estados
  Unidos (EEUU)
university universidad
unlock (phone) liberar;
  desbloquear
unlocked (phone) libre;
  desbloqueado
until hasta
up arriba
(to go) up subir
uphill cuesta arriba
upside-down al revés

upstairs de arriba
upward hacia arriba
urethra uretra
urgent urgente
urinary tract infection infección
  urinaria
us nosotros[as]
USB cable cable USB
use (v) usar
useful útil
useless inútil
username usuario
uterus útero

V

vacancy camas
vacancy, no completo
vacancy sign habitaciónes
vacant libre
vacation vacaciones
(to go on) vacation ir de
  vacaciones
vagina vagina
valid válido
validate validar
valley valle
value (worth) valor
van furgoneta
vase florero
Vaseline vaselina
VAT (Value-Added Tax) IVA
  (Impuesto al Valor Agregado)
vegetable verdura
vegetarian vegetariano[a]
velvet terciopelo
very muy
vest chaleco

video   vídeo
video camera   cámara de vídeo; videocámara
videogame   videojuego
view   vista
viewpoint   mirador
village   pueblo
village (tiny)   aldea
vineyard   viñedo
violence   violencia
violate   violar
virus   virus
visit (n)   visita
visit (v)   visitar
vitamin   vitamina
voice   voz
voicemail   buzón de voz
vomit (v)   vomitar

W

waist   cintura
wait   esperar
waiter   camarero
waiting room   sala de espera
waitress   camarera
wake up   despertarse
walk (n)   caminata
walk (v)   caminar; andar
wall, fortified   pared fortificada
wallet   cartera
want   querer
war   guerra
warm   caliente
warts   verrugas
wash   lavar
washcloth   toalla pequéna
washer   lavadora

waste (v)   gastar
watch (n)   reloj
watch (v)   mirar
watch over (guard)   vigilar
water   agua
water, carbonated   agua con gas
water, drinkable   agua potable
water, mineral   agua mineral
water, non-carbonated   agua sin gas
water, tap   agua del grifo
water, undrinkable   agua no potable
waterfall   cascada
waterskiing   esquí acuático
wave (water)   ola
wavy   ondulado
way (street)   camino
we   nosotros[as]
weak   débil
wear   llevar
weather   tiempo
webcam   webcam
website   página web
wedding   boda
Wednesday   miércoles
week   semana
weekend   fin de semana
weight   peso
(to gain) weight   subir de peso
(to lose) weight   bajar de peso
weight limit   peso máximo
welcome   bienvenido
well (so)   pues
well (well-being, manner)   bien
Well!   ¡Vaya!
well-being   bienestar

west oeste
wet mojado
What? ¿Qué?
whatever (anything) cualquier cosa
whatever (expression) como quiera
wheat trigo
wheel rueda
wheelchair silla de ruedas
wheelchair-accessible acceso de silla de ruedas
when (conjunction) cuando
When? ¿Cuándo?
whenever cuando sea
where donde
Where? ¿Dónde?
wherever donde sea
which (pronoun) que
Which? ¿Cuál?; ¿Qué?
whichever cualquiera
whine (v) quejarse
whine / whining quejido
white blanco
who quien; que
Who? ¿Quién?
whoever quienquiera
Whom? ¿A quién?
(for) whom? ¿Para quién?
whose cuyo
Whose? ¿De quién?
Why? ¿Por qué?
widow viuda
widower viudo
wife esposa
Wi-Fi Wi-Fi
Wi-Fi hotspot zona Wi-Fi

wild salvaje
win ganar
winner ganador[a]
wind viento
windmill molino
window ventana
windshield wipers limpiaparabrisas
windsurfing windsurfing
windy ventoso
wine vino
wine, red vino tinto
wine, white vino blanco
wine shop tienda de vinos
wing ala
winter invierno
wipes, diaper toalletas húmedas (para bebés)
wisdom sabiduría
wise sabio
wish (n) deseo
wish (v) desear
with con
withdraw retirar
without sin
woman mujer; dama (formal)
woman (young) maja
women mujeres; damas (formal)
wood madera
wool lana
word palabra
work (n) trabajo
work (v) trabajar
work (of art, theater) obra
world mundo
worried preocupado
worry preocuparse

worse / worst peor
worth (n) valor
worth (v) valer
Wow! ¡Guau!; ¡Vaya!
wrap envolver
wrapped envuelto
wrestling lucha libre
wrist muñeca
write escribir
writer escritor

X

X-ray rayos x

Y

year año
yellow amarillo
yes sí
yet (still) todavía
yesterday ayer
yoga (n) yoga
yoga (v) hacer yoga
yogurt yogur
you (formal) usted (Ud.)
you (formal, plural) ustedes (Uds.)
you (informal) tú

you (informal, plural) vosotros[as]
you (direct / indirect object) te
you (prep. pronoun) ti
your (formal) su
your (informal) tu
your (informal, plural) vuestro
yours (formal) suyo
yours (informal) tuyo
yours (informal, plural) vuestro
young joven
youth (young person) joven
youth (era) juventud
youth hostel albergue de juventud
youth hostel membership card carné de alberguista
youths jóvenes
Yuck! ¡Qué asco!

Z

zero cero
zip code código postal
zip-lock bag bolsa de cremallera
zipper cremallera
zoo zoo

TIPS FOR HURDLING THE LANGUAGE BARRIER

A fear of the language barrier keeps many people (read: English speakers) out of Europe, but the "barrier" is getting smaller every day. English really has arrived as Europe's second language. That said, having an interest in the native language wins the respect of those you'll meet. Start conversations by asking politely in the local language, "Do you speak English?" Remember that you're surrounded by expert tutors, and try not to let your lack of foreign language skills isolate you.

Creative Communication

Speak slowly, clearly, and with carefully chosen words. When speaking English, choose easy words and clearly pronounce each syllable (po-ta-toes). Avoid contractions. Be patient—speaking louder and tossing in a few extra words doesn't help.

Keep your messages grunt-simple. Make single nouns work as entire sentences. A one-word question ("Photo?") is just as effective as something grammatically correct ("May I take your picture, sir?"). Things go even easier if you include the local "please" (e.g., "Toilet, *por favor*?").

Can the slang. Someone who learned English in a classroom will be stumped by American expressions such as "sort of like," "pretty bad," or "Howzit goin'?"

Risk looking goofy. Butcher the language if you must, but communicate. I'll never forget the clerk in a European post office who flapped her arms and asked, "Tweet, tweet, tweet?" I answered with a nod, and she gave me the airmail stamps I needed.

Be melodramatic. Exaggerate the native accent. The locals won't be insulted; they'll be impressed. English spoken with an over-the-top sexy Spanish accent makes more sense to the Spanish ear.

A notepad works wonders. Written words and numbers are much easier to understand than their mispronounced counterparts. Bring a notepad. To repeatedly communicate something difficult or important (such as medical instructions, "I'm a strict vegetarian," etc.), write it in the local language.

Assume you understand and go with your gut. Treat most problems as multiple-choice questions, make an educated guess at the meaning, and proceed confidently. I'm correct about 80 percent of the time—and even when I'm wrong, I usually never know it. I only blow it about 10 percent of the time. By trusting my judgment, my trip becomes easier—and occasionally much more interesting.

International Words

As our world shrinks, more and more words leap their linguistic boundaries and become international. Sensitive travelers choose words most likely to be universally understood ("auto" instead of "car"; "holiday" for "vacation"; "kaput" for "broken"; "photo" for "picture"). They also internationalize their pronunciation: "University," if you play around with its sound (oo-nee-vehr-see-tay), can be understood anywhere.

Here are a few internationally understood words. Remember, cut out the Yankee accent and give each word a pan-European sound ("autoboooos," "Engleesh").

Hello	Bank	Toilet
No	Hotel	Police
Stop	Post (office)	English
Kaput	Camping	Telephone
Ciao	Auto	Photo
Bye-bye	Autobus	Photocopy
OK	Taxi	Computer
Mañana	Tourist	Sport
Pardon	Beer	Internet
Rock 'n' roll	Coke, Coca-Cola	Central
Mamma mia	Tea	Information
No problem	Coffee	University
Super	Vino	Passport
Sex / Sexy	Chocolate	Holiday (vacation)
Oo la la	Picnic	Gratis (free)
Moment	Self-service	America's favorite
Bon voyage	Yankee, Americano	four-letter words
Restaurant	Amigo	

Accent on Accents

Accent marks in Spanish serve several purposes. Not only do they indicate a stressed syllable, but they can also be used over a vowel to distinguish between two words that are spelled (and pronounced) the same yet have different meanings.

Sometimes the differences are small, as with these word pairs that sound the same: *mi* (my) and *mí* (me), *tu* (your) and *tú* (you), *el* (the) and *él* (he). Other times the differences are greater, as when the accent mark indicates a stressed syllable and alters the meaning of a word. It's natural to say you love your *mamá* (mom), but if you say you love your *mama*, people may wonder why you love your breast. Spanish speakers will understand if you talk to your *papá* (dad) every day, but saying you talk to your *papa* (potato) will raise some eyebrows!

While some English-looking Spanish words do indeed communicate the same thing in both languages, others have completely different meanings. Saying you're *embarazada* doesn't mean you're embarrassed—it means you're pregnant. You'd think a pie would be something yummy, but in Spanish *pie* means foot. And if you tell someone you're *exitado*, you're not emotionally moved, but sexually excited.

Spanish Verbs

These conjugated verbs will help you construct a caveman sentence in a pinch.

Spanish has two different verbs that correspond to the English "to be"—*ser* and *estar.* Generally speaking, *ser* is used to describe a condition that is permanent or longer-lasting, and *estar* is used for something that is temporary. Which verb you use can determine the meaning of the sentence. For example, *Ricardo es contento,* using *ser,* means that Ricardo is a happy, content person (as a permanent personality trait). *Ricardo está contento,* using *estar,* means that Ricardo is currently happy (temporarily in a good mood).

TO GO	IR	eer
I go	yo voy	yoh boy
you go (formal)	usted va	oo-**stehd** bah
you go (informal)	tú vas	too bahs
he / she goes	él / ella va	ehl / **ay**-yah bah
we go	nosotros vamos	noh-**soh**-trohs **bah**-mohs
you go (plural formal)	ustedes van	oo-**stehd**-ehs bahn
they (m / f) go	ellos / ellas van	**ay**-yohs / **ay**-yahs bahn

TO BE (permanent)	SER	sehr
I am	yo soy	yoh soy
you are (formal)	usted es	oo-**stehd** ehs
you are (informal)	tú eres	too **eh**-rehs
he / she is	él / ella es	ehl / **ay**-yah ehs
we are	nosotros somos	noh-**soh**-trohs **soh**-mohs
you are (plural formal)	ustedes son	oo-**stehd**-ehs sohn
they (m / f) are	ellos / ellas son	**ay**-yohs / **ay**-yahs sohn

TO BE (temporary)	ESTAR	ay-**star**
I am	yo estoy	yoh eh-**stoy**
you are (formal)	usted está	oo-**stehd** eh-**stah**
you are (informal)	tú estás	too eh-**stahs**
he / she is	él / ella está	ehl / **ay**-yah eh-**stah**
we are	nosotros estamos	noh-**soh**-trohs eh-**stah**-mohs
you are (plural formal)	ustedes están	oo-**stehd**-ehs eh-**stahn**
they (m / f) are	ellos / ellas están	**ay**-yohs / **ay**-yahs eh-**stahn**

TIPS

TO DO / TO MAKE	HACER	ah-**thehr**
I do	yo hago	yoh **ah**-goh
you do (formal)	usted hace	oo-**stehd** ah-thay
you do (informal)	tú haces	too **ah**-thehs
he / she does	él / ella hace	ehl / **ay**-yah **ah**-thay
we do	nosotros hacemos	noh-**soh**-trohs ah-**theh**-mohs
you do (plural formal)	ustedes hacen	oo-**stehd**-ehs **ah**-thehn
they (m / f) do	ellos / ellas hacen	**ay**-yohs / **ay**-yahs **ah**-thehn

TO HAVE	TENER	teh-**nehr**
I have	yo tengo	yoh **tehn**-goh
you have (formal)	usted tiene	oo-**stehd** tee-**ehn**-ay
you have (informal)	tú tienes	too tee-**ehn**-ehs
he / she has	él / ella tiene	ehl / **ay**-yah tee-**ehn**-ay
we have	nosotros tenemos	noh-**soh**-trohs tay-**neh**-mohs
you have (plural formal)	ustedes tienen	oo-**stehd**-ehs tee-**ehn**-ehn
they (m / f) have	ellos / ellas tienen	**ay**-yohs / **ay**-yahs tee-**ehn**-ehn

TO SEE	VER	behr
I see	yo veo	yoh **bay**-oh
you see (formal)	usted ve	oo-**stehd** bay
you see (informal)	tú ves	too bays
he / she sees	él / ella ve	ehl / **ay**-yah bay
we see	nostros vemos	noh-**soh**-trohs **beh**-mohs
you see (plural formal)	ustedes ven	oo-**stehd**-ehs behn
they (m / f) see	ellos / ellas ven	**ay**-yohs / **ay**-yahs behn

TO SPEAK	HABLAR	ah-**blar**
I speak	yo hablo	yoh **ah**-bloh
you speak (formal)	usted habla	oo-**stehd ah**-blah
you speak (informal)	tú hablas	too **ah**-blahs
he / she speaks	él / ella habla	ehl / **ay**-yah **ah**-blah
we speak	nosotros hablamos	noh-**soh**-trohs ah-**blah**-mohs
you speak (plural formal)	ustedes hablan	oo-**stehd**-ehs **ah**-blahn
they (m / f) speak	ellos / ellas hablan	**ay**-yohs / **ay**-yahs **ah**-blahn

TO LIKE	GUSTAR	goo-**star**
I like	me gusta	may **goo**-stah
you like (formal)	le gusta	lay **goo**-stah
you like (informal)	te gusta	tay **goo**-stah
he / she likes	le gusta	lay **goo**-stah
we like	nos gusta	nohs **goo**-stah
you like (plural formal)	les gusta	lehs **goo**-stah
they like	les gusta	lehs **goo**-stah

TO WANT ("would like")	GUSTARÍA	goo-stah-**ree**-ah
I would like	me gustaría	may goo-stah-**ree**-ah
you would like (formal)	le gustaría	lay goo-stah-**ree**-ah
you would like (informal)	te gustaría	tay goo-stah-**ree**-ah
he / she would like	le gustaría	lay goo-stah-**ree**-ah
we would like	nos gustaría	nohs goo-stah-**ree**-ah
you would like (plural formal)	les gustaría	lehs goo-stah-**ree**-ah
they would like	les gustaría	lehs goo-stah-**ree**-ah

TO WANT	QUERER	kay-**rehr**
I want	yo quiero	yoh kee-**ehr**-oh
you want (formal)	usted quiere	oo-**stehd** kee-**ehr**-ay
you want (informal)	tú quieres	too kee-**ehr**-ehs
he / she wants	él / ella quiere	ehl / **ay**-yah kee-**ehr**-ay
we want	nosotros queremos	noh-**soh**-trohs kay-**reh**-mohs
you want (plural formal)	ustedes quieren	oo-**stehd**-ehs kee-**ehr**-ehn
they (m / f) want	ellos / ellas quieren	**ay**-yohs / **ay**-yahs kee-**ehr**-ehn

TO NEED	NECESITAR	nay-theh-see-**tar**
I need	yo necesito	yoh nay-theh-**see**-toh
you need (formal)	usted necesita	oo-**stehd** nay-theh-**see**-tah
you need (informal)	tú necesitas	too nay-theh-**see**-tahs
he / she needs	él / ella necesita	ehl / **ay**-yah nay-theh-**see**-tah
we need	nostros necesitamos	noh-**soh**-trohs nay-theh-see-**tah**-mohs
you need (plural formal)	ustedes necesitan	oo-**stehd**-ehs nay-theh-**see**-tahn
they (m / f) need	ellos / ellas necesitan	**ay**-yohs / **ay**-yahs nay-theh-**see**-tahn

TO HAVE TO	TENER QUE	teh-**nehr** kay
I have to	yo tengo que	yoh **tehn**-goh kay
you have to (formal)	usted tiene que	oo-**stehd** tee-**ehn**-ay kay
you have to (informal)	tú tienes que	too tee-**ehn**-ehs kay
he / she has to	él / ella tiene que	ehl / **ay**-yah tee-**ehn**-ay kay
we have to	nosotros tenemos que	noh-**soh**-trohs tay-**neh**-mohs kay
you have to (plural formal)	ustedes tienen que	oo-**stehd**-ehs tee-**ehn**-ehn kay
they (m / f) have to	ellos / ellas tienen que	**ay**-yohs / **ay**-yahs tee-**ehn**-ehn kay

TIPS

Spanish Tongue Twisters

Tongue twisters are a great way to practice a language and break the ice with locals. Here are a few Spanish tongue twisters that are sure to challenge you and amuse your hosts.

Pablito clavó un clavito.	Paul stuck in a stick.
¿Qué clavito clavó Pablito?	What stick did Paul stick in?

Un tigre, dos tigres, tres tigres	One tiger, two tigers, three tigers
comían trigo en un trigal.	ate wheat in a wheat field.
Un tigre, dos tigres, tres tigres.	One tiger, two tigers, three tigers.

El cielo está enladrillado.	The sky is bricked up.
¿Quién lo desenladrillará?	Who will unbrick it?
El desenladrillador que lo	He who unbricks it,
desenladrille un buen	what a fine unbricker he will be.
desenladrillador será.	

English Tongue Twisters

After your Spanish friends have laughed at you, let them try these tongue twisters in English.

If neither he sells seashells,
nor she sells seashells,
who shall sell seashells?
Shall seashells be sold?

Peter Piper picked a peck
of pickled peppers.

Rugged rubber baby
buggy bumpers.

The sixth sick sheik's
sixth sheep's sick.

Red bug's blood and
black bug's blood.

Soldiers' shoulders.

Thieves seize skis.

I'm a pleasant mother
pheasant plucker. I pluck
mother pheasants. I'm
the most pleasant mother
pheasant plucker that ever
plucked a mother pheasant.

APPENDIX

LET'S TALK TELEPHONES

Smart travelers use the telephone to reserve or reconfirm rooms, get tourist information, reserve restaurants, confirm tour times, or phone home.

Dialing Within Spain

Spain has a direct-dial phone system (without area codes). All of Spain's phone numbers are nine digits long and can be dialed direct throughout the country. For example, the phone number of one of my recommended Madrid hotels is 915-212-941. That's exactly what you dial, whether you're calling the hotel from the Madrid train station or from Barcelona. Spain's landlines start with 9, and mobile lines start with 6. Numbers that begin with 900 are toll-free, though numbers starting with 901 and 902 can be expensive toll lines. Directory assistance is also pricey (tel. 11811 or 11818).

For more information, see www.ricksteves.com/phoning.

Dialing Internationally

If you want to make an international call, follow these steps:

• Dial the international access code (00 if you're calling from Europe, 011 from the US or Canada). If you're dialing from a mobile phone, you can replace the international access code with +, which works regardless of where you're calling from. (On many mobile phones, you can insert a + by pressing and holding the 0 key.)

• Dial the country code *(código de país)* of the country you're calling (for example, 34 for Spain, or 1 for the US or Canada).

• For Spain, dial the local number. For countries that use area codes, first dial the area code *(prefijo)*, then the local number, keeping in mind that calling many countries requires dropping the initial zero of the phone number. The European calling chart in this chapter lists specifics per country.

Calling from the US to Spain: Dial 011 (the US international access code), 34 (Spain's country code), then the nine-digit number.

For example, if you're calling the Madrid hotel cited earlier, you'd dial 011-34-915-212-941.

Calling from any European country to the US: To call my office in Edmonds, Washington, from anywhere in Europe, I dial 00 (Europe's international access code), 1 (the US country code), 425 (Edmonds' area code), and 771-8303.

Embassies

American Embassy: Tel. 915-872-200; Calle Serrano 75, Madrid; http://madrid.usembassy.gov

Canadian Embassy: Tel. 914-233-250; Paseo de la Castellana 259D, Madrid; www.espana.gc.ca

NUMBERS AND STUMBLERS

Here are a few things to keep in mind:

- Europeans write a few of their numbers differently than we do. $1 = 1$, $4 = 4$, $7 = 7$.
- In Europe, dates appear as day/month/year.
- Commas are decimal points, and decimal points are commas. A dollar and a half is $1,50; one thousand is 1.000; and there are 5.280 feet in a mile.
- When counting with fingers, start with your thumb. If you hold up your first finger to request one item, you'll probably get two.
- What Americans call the second floor of a building is the first floor in Europe.
- On escalators and moving sidewalks, Europeans keep the left "lane" open for passing. Keep to the right.

Metric Conversions

A kilogram is 2.2 pounds, and l liter is about a quart, or almost four to a gallon. A kilometer is six-tenths of a mile. I figure kilometers to miles by cutting the kilometers in half and adding back 10 percent of the original (120 km: 60 + 12 = 72 miles; 300 km: 150 + 30 = 180 miles).

European Calling Chart

Just smile and dial, using this key:
AC = Area Code, LN = Local Number.

European Country	Calling long distance within ...	Calling from the US or Canada to ...	Calling from a European country to ...
Austria	AC + LN	011 + 43 + AC (without the initial zero) + LN	00 + 43 + AC (without the initial zero) + LN
Belgium	LN	011 + 32 + LN (without initial zero)	00 + 32 + LN (without initial zero)
Britain	AC + LN	011 + 44 + AC (without initial zero) + LN	00 + 44 + AC (without initial zero) + LN
France	LN	011 + 33 + LN (without initial zero)	00 + 33 + LN (without initial zero)
Germany	AC + LN	011 + 49 + AC (without initial zero) + LN	00 + 49 + AC (without initial zero) + LN
Gibraltar	LN	011 + 350 + LN	00 + 350 + LN
Ireland	AC + LN	011 + 353 + AC (without initial zero) + LN	00 + 353 + AC (without initial zero) + LN
Italy	LN	011 + 39 + LN	00 + 39 + LN

European Country	Calling long distance within ...	Calling from the US or Canada to ...	Calling from a European country to ...
Morocco	LN	011 + 212 + LN (without initial zero)	00 + 212 + LN (without initial zero)
Netherlands	AC + LN	011 + 31 + AC (without initial zero) + LN	00 + 31 + AC (without initial zero) + LN
Portugal	LN	011 + 351 + LN	00 + 351 + LN
Spain	LN	011 + 34 + LN	00 + 34 + LN
Switzerland	LN	011 + 41 + LN (without initial zero)	00 + 41 + LN (without initial zero)

- The instructions above apply whether you're calling to or from a European landline or mobile phone.

- If calling from any mobile phone, you can replace the international access code with "+" (press and hold 0 to insert it).

- The international access code is 011 if you're calling from the US or Canada.

- To call the US or Canada from Europe, dial 00, then 1 (country code for US and Canada), then the area code and number. In short, 00 + 1 + AC + LN = Hi, Mom!

Temperature Conversion

For a rough conversion from Celsius to Fahrenheit, double the number and add 30. For weather, remember that 28°C is 82°F—perfect. For health, 37°C is just right.

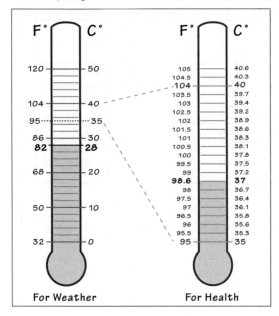

For Weather   For Health

FILLING OUT FORMS

If you need to decipher paperwork or forms, the following will help.

Sr. / Sra. / Srta.	Mr. / Mrs. / Miss
nombre	first name
apellido	last name
dirección	address
domicilio	address
calle	street
ciudad	city
estado	state
país	country
nacionalidad	nationality
origen / destino	origin / destination
edad	age
fecha de nacimiento	date of birth
lugar de nacimiento	place of birth
sexo	sex
masculino	male
femenino	female
casado / casada	married man / married woman
soltero / soltera	single man / single woman
divorciado / viudo	divorced / widowed
profesión	profession
adulto	adult
niño / niña	boy / girl
niños	children
familia	family
firma	signature
fecha	date

When filling out dates, do it European-style: day/month/year.

TEAR-OUT CHEAT SHEETS

Basics

Tear out this sheet of Spanish survival phrases and keep it in your pocket to use in case you're caught without your phrase book.

Hello.	Hola. **oh**-lah
Mr.	Señor sehn-**yor**
Mrs.	Señora sehn-**yoh**-rah
Miss	Señorita sehn-yoh-**ree**-tah
Do you speak English?	¿Habla usted inglés? **ah**-blah oo-**stehd** een-**glays**
Yes. / No.	Sí. / No. see / noh
I don't understand.	No comprendo. noh kohm-**prehn**-doh
I'm sorry.	Lo siento. loh see-**ehn**-toh
Please.	Por favor. por fah-**bor**
Thank you.	Gracias. **grah**-thee-ahs
You're welcome.	De nada. day **nah**-dah
Excuse me.	Perdone. pehr-**doh**-nay
OK?	¿Vale? **bah**-leh
It's (not) a problem.	(No) hay problema. (noh) ī proh-**bleh**-mah
Good.	Bueno. **bweh**-noh
Goodbye.	Adiós. ah-dee-**ohs**
How much is it?	¿Cuánto cuesta? **kwahn**-toh **kweh**-stah
Write it?	¿Me lo escribe? may loh eh-**skree**-bay
euro (€)	euro **yoo**-roh
zero	cero **thehr**-oh
one / two	uno / dos **oo**-noh / dohs
three / four	tres / cuatro trehs / **kwah**-troh
five / six	cinco / seis **theen**-koh / says
seven / eight	siete / ocho see-**eh**-tay / **oh**-choh
nine / ten	nueve / diez **nweh**-bay / dee-**ehth**

Can you help me?	¿Puede ayudarme? **pweh**-day ī-yoo-**dar**-may
I'd like / We'd like...	Me / Nos gustaría... may / nohs goo-stah-**ree**-ah
...this.	...esto. **eh**-stoh
...a ticket.	...un billete. oon bee-**yeh**-tay
...the bill.	...la cuenta. lah **kwehn**-tah
Where is a cash machine?	¿Dónde hay un cajero automático? **dohn**-day ī oon kah-**hehr**-oh ow-toh-**mah**-tee-koh
Where are the toilets?	¿Dónde están los servicios? **dohn**-day eh-**stahn** lohs sehr-**bee**-thee-ohs
men	hombres **ohm**-brehs
women	mujeres moo-**heh**-rehs
Is it free?	¿Es gratis? ehs **grah**-tees
Is it included?	¿Está incluido? eh-**stah** een-kloo-**ee**-doh
Is it possible?	¿Es posible? ehs poh-**see**-blay
entrance / exit	entrada / salida ehn-**trah**-dah / sah-**lee**-dah
What time does this open / close?	¿A qué hora abren / cierran? ah kay **oh**-rah **ah**-brehn / thee-**ehr**-ahn
Just a moment.	Un momento. oon moh-**mehn**-toh
now / soon	ahora / pronto ah-**oh**-rah / **prohn**-toh
later	más tarde mahs **tar**-day
today / tomorrow	hoy / mañana oy / mahn-**yah**-nah
Sunday	domingo doh-**meen**-goh
Monday	lunes **loo**-nehs
Tuesday	martes **mar**-tehs
Wednesday	miércoles mee-**ehr**-koh-lehs
Thursday	jueves **hweh**-behs
Friday	viernes bee-**ehr**-nehs
Saturday	sábado **sah**-bah-doh

Restaurants

I'd like / We'd like...	Me / Nos gustaría... may / nohs goo-stah-**ree**-ah
...to reserve...	...reservar... reh-sehr-**bar**
...a table for one / two.	...una mesa para uno / dos. **oo**-nah **meh**-sah **pah**-rah **oo**-noh / dohs
Is this table free?	¿Está libre esta mesa? eh-**stah** lee-bray **eh**-stah **meh**-sah
How long is the wait?	¿Cuánto tiempo hay que esperar? **kwahn**-toh tee-**ehm**-poh ī kay eh-speh-**rar**
The menu (in English), please.	La carta (en inglés), por favor. lah **kar**-tah (ehn een-**glays**) por fah-**bor**
breakfast	desayuno deh-sah-**yoo**-noh
lunch	almuerzo / comida ahlm-**wehr**-thoh / koh-**mee**-dah
dinner	cena **theh**-nah
service (not) included	servicio (no) incluido sehr-**bee**-thee-oh (noh) een-kloo-**ee**-doh
cover charge	precio de entrada **preh**-thee-oh day ehn-**trah**-dah
to go	para llevar **pah**-rah yeh-**bar**
with / without	con / sin kohn / seen
and / or	y / o ee / oh
fixed-price meal (of the day)	menú (del día) meh-**noo** (dehl **dee**-ah)
specialty of the house	especialidad de la casa eh-speh-thee-ah-lee-**dahd** day lah **kah**-sah
combination plate	plato combinado **plah**-toh kohm-bee-**nah**-doh
What do you recommend?	¿Qué recomienda? kay reh-koh-mee-**ehn**-dah
appetizers	tapas **tah**-pahs
bread	pan pahn

cheese	queso	**keh**-soh
sandwich	bocadillo	boh-kah-**dee**-yoh
soup	sopa	**soh**-pah
salad	ensalada	ehn-sah-**lah**-dah
meat	carne	**kar**-nay
poultry	aves	**ah**-behs
fish	pescado	peh-**skah**-doh
seafood	marisco	mah-**ree**-skoh
vegetables	verduras	behr-**doo**-rahs
fruit	fruta	**froo**-tah
dessert	postres	**poh**-strehs
tap water	agua del grifo	**ah**-gwah dehl **gree**-foh
mineral water	agua mineral	**ah**-gwah mee-neh-**rahl**
milk	leche	**leh**-chay
(orange) juice	zumo (de naranja)	**thoo**-moh (day nah-**rahn**-hah)
coffee / tea	café / té	kah-**fay** / tay
wine	vino	**bee**-noh
red / white	tinto / blanco	**teen**-toh / **blahn**-koh
glass / bottle	vaso / botella	**bah**-soh / boh-**teh**-yah
beer	cerveza	thehr-**beh**-thah
Cheers!	¡Salud!	sah-**lood**
More. / Another.	Más. / Otro.	mahs / **oh**-troh
The same.	El mismo.	ehl **mees**-moh
Finished.	Terminado.	tehr-mee-**nah**-doh
The bill, please.	La cuenta, por favor.	lah **kwehn**-tah por fah-**bor**
Do you accept credit cards?	¿Se aceptan tarjetas de crédito?	say ah-**thehp**-tahn tar-**heh**-tahs day **kray**-dee-toh
tip	propina	proh-**pee**-nah
Delicious!	¡Delicioso!	deh-lee-thee-**oh**-soh

The perfect complement to your phrase book

Travel with Rick Steves' candid, up-to-date advice on the best places to eat and sleep, the must-see sights, getting off the beaten path—and getting the most out of every day and every dollar while you're in Europe.

Audio Europe™

Rick's Free Travel App

Get your FREE **Rick Steves Audio Europe**™ app to enjoy...

- Dozens of self-guided tours of Europe's top museums, sights and historic walks

- Hundreds of tracks filled with cultural insights and sightseeing tips from Rick's radio interviews

- All organized into handy geographic playlists

- For iPhone, iPad, iPod Touch, Android

With Rick whispering in your ear, Europe gets even better.

Find out more at ricksteves.com

Join a Rick Steves tour

Enjoy Europe's warmest welcome... with the flexibility and friendship of a small group getting to know Rick's favorite places and people. It all starts with our free tour catalog and DVD.

Great guides, small groups, no grumps.

See more than three dozen itineraries throughout Europe
ricksteves.com

Start your trip at

Free information and great gear to

▶ Plan Your Trip

Browse thousands of articles and a wealth of money-saving tips for planning your dream trip. You'll find up-to-date information on Europe's best destinations, packing smart, getting around, finding rooms, staying healthy, avoiding scams and more.

▶ Travel News

Subscribe to our free Travel News e-newsletter, and get monthly updates from Rick on what's happening in Europe.

▶ Graffiti Wall & Travelers Helpline

Learn, ask, share—our online community of savvy travelers is a great resource for first-time travelers to Europe, as well as seasoned pros.

Rick Steves' Europe Through the Back Door, Inc.

ricksteves.com

turn your travel dreams into affordable reality

▸ Rick's Free Audio Europe™ App

The Rick Steves Audio Europe™ app brings history and art to life. Enjoy Rick's audio tours of Europe's top museums, sights and neighborhood walks—plus 200 tracks of travel tips and cultural insights from Rick's radio show—all organized into geographic playlists. Learn more at ricksteves.com.

▸ Great Gear from Rick's Travel Store

Pack light and right—on a budget—with Rick's custom-designed carry-on bags, wheeled bags, day packs, travel accessories, guidebooks, journals, maps and DVDs of his TV shows.

130 Fourth Avenue North, PO Box 2009 • Edmonds, WA 98020 USA
Phone: (425) 771-8303 • Fax: (425) 771-0833 • www.ricksteves.com

Rick Steves® www.ricksteves.com

Avalon Travel
a member of the Perseus Books Group
1700 Fourth Street, Berkeley, CA 94710, USA

Text © 2013, 2009 by Rick Steves. All rights reserved.
Cover © 2013 by Avalon Travel.
All rights reserved.
Maps © 2013, 2009 by Europe Through the Back Door.
All rights reserved.

Printed in China by RR Donnelley
First edition. First printing January 2013.

ISBN-13: 9781612382050

For the latest on Rick's lectures, guidebooks, tours,
and public television series, contact Europe Through
the Back Door, Inc., Box 2009, Edmonds, WA 98020,
tel. 425/771-8303, fax 425/771-8383, www.ricksteves
.com, rick@ricksteves.com.

Europe Through the Back Door
Managing Editor: Risa Laib
Series Manager: Cathy Lu
Project Editor: Cara Erickson
Editors: Jennifer Madison Davis, Tom Griffin, Cameron
Hewitt, Suzanne Kotz, Sarah McCormic, Carrie Shepherd
Intro Editor: Ari Bradshaw
Editorial Assistant: Jessica Shaw
Graphic Content Director: Laura VanDeventer
Researchers: Rebecca Shortuck, Cameron Hewitt,
Amanda Zurita

Avalon Travel
a member of the Perseus Books Group
1700 Fourth Street, Berkeley, CA 94710, USA

Printed in China by RR Donnelley.
Third edition. First printing January 2014.

ISBN-13: 978-1-61238-205-0

For the latest on Rick's lectures, guidebooks, tours,
and public television series, contact Europe Through
the Back Door, P.O. Box 2009, Edmonds, WA 98020,
tel. 425/771-8303, fax 425/771-0833, www.ricksteves
.com, rick@ricksteves.com.

Europe Through the Back Door
Managing Editor: Risa Laib
Series Manager: Cathy Lu
Project Editor: Glenn Eriksen
Editors: Jennifer Madison Davis, Tom Griffin, Cameron
    Hewitt, Cathy McDonald, Suzanne Kotz, Carrie Shep-
    herd, Gretchen Strauch
Editorial Assistant: Jessica Shaw
Editorial Interns: Emily Dugdale, Andrés Garza, Val-
    erie Gilmore, Rebekka Shattuck, Candace Winegrad,
    Amanda Zurita

Translation: Amanda Buttinger, Patricia Feaster,
  Nygil Murrell, Inma Raneda, Vanessa Valles, Gloria
  Villaraviz Weeden
Lead Researcher: Cameron Hewitt
Research Assistance: Cristina Cabrera, Julie Coen,
  Carlos Galvin, Inés Muñiz
Graphic Content Director: Laura VanDeventer
Maps & Graphics: David C. Hoerlein, Twozdai Hulse,
  Lauren Mills, Dawn Tessman Visser

Avalon Travel
Senior Editor and Series Manager: Madhu Prasher
Editor: Jamie Andrade
Associate Editor: Nikki Ioakimedes
Proofreader: Kelly Lydick
Production & Typesetting: McGuire Barber Design
Cover Design: Kimberly Glyder Design
Maps & Graphics: Kat Bennett, Mike Morgenfeld

Photography: Dominic Bonuccelli, Rick Steves
Front Cover Photo: Madrid, Spain © Mira / Alamy